DATE DUE

DEMCO 38-296

the FUTURE
of SOUTHERN
LETTERS

---

edited by
JEFFERSON HUMPHRIES
& JOHN LOWE

New York   Oxford
Oxford University Press
1996

Oxford University Press

Oxford   New York
Athens   Auckland   Bangkok   Bogota   Bombay
Buenos Aires   Calcutta   Cape Town   Dar es Salaam
Delhi   Florence   Hong Kong   Instanbul   Karachi
Kuala Lumpur   Madras   Madrid   Melbourne
Mexico City   Nairobi   Paris   Singapore
Taipei   Tokyo   Toronto

and associated companies in
Berlin   Ibadan

Copyright © 1996 by Oxford University Press

Published by Oxford University Press, Inc.,
198 Madison Avenue, New York, New York 10016

Oxford is a registered trademark of Oxford University Press

Library of Congress Cataloging-in-Publication Data
The future of southern letters / edited by Jefferson Humphries and John Lowe.
    p.   cm.
Includes index.
ISBN 0-19-509781-5 — ISBN 0-19-509782-3 (pbk.)
1. American literature — Southern States — History and criticism — Theory, etc.   2. Southern
States — Intellectual life — 1865–   3. Southern States — In literature.   4. Canon (Literature)
I. Humphries, Jefferson.   II. Lowe, John.
PS261.F88   1996
810.9'975 — dc20   95-40297

1 2 3 4 5 6 7 8 9
Printed in the United States of America
on acid-free paper

*For Jack Murrah
and the officers and staff of
the Lyndhurst Foundation,
whose moral and financial support
made this book possible.*

Contents

Contributors

JAMES APPLEWHITE, a professor of English at Duke University and former director of Duke's Institute for the Arts, has published six volumes of poetry, including *Statues of the Grass, Following Gravity,* and *Foreseeing the Journey.* He is the recipient of writing fellowships from both the Guggenheim Foundation and the National Endowment for the Arts.

JACK BUTLER is the author of *Jujitsu for Christ* and *Living in Little Rock with Miss Little Rock* and of other works of poetry and fiction. He is director of the Program in Creative Writing at the College of Santa Fe.

FRED CHAPPELL, a professor of English at the University of North Carolina at Greensboro, has received the Bollingen Prize for Poetry and the Best Foreign Book Award from the Académie Française. He is the author of six books of fiction and seven of poetry, including *Midquest, Source* (both poetry), and *I Am One of You Forever* and *Dagon* (novels).

RODGER CUNNINGHAM, Appalachian writer and critic and professor at Sue Bennett College in Kentucky, is the author of *Apples in the Flood* and of numerous essays and stories.

KATE DANIELS is poet-in-residence at Vanderbilt University Medical Center, a member of the graduate faculty in creative writing at Bennington College, and the author of two volumes of poetry, *The White Wave* (which received the Agnes Lynch Starrett Prize in Poetry) and *The Niobe Poems.* She was a founding editor of *Poetry East.*

FRED HOBSON is a professor of English at the University of North Carolina at Chapel Hill, the editor of the *Southern Literary Journal,* and the author of *Tell About the South: The Southern Rage to Explain, The Short Reign of Southern*

Realism: The Fiction of the 1920s, and many other books and essays. He has just published *Mencken,* the definitive biography of H. L. Mencken.

JEFFERSON HUMPHRIES's poetry, short fiction, and essays have appeared in many journals and anthologies. His books include *A Bestiary* (poems), *Metamorphoses of the Raven,* and *The Puritan and the Cynic.* He also edited *Conversations with Reynolds Price.* He teaches at Louisiana State University.

JOHN W. LOWE, currently Fulbright professor at the University of Munich, is professor of English at Louisiana State University and the author of *Jump at the Sun: Zora Neale Hurston's Cosmic Comedy.* He edited *Conversations with Ernest Gaines* and has published many essays on humor and on southern, African-American, and ethnic literature.

JIM WAYNE MILLER is a professor emeritus of languages at Bowling Green University and a well-known Appalachian novelist and poet. His volumes of poetry include *Copper Head Cane* and *Dialogue with a Dead Man.*

JAMES OLNEY, Voorhies professor of English at Columbia University, is coeditor of *The Southern Review,* author of *Metaphors of Self: The Meaning of Autobiography, Tell Me Africa: An Approach to African Literature, The Rhizome and the Flower: The Perennial Philosophy—Yeats and Jung,* and many other books, essays, and scholarly articles.

BRENDA MARIE OSBEY is writer-in-residence at Loyola University and the author of three volumes of poetry: *Ceremony for Minneconjoux, In These Houses,* and *Desperate Circumstance, Dangerous Woman.*

MICHAEL SARTISKY is the executive director of the Louisiana Endowment for the Humanities.

DAVE SMITH is the author of many volumes of poetry, including *Cuba Nights, Cumberland Station,* and *The Fisherman's Whore.* He has twice been a runner-up for the Pulitzer Prize in Poetry. Since 1990, he has coedited the *Southern Review.*

STEPHEN A. SMITH, professor of communication at the University of Arkansas, Fayetteville, was formerly director of communications for then-governor Bill Clinton. He is the author of *Myth, Media, and the Southern Mind.*

the FUTURE
of SOUTHERN
LETTERS

JOHN LOWE

Introduction

It is never, as one knows, the subject, *but only the*
treatment *that distinguishes the artist and poet.*

Friedrich Schiller, "On Matthison's Poems" (1794)

We talk real funny down here
We drink too much and we laugh too loud
We're too dumb to make it in no northern town . . .
We got no-necked oilmen from Texas
And good ol' boys from Tennessee
And college men from L.S.U.
Went in dumb. Come out dumb too
Hustlin' 'round Atlanta in their alligator shoes
Gettin' drunk every weekend at the barbecues—
We're Rednecks, we're rednecks
And we don't know our ass from a hole in the ground.

Randy Newman, "Rednecks" (1974)

W hen Randy Newman's "Rednecks" came out two decades ago it seemed
to speak for a moment when the South had one foot in its moonlit, mag-
nolia-scented, but racist past, and the other in the age of pickup trucks, Sunbelt cities, and country rock. Today, even that moment seems dated. Although
the racial agonies the song also speaks of still exist in all areas of the country,
the southern "good old boy" has had to make room for professional women,
educated African-Americans, and new immigrants like the Vietnamese, Cam-
bodians, and Haitians. The rural past has been eclipsed by an ever-expanding
urban present, centered on high-finance, high-tech wheeling-dealing, which

takes place in high-rise postmodern skyscrapers, hub airports, and gigantic shopping malls. At the same time, the South still seems haunted by the gothic ghosts of its past, and religion's sway is as strong as ever, despite the development of a new southern hedonism. Maybe that accounts for the heavy irony in Newman's voice, as he initially seems to accept the stereotype; later he appears to be fighting it tooth and nail, waging a double-front deconstruction, first on the mythology of the South (much of it self-generated) and next on the secondary mythology, much of it negative, that continues to widely circulate in other regions of the country and abroad as well. And yet Newman, like most of our writers, finds much to celebrate too, even as he criticizes, and he seems to think that this cauldron of symbols and markers, bubbling over with a new brew of southern identity, offers much vitality, humor, and hope.

Newman's song attracted attention when it came out, sometimes not so much for what he was saying as for how he said, sang, and accompanied it. Perhaps Schiller's general principle about style fits many readers, including Newman's; it isn't the *South* they care about so much, but the stylistics of those who make it their subject. But I would hazard a guess that most of the writers in this volume, at any rate, and most *southern* readers, if not the majority of general readers, would quarrel with that. Content, when it has a stranglehold on the heart, *does* matter. What Newman is really addressing is the age-old southern rage against hypocritical attacks on southern culture, a rage surprisingly shared on occasion by southern women, African-Americans, and Jews, who have all on occasion risen to defend their region.

A Southern Grammatology

The most prominent voices in this debate have always been those of the South's artists. Subject and style are somewhat dictated by the times and the culture, but artists make conscious choices. Such a gift is accompanied by responsibility, so as dedicated South-watchers and aficionados of the literature that reflects it, we should continually ask this question: who writes down—or makes up—the image of the South for us today? Is it simply mirrored back to us from the ever-slicker news reports of our local TV station? If, as some suggest, the best images are found in the narratives of our native writers, are these authors faithful to the reality of life as we know it, or are they catering to the stereotypes they think a national audience (including southerners themselves) requires? Finally, who will be writing southern literature tomorrow, and about what, and why?

This volume seeks to answer these and other questions by letting many of our younger and more interesting writers speak for themselves, and for a region and a people whose contours and ticks they feel a need to chart. They may have other, more prominent concerns, too, but this charting and mapping of the culture inevitably follows, as a matter of course, because of who these writers have been, are, and will be: southerners. We also take some looks backward, at our joint past, which, despite the modernist and postmodernist zeitgeists, all too often dictates the future.

Books like these of course have to ponder definitions. Superficially, there has always been a debate about what states qualify as southern. In the nineteenth century, Maryland certainly would have been included; today, probably not. Most would be content to say the South consists of the former Confederacy plus Kentucky and Oklahoma, but we're still asking ourselves, is Texas part of the South? If not, are we willing to deny the profoundly southern qualities of the thoughtful and intricate writing in the novels of Beverly Lowry, the plays of Horton Foote, or the epics and bittersweet comedies of Larry McMurtry?

Then there's the question of permanence. Is being southern a category fixed for life? What do you do with the southern writer who leaves the South, both physically *and* in her fiction? One might ask, for instance, whether Richard Ford is really a southern writer. Most of his works unfold in distant places and concern easterners or Rocky Mountain folk. Nonetheless, does he—do they—speak under this patina with a southern nuance? Are the places they inhabit really metaphors for southern climes? Then there's the case of James Wilcox, a gifted comic writer who's been compared to Chekhov. His first four novels were set in Louisiana, but he's been using New York for most of his locales since then, probably because he's been living in Gotham for some time now. Yusef Komunyakaa now writes poetry in Indiana, not Louisiana. Cormac McCarthy recently won the National Book Award for his wonderful *All the Pretty Horses*, but much of it is set in Mexico. Gail Godwin has been confusing label-pasters for years with her shifting subjects and locales. Southern or not?

This is an old debate, after all; we've driven out some of our best writers, including Edgar Allan Poe, George Washington Cable, Charles Chesnutt, Carson McCullers, Robert Penn Warren, Allen Tate, and many others, and most of them began to write some non-southern narratives. Others, however, seemed relatively unaffected. Warren, to cite the most salient example, spent much of his life in Connecticut, but would anyone challenge the profoundly southern essence of his writing? But even those who chose to stay put can and do venture outside "southern" waters. What then? Do we include these texts in surveys, anthologies, and studies of southern literature? It seems likely we'll see many more examples of this syndrome in the future, as Americans in general and writers, perhaps, in particular, become more mobile and less fastened to their cultural bases. No doubt, however, as always, we'll see just as many writers *returning* to their "roots." Tony Kushner, a Louisianan, won the Pulitzer Prize for *Angels in America*, but there is little that is southern about the play. But does that necessarily mean that Kushner's future works won't be about the South? Other recent dramas have proved the vitality southern subjects have for the region's playwrights, such as Beth Henley, Marsha Norman, Tom Dent, Robert Harling, and Alfred Uhry, yet many of them have slipped easily in and out of southern themes.

Similarly, we have to ask ourselves what we mean when we say "literature." Does it include popular but definitely schlock productions—sex-grits-and-skyscrapers paperbacks with titles like *Atlanta* or *B'ham Ala*? Typically, a blurb for the former reads, "The inside story of the thundering emergence of a city of glass and steel—the men who built it, the women who bathed in its glamour, and loved in its shadows, and the shocking power-play that threatened to engulf their glittering dreams."

More problematic are the compelling narratives by talented storytellers that all the same seem calculated for a mass audience, especially in their obliging redecking of old stereotypes in new guises. I am thinking here of the work of Harry Crews, Pete Dexter, or, distressingly, much of Pat Conroy's wildly popular *Prince of Tides*. Catering to an audience-determined formula? Looking for the movie contract? Or are these necessarily compromising factors? What about novelist Lee Smith's recent foray into Nashville's music scene, surely one of the most interesting aspects of contemporary southern culture? A sellout, or an expansion of her natural canvas? And how does it compare with Harry Crews's similar mining of another musical realm in *The Gospel Singer*, a novel that garnered the praise of a master craftsman of the old school, Andrew Lytle?

One thing seems certain: most of today's southern narratives, highbrow or low, aspire to mirror a culture in the throes of dynamic and dramatic change, a condition that has often led to some of the greatest achievements in southern literature, such as *Cane*, *The Sound and the Fury*, *All the King's Men*, and *Meridian*.

As the outpouring of books like *Atlanta* reveals, however, not all of our musings on change have been of this gravity. In addition to the page-turners, what are we to do with the vastly popular books of southern good-old-boy humorists like the late Lewis Grizzard and Roy Blount Jr.? Their witticisms grew out of the fertile soil of change too; do such writers have any affinity with, or (gasp!) an actual influence on, "serious" comic writers like Clyde Edgerton, Barry Hannah, Larry Brown, Lewis Nordan, or Allan Gurganus? And for that matter, the new southern woman has a comic persona too, in the delightful fictions of Alice Childress, Ellen Gilchrist, Fannie Flagg, Rita Mae Brown, and Kaye Gibbons. Do we draw a strict line of separation between them and more commercially thinking women writers? And the debate still rages about John Kennedy Toole's *Confederacy of Dunces*; can such a popular, wildly funny book really be any good?

Once again, this is hardly a new conundrum. Southern readers and critics have always wondered what to do with "popular writers," especially when their works indubitably satisfy basic human yearnings for warmth, humor, and tenderness, without necessarily providing great art. The frontier humorists had to wait outside the academy for some time, and so did their heir, Mark Twain.

Popular *women* writers must face the charge of being melodramatic, sentimental, or both. This charge has its most obvious example in Margaret Mitchell, but one sees it again today in the chilly critical reception of a work such as Olive Ann Burns's runaway best-seller, *Cold Sassy Tree*. The current holder of the "popular" southern historical novel crown, however, is surely Anne Rivers Siddons, whose *Peachtree Road* not only limns her own native culture but also sets out a basic pattern (some would say formula) followed in her other romances, such as *The Outer Banks*, about North Carolina. Yet on reading V. S. Naipaul's interview with her in *A Turn in the South*, one is struck by her honesty, her concern for justice, and her constant examination of the implications of being southern, female, and an artist.

Burns and Siddons clearly loom far above the many hack writers who combine ample portions of sex and glitter with southern stereotypes. But again, how do we draw the line? Quo vadis, southern writer?

Resetting the Table

As my remarks already suggest, the future of southern letters won't lie entirely in the hands of white male southerners. The *greatest* change in southern letters has come in with the new canon. Without question, many of the very best and/or most popular contemporary writers from the region are female, African-American, or both. Ernest Gaines and Alice Walker are surely candidates, along with Reynolds Price, for recognition as the greatest currently active southern writers.

But as always, the *living* canon—our current supply of active writers—shifts regularly, in unexpected ways. Most obviously, we never know when commanding or merely intriguing voices will be stilled, either by premature death, illness, or writer's block. We lost Henry Dumas, John Kennedy Toole, John O. Killens, and Raymond Andrews all too soon. Many regret that Ralph Ellison, Harper Lee, and others never followed up their brilliant first novels with others.

Some of the greatest writers in the tradition have continued to write well into old age; surviving and productive figures here include Elizabeth Spencer, Reynolds Price, Albert Murray, Shirley Ann Grau, Wendell Berry, David Madden, Maya Angelou, and Mary Lee Settle, and one devoutly hopes that our literary future will include new works by them. Often, writers we think we know well astonish us with something entirely new, unexpected, and utterly true, as in Peter Taylor's magnificent *Summons to Memphis*, or Douglas's *Can't Quit You Baby*. So even when our writers die after a long, productive career, as was the case recently with Taylor, Robert Penn Warren, Etheridge Knight, Walker Percy, and Frank Yerby, we wonder if they took a final manuscript with them. On the other hand, other great living writers, such as Eudora Welty and Margaret Walker Alexander, have seemingly halted their production.

The current state of southern letters, despite the losses mentioned above, is strong. The announcement of the 1993 Pulitzer Prizes in fiction and drama to two Louisiana natives follows the honors awarded to Allan Gurganus's *Oldest Living Confederate Widow Tells All* and Pete Dexter's *Paris Trout*. Ernest Gaines just received the prestigious MacArthur Award and, for *A Lesson before Dying*, the National Book Critics' Circle Award. Such acclaim and attention can only encourage and challenge developing and struggling writers of the South to press on.

Writers of the contemporary South differ dramatically from their predecessors; how could they not? In their lifetime the region has changed more than it had in all its previous history. But somehow southern writers, moving with the flow, see some kind of constant, enduring presence in southern settings. Place, despite dramatic changes, still casts the same old spell in many ways. New Orleans, in the works of poet Brenda Marie Osbey, novelist John Kennedy Toole, or short story writer Ellen Gilchrist, seems eternal and unique. The rippling fields and forests emerge with a contemporary menace but an ageless essence in the works of Cormac McCarthy, while Louise Shivers finds a sensual, smoky setting for her tale of contemporary passion in the North Carolina tobacco country. Charleston has never seemed so hip, so vibrant, but yet so traditional and tropical too, as in the fiction of Josephine Humphreys or Pat Conroy. Other writers from other places have added to this tradition recently. Peter Matthiessen's brooding, brutal, and beautiful depiction of the Florida frontier in *Killing Mr. Watson* reminds us that transplanted "Yankees" have frequently added to our store of verbal landscapes. Who can forget Marjorie Kinnan Rawlings's equally compelling vision of her beloved Florida?

Resetting the table has meant playing with some recipes as well. An often-overlooked component of Faulkner's continuing influence on southern letters has been evident in the experimental nature of much of southern fiction of the last few decades. One of the most impressive achievements here has been Jack Butler's *Jujitsu for Christ*, to my mind one of the true classics in the tradition. Another writer willing to take on almost any aesthetic dare is Barry Hannah, whose real achievement sometimes gets obscured by his occasional, inevitable failures. The women's movement and its focus on gender has undoubtedly encouraged writers to experiment in exploring issues that matter to their opposite sex, often in that sex's voice. Clyde Edgerton's *Raney*, Reynolds Price's *Kate Vaiden*, Ellen Douglas's *Rock Cried Out*, and Alice Walker's *Third Life of Grange Copeland* all fit this welcome pattern and seem to promise more to come. Writers have shown a willingness to cross ethnic and racial boundaries: Robert Olen Butler's *Good Scent from a Strange Mountain* concerns Vietnamese-Americans; Shirley Ann Grau has returned to the literary scene with her striking new novel *Roadwalkers*, about African-Americans caught in the Great Depression.

Similarly, recent attention in society at large to abused children and children's rights has coincided with a new interest in child narrators and characters in southern fiction; imaginative rethinking of southern classics such as *Huckleberry Finn* have lately emerged in works such as Padgett Powell's *Edisto*, Kaye Gibbons's *Ellen Foster*, and Dori Sanders's *Clover*.

As this collection's several essays on southern poetry demonstrate, innovation and experimentation continue to vitalize southern poetry. I would add that the lyrical tradition of poetry lives on, especially in Louisiana, where one finds Pinkie Gordon Lane, Mona Lisa Saloy, Tom Dent, Brenda Marie Osbey, and many others. Louisiana now also boasts Dave Smith, whose muscular, dark, and brooding work brings a contemporary resonance to an equally venerable tradition of masculine poetry, epitomized by Donald Davidson, Allen Tate, James Dickey, Jerry W. Ward Jr., Fred Chappell, Alvin Aubert, and, of course, Robert Penn Warren.

The elegant patterns of malaise charted by the late Walker Percy have found a more pedestrian expression in the recent and creative neorealism of writers such as Bobbie Ann Mason, Valerie Sayers, Larry Brown, Richard Ford, and Josephine Humphreys. And yet one of our contributors, Jack Butler, claims that the most uninteresting literature of all is that which seeks to expose the "essential meaningless and vapidity of life," a sentiment others surely share. Clearly, although certain threads appear to run in common through southern texts, attitudes and approaches toward them differ widely.

At least one sign of the newly catholic nature of southern studies may be found in the emerging courses, anthologies, and critical studies that reflect the new canon of southern literature and cultural studies. *The History of Southern Literature* (1985), edited by an older generation of scholars, offered the first proof of the paradigm shift. A more dramatic example, in the broader field of southern cultural studies, emerged in the best-selling and widely honored *Encyclopedia of Southern Culture* (1989), edited by Charles Reagan Wilson and William Ferris, which attempted to honor every aspect of the region's life and thought, from hushpuppies, kudzu, possums, and air-conditioning to architectural styles, dialect, recreation, and women's lives. Although the hundred-page section on "Black Life" is impressive, references to African-American culture appear throughout the many entries. Even more space is devoted to "Ethnic Life" and "Folklife." One is surprised and disappointed to find that only three of the forty writers identified as "major" in the folklife section are African-Americans. But the study as a whole constitutes a watershed in rethinking what southern "culture" is, incorporating much previously scorned material and peoples, and placing folk culture's value much higher in our collective consciousness. The *Encyclopedia* in many ways reflects a sea change in the academy, where the South's peoples and cultures are studied in interdisciplinary, multicultural ways undreamed of only a few decades ago. Within literature, previously dismissed genres such as diaries, journals, cookbooks, autobiographies, work songs, spirituals, and the like now are studied alongside long-revered poems, novels, plays, essays, and sermons. The *Encyclopedia*'s writers and other "New New South" scholars practice a revisionist history, one that looks with a jaundiced eye on the old accounts of southern history while eagerly seeking out documents, photographs, maps, and any literary artifacts that point to a broader portrait of our past than we have previously suspected. This scholarship, with its attendant panels, symposia, festivals, and the like, which often involve the region's writers, has gradually fed into the creation of a new southern literature and will surely continue to have its effect in the decades to come.

Reaccentuating the Past

The future of southern letters will always be partly dependent on our changing perceptions of its past. Twenty-five years ago, most southern literature courses focused on white male writers; even Eudora Welty and Flannery O'Connor were considered "minor" writers and not worthy of study, and the only black writer who made the list from time to time was Booker T. Washington, for obvious reasons. One often heard the argument that this was simply the result of an aesthetic evaluation; the "best" writers just turned out to be male. But of course literary hierarchies, which in turn led to literary histories, paralleled the old patterns of history. The record of the past was assumed to be a linear progression of "great events," which inevitably starred "great men."

Sweeping change in historiography, partly brought about by European historians such as Febvre, Bloch, and, most important, Braudel, has made history less a stitching together of great events than a mining of what Braudel calls "the structure of everyday life." Coincidentally or not, seismic forces operating in literary studies have had much the same effect. In 1996, southern literature courses often devote at least a third of their syllabi to African-American writers, and many works by women, black and white, have been brought into the classroom as well. The list of previously unknown—rather than merely neglected—writers grows apace. The remarkable *Civil War Diary of Sarah Morgan* has not only presented us with a memorable voice from the past but has also radically reshaped our sense of important moments in southern history, notably the Battle of Baton Rouge, the Battle of Port Hudson, and the Siege of Vicksburg. Morgan's reportage contrasts dramatically with Mary Chesnut's and complements the important work currently being done on the role women played in mourning practices, southern art, and the cult of the Lost Cause, a subject that has been brought to our attention in the important *The Confederate Image: Prints of the Lost Cause*, which in turn extends the ground-breaking (and somewhat opposed) work of Charles Reagan Wilson's *Baptized in Blood: The Religion of the Lost Cause, 1865-1920*, and Gaines Foster's *Ghosts of the Confederacy: Defeat, the Lost Cause, and the Emergence of the New South*.

These works of course represent only a fragment of important new studies coming out of southern history, women's studies, multicultural studies, American art history, and many other dynamic disciplines. One might argue that southern writers are unlikely to read such academic texts, but they certainly know when the public's tastes are being steered back toward regional literature, history, and culture, whether directly or indirectly, through a kind of "trickle-down" effect brought about by local newspapers, book reviews, or even magazine articles in *Southern Living, Southern Accents*, and the like.

One of the things that needs to be said here is that despite the changes listed above, the South in many ways continues to be a very conservative region, and it would be foolish to pretend that conservative elements in southern literature—and, indeed, literary criticism—have disappeared. Several of the essays in this book reflect that reality—particularly Fred Hobson's and Jefferson Humphries's.

Certainly many writers native to the region and from outside it have been turning to historical fiction lately. Many African-American writers have done so; southerners Margaret Walker Alexander and Alex Haley paved the way with *Jubilee* and *Roots*, respectively, following the lead of Frank Yerby, whose *Foxes of Harrow* ought to have been seen in that light too, and would have, if more people had realized that its author was black. All three of these novels went back in time to examine slavery from a black perspective, a venerable tradition that of course began with yet another southern genre, the slave narrative. In our time this tradition, recast in the historical novel, has found one of its greatest expressions in Ohio's Toni Morrison, in her Pulitzer Prize–winning *Beloved*. Another non-southerner, Sherley Anne Williams, preceded Morrison in searching out another vision of southern slavery in *Dessa Rose*. Nor is slavery the only time frame subject to inspection. Georgia's Alice Walker chose the 1930s (*The Color Purple*) and the 1960s of the civil rights movement (*Meridian*) for examination under her literary microscope. Similarly, Ernest Gaines has set most of his work in the past, most obviously in *The Autobiography of Miss Jane Pittman*, which examines both of the heroic epochs (emancipation and the civil rights movement) through the life of its title character. His magnificent new novel, *A Lesson before Dying*, goes back to a 1948 execution to help us ponder why so many young, black American men continue to be warehoused and put to death in today's up-to-date prisons. Gloria Naylor, who is no southerner but was conceived, she reminds us, in Mississippi, went to the legendary Georgia/South Carolina coast for her hit novel *Mama Day*, a book that shuttles easily between the legendary past and a disillusioning present.

Rita Mae Brown's Civil War novel *High Hearts* is a key example of how a writer associated with one school—in this case, comic "feminist" fiction—can easily switch gears in order to mine and rethink a classic southern genre. Something rather similar may be found in various pieces by the good-old-boy *enfant terrible* of southern letters, Barry Hannah, particularly in his justly famous short stories involving Jeb Stuart.

In his recent study *The Southern Writer in the Postmodern World*, Fred Hobson has made an interesting observation about Bobbie Ann Mason, who has frequently been criticized for writing a kind of "Kmart" realism, even when ostensibly pondering historical issues, such as Vietnam, in books like *In Country*. Hobson gives Mason credit for engaging such matters; argues that she shouldn't be expected to write historical fiction the way Warren or Faulkner would; and, most revealingly, notes the difficulty of coupling what he calls a "minimalist" style with historical subject matter. Hobson suggests, "Perhaps mythology—and a way to order one's life—can come from *M*A*S*H* as well as *The Golden Bough*" (Hobson 19–20).

Hobson seems on the verge of proclaiming folklore the successor of mythology. One of the great things about the rediscovery of Zora Neale Hurston and her work has been a renewed respect for southern folk culture (heretofore labeled "low culture"), and not just that of African-Americans. High-minded critics such as Mencken and others always blasted the South for its lack of "high culture"; recent literary criticism — certainly of African-American southern literature, but also of women's writing in the South (like that focused on Augusta Jane Evans in the nineteenth century, for instance, or the work of Ellen Douglas or Elizabeth Spencer in our own time) — has revealed a rich vein of folk culture that runs prominently through classic and little-known works of southern literature. One finds it in unexpected places, as in the description of the way southern belles fastened the buttons of Confederate soldier's uniforms onto their dresses in Thomas Nelson Page's Reconstruction novel, *Red Rock*, or the lovingly detailed quotidean rituals Welty provides in *Delta Wedding*, or the African-American folklore one finds in Raymond Andrews's or John Killens's fictional small towns. Will critical appreciation of these neglected aspects of southern writing encourage more of it?

New Southern Dialogics

All these issues and many more are taken up by the authors we have assembled here. In our lead essay, James Applewhite reveals the prominence and significance of the unsatisfactory father motif in southern letters; surely one extension of his theory would be that many of today's southern artists find the old approaches and stereotypes of their literary tradition moldy at best and are constantly seeking to replace outworn symbols with newer ones, while simultaneously trying to restore that sense of fidelity to the South's body and mind that originally animated the old symbols when they were generated.

In his apt metaphor describing the differentiation between writers and critics, Jack Butler suggests that the critics map the coastline, while the writers *are* the coastline. But this image also suggests that the real way we define the body of the South and its culture is through its boundaries and what they touch, a theory quite similar, in fact, to Fredrik Barth's formulation of what constitutes an ethnic group: not content but boundary, a constantly shifting line. And as Jefferson Humphries asserts in his essay here, any regional or national identity stems from at least two conflicting needs — the desire to create a narrative from within that codifies identity but also by the narrative constructed *without* that the first narrative inevitably responds to.)

Butler proclaims the need to be not just southern but "southern modern," to bring a novelty into the equation of rendering the New New South. But he, like Applewhite and many others in this volume, conjures up that old genie William Faulkner in the same breath, blending the present and the past to cast a new formula for southern writing, albeit set in his own vital language: "We think of a place; we think of the darkness and splendor of families; we think of a way of talking; we think of the Bible; and we think of black and white locked into a mutual if inharmonious fate."

And yet, as our writers constantly demonstrate, most of the changes — even the seismic eruption of postmodern southern humor have antecedents. Stephen

Smith's jaunty ride through the trickster show of our literary humor demonstrates that that other rude, irreverent South, just back of the big house, lives on and on and on, even if it has to pitch its sideshow tent in Kmart's parking lot. His open eye for popular culture's role in this ongoing carnival makes for some joyful reading and some careful rethinking.

The ubiquitous presence of humor in southern discourse finds ample display in two other pieces in our collection. Fred Chappell's hilarious sendup of books such as this one displays, if nothing else, the boisterous survival of southern academic humor. He also wickedly skewers the expectations we and publishers have of southern writers. The fact that "Wil Hickson" speaks to us from 2001 (a "South Odyssey"?) confirms not only that there will be a future for southern letters but also that the quest for it will remain ever elusive, endless, and, one hopes, joyful. Ole Wil's short history of the Appal Lit Insurrection furnishes a kind of microcosm of the broader history of the set it seeks to separate from—"Grit Lit," southern literature itself.

Similarly, Jim Wayne Miller resurrects the legendary and irreverent Sut Lovingood to poke fun at our academic landmark, *The History of Southern Literature*, which is eloquently defended elsewhere in this volume by Fred Hobson. Nobody ever said that southern writers and scholars tend to agree!

The hip-flip mask of Chappell finds its counterpart in the dramatic jeremiad of Rodger Cunningham, who makes a startling application of postcolonialist theorists such as Edward Said to help us posit a different kind of future for Appalachia. In reaching out to the methodologies of other fields, Cunningham encourages us to remap what we think is familiar terrain.

Poet Kate Daniels employs a luminous prose to demonstrate how the postmodern writer's identity stems from a personal task: commemorating one's family. For in her brief memoir of a Richmond childhood, she locates the origins of narratives in the structures of everyday life, as they pass, as Zora Neale Hurston might say, from "mouth almighty" as it whiles away a summer's night on dimly lit front porches. Daniels shows us how these voices helped her both write and read poetry years later, in the North (where, like many, she finds out what it *really* means to be southern) and, later, in Louisiana.

Fred Hobson and Jefferson Humphries offer varying views of our subject from very different academic perches. Hobson, once a Pulitzer Prize–winning journalist and for many years an editor, teacher, and historian/scholar of southern literature, provides us with a shrewd and true-to-the-bone assessment of what the patterns mean in the long history of the southern literary canon. Among its many other virtues, Hobson's essay demonstrates decisively that academic critics have an extremely important role to play in identifying, supporting, and, yes, criticizing future southern writers. Understanding the errors of past scholars (especially their racism and sexism) plays a key role here, but Hobson takes pains to temper some recent and, he would say, unwarranted attacks on the elder generation's critical legacy. Hobson's even-handed and courageous approach skillfully untangles some knotted clusters of aesthetics and ideology, and coincidentally equips us with some valuable clues about how best to examine similar knots in our critical and literary discourse about contemporary and future writers. His piece is also a tribute to magnificent scholars such as Louis Rubin and Lewis Simpson, who in transforming their approaches to southern letters—most memorably in their seminal *History of Southern Literature* (1985)—helped steer us toward the multicultural, interdisciplinary position the field now seems to favor. Hobson's essay offers a reminder, too, that no consideration of the South's literary future will be successful in effacing its past.

Jefferson Humphries appears to contradict much of what some other essayists here have written in his emphasis on the South as story, as idea, but in fact he usefully complements many of their pronouncements, particularly those of Fred Hobson. Humphries uses an adroit blend of contemporary theory and literary history (much of it drawn from the nineteenth century) to create a surprising congruence between Old South intellectual activity and recently fashionable theories of narrative. His employment of "narrative exigency" ties together many apparently disparate observations in this collection, and like Hobson and Olney, Humphries mines the past in order to understand the future.

No section of this volume speaks more eloquently of the continuing hold of place than the interview with Brenda Marie Osbey. Her comments on New Orleans offer proof of at least one area of traditional southern resonance that continues to pulse with generating, creative power. And yet Osbey speaks perceptively about the "quilt" of the South, noting the other distinct "patches" that have also retained a certain unique quality. She sees religion, a preoccupation with death and loss, remembrance, and a love for the land as common threads that hold the quilt together.

Osbey's meditations and wry comments find a contrast in Robert Olen Butler's conversation with Michael Sartisky. Butler provides fascinating insights on how it feels for a southern writer to achieve virtually overnight fame, as he did when he won the Pulitzer Prize. He also offers up quite a detailed autobiography, one that explains why writing about "the collision of cultures"—especially those of Vietnam and America—comes naturally to him, as it does for many southern writers. Readers pondering the question of who actually belongs in this latter group, or what makes an outsider a "southern writer," will find a compelling case study in Butler, who grew up in St. Louis, lived in New York for years, and then went to Vietnam. Ultimately, when his interviewer asks him to name the "place" that he identifies with most closely, he names Louisiana, his home for the last eight years.

Butler's musings on the influences and patterns in his life suggest the importance of autobiography in southern letters. James Olney brings his impressive expertise in this field to bear on the peculiarities of the southern "life narrative." His essay also typifies some of the most encouraging comparative work now being done, particularly in his pairing of works by a black man and a white woman—Mississippi's native son and daughter Richard Wright and Eudora Welty.

Olney's remarks may seem to address only the past, yet they are especially apropos now, when the personal memoir has been coming more to the fore of southern letters. Surely the civil rights–era witnessing of James Farmer, Anne Moody, Howell Raines, and many others has played a large role in establishing a contemporary version of the venerable tradition of the classic slave narratives, Washington's *Up from Slavery*, or Mary Chesnut or Sarah Morgan's Civil War diaries. Writers such as Reynolds Price, Maya Angelou, Albert Murray, and the many others collected in anthologies such as *A World Unsuspected* continue to write in this genre. Fiction itself has adapted this mode in make-believe memoirs, such as Gaines's memorable *Autobiography of Miss Jane Pittman*, or Allan Gurganus's best-seller, *Oldest Living Confederate Widow Tells All*. We can hardly speculate about the future of these traditions without meditating at length on their origins.

Dave Smith's musings over the problem of defining a "southern poet" rehearses many of the issues raised here by his fellow versifiers, James Applewhite, Fred Chappell, Kate Daniels, and Brenda Marie Osbey. But Smith also profitably zeroes in on a kind of "attitude of obligation, of piety, of something like a sacred respect" that one indeed notices both in the poems of this group and in their pronouncements about those poems.

Problems and Prospects in Southern Letters

This discussion would be incomplete without word of some exciting developments in southern letters that complement the suggestions of the writers in this volume. Jefferson Humphries's ongoing task of employing contemporary, frequently European criticism toward a rereading of southern letters is by no means unique. The dynamic Society for the Study of Southern Literature's bulging and informative newsletters offer eloquent testimony to the exciting new approaches to the field now being mounted by feminists, African-Americanists, Marxists, Hispanic-Americanists, deconstructionists, postcolonialists, and all other types of critics.

But much work remains to be done. Several essayists in this collection chide critics for neglecting Appalachian literature and culture. Someone should concurrently urge southernists to pay more attention to the South's French and Spanish legacies, especially the Cajun and Creole cultures in Louisiana. And then what about the new literature now being written by recent immigrants to the South from other countries such as Cuba, Vietnam, Haiti, and, more recently, China and India? Miami's scintillating Little Havana has already produced some original new writers, such as Virgil Suarez, and the Hispanic-American Renaissance in Texas, typified by the writing of Rolando Hinojosa, has been thriving for some time. More is sure to come as other groups coalesce and find their "southern" voice. One preliminary effect has been the Pulitzer Prize–winning novel *A Good Scent from a Strange Mountain*, by Louisiana's Robert Olen Butler, a group of stories centering on Vietnamese Americans on the Gulf Coast. Surely this community will be speaking in its own voice shortly, and we will need critics who know how to properly hear it and integrate it with the broader dialogic of the region.

These "emerging southerners," after all, are undergoing a more severe form of the "future shock" all southerners are experiencing, and all southern writers, regardless of their other affiliations, must come to grips with the literary traditions of the past that continue to inform and influence the future. As I have suggested, this has meant rethinking and reinventing all the subgenres of southern writing, including the historical novel, a subgenre explored by Rita Mae Brown, Ernest Gaines, Alice Walker, and others. This too is nothing new; as Mikhail Bakhtin usefully tells us,

> Every age re-accentuates in its own way the works of its most immediate past. The historical life of classic works is in fact the uninterrupted process of their social and ideological re-accentuation. Thanks to the intentional potential embedded in them, such works have proved capable of uncovering in each era and against ever new dialogizing backgrounds ever newer aspects of meaning; their semantic content literally continues to grow, to further create out of itself. Likewise their influence on subsequent creative works inevitably includes re-accentuation. New images in literature are very often created through a re-accentuation of old images, by translating them from one accentual register to another (from the comic plane to the tragic, for instance, or the other way around). (Bakhtin 421)

Richard Wright, in detailing the development of an authentic and southern African-American voice, affirmed the validity of Bakhtin's observation in a particular sense—that of liberation:

> We stole words from the grudging lips of the Lords of the Land, who did not want us to know too many of them or their meaning. And we charged this meager horde of stolen sounds with all the emotions and longings we had; we proceeded to build our language in inflections of voice, through tonal variety, by hurried speech, in honeyed drawls, by rolling our eyes, by flourishing our hands, by assigning to common, simple words new meanings, meanings which enable us to speak of revolt in the actual presence of the Lords of the Land without their being aware! Our secret language extended our understanding of what slavery meant and gave us the freedom to speak to our brothers in captivity; we polished our new words, caressed them, gave them new shape and color, a new order and tempo, until, though they were the words of the Lords of the Land, they became *our* words, *our* language. (Wright 40)

In another passage, Wright suggested that this process demanded of African-American southerners the qualities always exacted of "mighty artists." I do not wish to subtract one iota from the specificity this observation must continue to have in relation to the struggles of African-Americans; but the broader ramifications of dealing with a view imposed from outside a culture has been a problem for *all* southerners for some time now. Secondly, Wright's reference to "mighty artists" powerfully indicates the connection he sees between aesthetics and ideology. Many southern critics—most notably the Fugitives, but including many critics writing today—have denied this link. It is time, though, for this artificial barrier to come down.

This book attempts to demonstrate our own time's attempt to reaccentuate our traditions, while simultaneously building our own language and literature to fit today's needs and realities. Thankfully, the walls separating southerners from one another have been tumbling down; those that remain may be breached, paradoxically, by embracing each other's "secret language," by learning to listen on *all* the broadcasting frequencies. Our writers have preceded us in this endeavor; one of the things this collection proves is that southern writers read each other avidly and appreciatively. No "Melville never meeting Whitman" here. Praise gets heaped on quite a number of writers we weren't able to corral for this gathering, such as Lewis Nordan, Reynolds Price, Anne Tyler, Clyde Edgerton, James Alan McPherson, Louis Rubin, Cormac McCarthy, Robert Morgan, Ernest Gaines, Cleanth Brooks, David Bottoms, Charles Wright, William Styron, Gayl Jones, Willie Morris, Alice Walker, Barry Hannah, Bobbie Ann Mason, Lewis Simpson, and, especially often, Lee Smith, whose work places her in several camps.

What do writers look for in their peers? No doubt sheer pleasure and wonder lead the list, but they also find warnings of things to come, things hidden, things festering, that may be just beneath the surface of their own work as well. Writers prophesy to each other as well as to their general readers.

During his first presidential campaign, Jimmy Carter sounded a refrain that he had utilized frequently during his dynamic stint as governor of Georgia: namely, that the passage of the Civil Rights Act in the 1960s was the greatest thing that had ever happened to the South. Equally dramatic change followed as the nation experienced its first military defeat in Vietnam, bringing it in line with the South, which until then had labored under the heavy penumbra of a civil war that in many ways should have been forgotten. "The defeated South," already flexing its Sunbelt power, was now part of a "defeated" nation. As James Applewhite remarks in this volume, "Much tragedy is encoded, for the South and for the nation, in that allegiance beyond logic, beyond reason."

And now in the 1990s, with another southern president in the White House, with African-American mayors in place in most large southern cities, and a woman newly elected in her own right to the Senate from Texas (which already, like Kentucky before it, had elected a woman governor), the South, relocating its mythical allegiances, indeed sets many standards for the nation to follow. A space-age Atlanta—presided over by Ted and Jane, the postmodern Rhett and Scarlett—prepares to host the Olympics. Florida's boom into the power-state category was only slightly slowed by Hurricane Andrew. Southern-hatched crazes have swept the nation, including Cabbage Patch dolls, the mania for Arkansas-born Wal-Mart, and the appetite for Cajun and Tex-Mex food, Vidalia onions, and pickled okra. Nashville has become the nation's music and recording center, for southern music—gospel, jazz, blues, rock and roll, bluegrass, zydeco, country—has surely become not only America's only unique cultural product but the music of the sphere itself.

And yet the proud new cities also harbor the homeless; newly affluent citizens may well be drug addicts, alcoholics, philanderers, and worse. Environmental and governmental scandals proliferate, and oil busts, plant closings, urban blight, and substandard schools continue to breed tragedies worth writing about. The news from the New New South isn't all good. But whatever the story, the South's special trappings give it a unique appeal and an opportunity to mount messages of national concern through compelling regional metaphor and narrative.

For despite the oft-bemoaned homogenization of the nation, the South continues to have a special identity quite apart from the rest of the nation, even when that identity sometimes seems just as different from the South's own past. To choose only one of many subjects, today, as much as ever, change, loss, and an effort to limn the contours of a vanishing world appear to be vital impulses for many southern writers. The difference lies in the subjects "lost": not just the old plantation but also the plantation quarters (Ernest Gaines); not just the isolation of the mountains but also their crafts and customs (Lee Smith); not just Old New Orleans but also its decency and honor (Nancy Lemann). And charting a world of loss, of course, goes all the way back to George Washington Cable, William Faulkner, Jean Toomer, and Katherine Anne Porter, to name but a few of our elegists. No doubt we (or more likely, our grandchildren) will someday hear about the vanished world of Houston's fabled Galleria, or Miami's Fontainebleu, or Charlotte's Coliseum.

To take this subject of loss to a broader dimension: if Fred Hobson is right that a certain power has been lost in southern letters, is that because the old agonies of the South—particularly those connected with race—have somewhat abated? Or is it merely that what used to be seen as local tragedy has passed into the realm of the nation? To put a more positive interpretation on it, perhaps southerners have at long last accepted what Richard Wright asserted long ago, in an utterance that has even more relevance to southerners in particular than to Americans as a whole: "The differences between black folk and white folk are not blood or color, and the ties that bind us are deeper than those that separate us. The common road of hope which we all have traveled has brought us into a stronger kinship than any words, laws, or legal claims" (Wright 146). As other barriers that divide us to continue to fall, and as long as our writers continue to travel this road of hope and to see the South as both a legacy and a challenge, there will always be a future for southern letters.

Works Cited

Bakhtin, Mikhail. *The Dialogic Imagination*. Ed. Michael Holquist. Trans. Caryl Emerson and Michael Holquist. Austin: U of Texas P, 1981.

Hobson, Fred C. *The Southern Writer in the Postmodern World*. Athens: U of Georgia P, 1991.

Wright, Richard. *Twelve Million Black Voices*. 1941; rpt. New York: Thunder's Mouth P, 1988.

1

JAMES APPLEWHITE

Southern Writing and
the Problem of the Father

My ideas about the future of southern writing are intimately bound up with certain qualities it has had in the past, as a result of its origins in a region with a particularly determining history. In order to forecast the future, I shall have to delve rather extensively into this past. I will begin by clarifying remarks about earlier twentieth-century southern poetry that I put forward in "The Poet at Home in the South" (*The Southern Review and Modern Literature* 1935–1985, Louisiana State University Press, 1988). Dave Smith, in his essay in the present volume, questions whether there *is* any recognizable distinctiveness among the poets I and others have treated as southern. I will respond to issues he raises.

At the heart of my earlier definition was the paradox I had felt in southern poetry from about the time of John Crowe Ransom and Allen Tate through the earlier James Dickey: that the enormous intelligence of such work was expressed largely in aesthetic terms, through the fused elements of irony, or narrative implication, and rhythm and musicality and formal invention. It was a mix that seemed to me analogous to the more extreme version one finds in Edgar Allan Poe, wherein the atmosphere surrounding the death of a beautiful woman was rendered with the most elaborate aesthetic calculation. I tried to locate this paradox of highly sophisticated artistic craft in the service of primordial, diffused (or atmospheric), predominantly emotional motives—hardly *ideas*—in a geographical region given to atavistic blood allegiances and to rhetoric in defense of indefensible causes.

The southern writer has struggled with a fuller and more boisterous attic or cellar of demons than is the average elsewhere, and these psychic entities have been not only the ghosts of idiosyncratic relatives or neighbors but also the products of unique historical circumstances. The emotional sweep of southern rhetoric, whether of the pulpit or of politics (and have the two ever been entirely separate in the South?), derived partly from the inarticulate, agonizing justification by place-possession—possessing place, being possessed by place—and by blood-lineages, by a deeply felt identity, by common suffering, all in the service of a *cause*, a way of life, that the rest of the nation could not, or would not, understand. Southerners could not explain their place, their style of living, could not mount a reasoned, analytic defense of it, because it was founded initially on slavery, then on an agrarian economy (in my region, one based on tobacco) that itself was identified with a continuing politics of race. In the older days, which continued even into the time of my own earlier experiences, southerners felt themselves good people, deeply justified by inhabitancy of a land holding generations of familial graveyards, but found themselves faced with the scorn and moral superiority of the rest of the nation. They could not answer the unanswerable question.

Their words therefore required an emotional, perhaps mystical, sweep and power. The small southern church (perhaps "tabernacle"), or the hamlet ("Mt. Gilead," "Troy," "Ebenezer"), might be justified by connection with earlier places of covenant. A country crossroads with white clapboard steeple might be named Mt. Sinai. I remember, as a child, deeply identifying with the struggles of a chosen people through a wilderness, toward a final preordained home soil. The preacher's words evoked the blazing flat fields of tobacco—paradoxically, both wilderness of trial and Promised Land. The fury of tobacco harvest led through each season of struggle to white, strict houses secure again in the shadow of oaks, with well and packhouse beside. The southerner simply *thought* in metaphoric, scriptural terms. "Land 'o Goshen," they'd say—Goshen being Egypt, place of captivity and release.

Politically, the Huey Long–Willie Stark appeal to a transcendental identification between articulating speaker and inarticulate masses produced a similar irrational and emotional rhetoric. The giving of voice to a downtrodden, furious or apathetic, long-denied people was an act far more atavistic than conventional politics. It carried religious overtones, saying, "In me will you be justified." It is operative today, released into the national arena in the coded racial politics of Jesse Helms and others.

But why do I characterize this southern predilection for a mythologized male leader as the problem of the father? It is partly because of the effect this overly idealized, and thus rigidified, pattern of leadership and fatherhood from the past has had on the present—on sons. These are the words of a Confederate soldier preserved at Appomattox Court House: "Appomattox and Gethsemane will always mean the same thing to me." The view of General Lee as a figure sacrificed in a tragically fated losing cause was apparently not the invention of Donald Davidson in his "Lee in the Mountains." But Davidson's poem constitutes one of the paradigmatic literary expressions of the Christlike southern leader and father figure, who is to be revered and admired from a distance, but whose status in extreme honor and defeat puts him almost beyond the bounds of ordinary human interaction. Perhaps because the honor of one so brilliant yet so defeated is especially fragile, Lee must be treated in hushed tones, as an icon, rather than as a real man. This is, of course, a very bad pattern for father-son relations. Psychologically, the Oedipal rival is given such unique circumstances—a role in a war as fabulous as that between the angels and God in *Paradise Lost*—and so religious an aura and justification as to be almost unavailable, too distant to allow any easy and healthy identification.

As Lee is seen walking the grounds of Washington College (later to be named Washington and Lee University) after the war, he is the subject of hushed commentary by the "boys"—who, in his shadow, will always be only boys. Lee must live out his remaining days, seeing his land "Ground by the heels of little men," waiting only for death, the final, soldierly "courier with his summons." Still he hears "the hoofbeats come and go and fade," waits for "a bugle call at dawn." He can leave only the consolation of "His might," who waits "Brooding within the certitude of time," an impossible, religious-secular justification in the figure of his own defeated, deified heroism, now at last in the mountains, a scriptural-sounding legacy (but not an available father) "Unto all generations of the faithful heart."

Allen Tate's great "Ode to the Confederate Dead" traces what is in effect the outcome for the later southern protagonist of this identity-fathering pattern of ancestral heroism in defeat. His narrator among the weathering stones and "inexhaustible bodies" (which feed the psyche as well as the grass "row after rich row") finds himself paralyzed, a victim of mute speculation, there next to such an "immoderate past": these demons that won't stay buried but rise again, an "inscrutable infantry," like a miasma up from the soil, to cloud imagination. No wonder that the catalogue of battle-names—Shiloh, Antietam, Malvern Hill, Bull Run—drowns the narrator's intellect in an overwhelming atmosphere.

> Lost in that orient of the thick-and-fast
> You will curse the setting sun.

Since this primordial Fall, this original sin of identity-engendering war, time has been both powerfully present and suspended. The reference to Zeno and Parmenides reinforces the paradox of this place of arrested conflagration, of dynamic stasis. The narrator is smothered, "a mummy, in time," and seems to himself almost underwater, as he feels the leaching, incremental, seasonal drift of the dead soldiers—as "the salt of their blood / Stiffens the saltier oblivion of the sea."

Tate's modern southerner is left in historic circumstances wherein he can only replay in imagination the earlier, definitive events of the Civil War. Just as a son suffering the diminishment of a powerful, unresolved Oedipal complex can only fantasize successful rivalries with the seemingly all-powerful father, so can this protagonist only reanimate the echoes of earlier poems, from Milton's elegiac, pastoral voice in "Lycidas," to Coleridge's lament for lost inspiration in his own "Dejection: An Ode," to Prufrock's paralysis in T. S. Eliot's "Love Song." But he feels himself quite unable to act. The power of these collective fathers is too great. Their historical moment is seen as unique, beyond rivalry. It can provide the material for the cycling repetition of elegiac memory, but not the basis for a successful life in the present. This is to say that the southern version of that classic, archetypal problem, the Oedipal conflict, is peculiarly conditioned in the South. The father (whether General Lee or some northern industrialist) cannot be rivaled. The contemporary southerner may meditate, furious and mute, like Quentin in Faulkner's *Sound and the Fury*. Or he may drive around in his big-wheeled pickup truck, Confederate battle flag on his bumper, rifle in his window-rack. He wants to fight the old war, but now he can only shoot rats at the Bibb County dump with David Bottoms.

Literary characters have been searching for their fathers since Telemachos in *The Odyssey*, as Joyce acknowledges, imitates, extends, and parodies in *Ulysses* — which was influential upon both the Faulkner of *The Sound and the Fury* and the Wolfe of *Look Homeward, Angel*. Among the world's most Oedipal novels, one would have also to include Goethe's *Sorrows of Young Werther*; and certainly, in American literature outside the South, the problem of the unsatisfactory father has been acute. One thinks of Whitman's father as portrayed in "There Was a Child Went Forth": "strong, self-sufficient, manly, mean, anger'd, unjust; / The blow, the quick loud word." Huck Finn's father, also, bequeathed him no firm ego-identification, leaving him free to raft the river with Jim and to enter others' lives. Hart Crane's hobos in *The Bridge*, "ranged in nomad raillery" behind his father's cannery, are vehicles of identification alternative to the successful businessman, and they take the poet's vision with them on their travels across the continent, finally to join the Mississippi, like Huck:

> *Down, down — born pioneers in time's despite,*
> *Grimed tributaries to an ancient flow —*
> *They win no frontier by their wayward plight,*
> *But drift in stillness, as from Jordan's brow.*

In more recent American poetry, the motif of unsatisfactory fathers extends from the Prussian-seeming Otto of Theodore Roethke, through Lowell's pathetic, retired Commander, to the Nazi-seeming Otto of Sylvia Plath. There are echoes, or parallels, in Berryman and Kunitz. But the unsatisfactoriness of the southern father or father-figure is of a peculiar sort and is to be found most paradigmatically in Faulkner. The short story "Barn Burning," for example, shows us the plight of young Sartoris Snopes in relation to a father whose enemies are passionately, pathetically his own enemies, because of the call of blood, but a father whose actions in defending his vicious dignity are utterly incomprehensible to the son, part of the furious past that has partly crippled this man (though he was not fighting for either side) — which helps make him a figure cut out of tin, his stiff foot coming down on porch boards and de Spain rug with ruthless, mechanical regularity. The point of this mechanical-man symbolism is, I think, that Sartoris Snopes's father has been wound up clock-like by his historical circumstances and cannot deviate from his determined course, even if it leads (as it does) to tragedy.

But it is *The Sound and the Fury* that represents most radically a vision of the present as almost entirely emptied of its own content by the past, and doomed to a diminished repetition of what has already occurred. And this is also Faulkner's most brilliantly atmospheric novel. The humid honeysuckle scent of Quentin's section is pure psychological miasma, like "that orient of the thick-and-fast" which blurs the narrator's vision in "Ode to the Confederate Dead." Benjy, Quentin and, in his own way, Jason spend their days on June 7, 1910, and the Easter weekend of 1928, reliving events from their childhood — events centered around their sister Caddy's loss of virginity. This was a definitive, damning Fall for all four children of the house of Compson, because it occurred in the context of a former, definitive Fall: that of the Old South. History, for people like this, has already been lost, and only an attempt to deny time, to cling to the illusory stasis of childhood, seems to hold hope. Ironically, it is Benjy the idiot, castrated, who can most "successfully" live in the past of a virgin Caddy. But even he must suffer her smell-marked loss (prefigured by perfume) over and over.

The Compson brothers' enclosure within an overwhelming atmosphere represents this psychological entrapment within a family romance wherein the mother has been replaced by sister as erotic center, and the forbidding father's prohibitions have become more metaphysical than sensual. Quentin's erotic rival is a fatherlike Dalton Ames, who can lift Caddy with one arm as a parent can a child, and who physically defeats Quentin with crushing ease. But it is Father who bequeaths to Quentin the watch and the symbolic burden of Time. Given what seems the fated fall of Caddy, Quentin can only move from immersion in honeysuckle smell and the drizzling atmosphere near Caddy, wet from the branch, to further immersion in the river where he drowns. Caught in the unconsciousness of regressive, obsessive memory, he can only go deeper into it. He has inherited a time without an *is* or *will be*. Everything important *was*. Any consideration of the future of southern writing must take note of how powerfully the historic forces in earlier poems and stories and novels have denied characters a future.

The best explanation of Quentin's despair comes in his last remembered dialogue with Father. He is attempting to convince Father that Caddy's "disgrace" and coming marriage to the ungentlemanly Herbert Head is a meaningful disaster, to which he will react definitively. Father is attempting to convince Quentin that it all means nothing, that Caddy's loss and Quentin's lie (that he was the seducer) is "a piece of natural human folly." But Father goes beyond a comforting naturalism, into a nihilism that sees man as contending with a "dark diceman" to whom one's "despair or remorse or bereavement is not particularly important." Father's vision of the meaninglessness of events is significantly connected to both Christianity and history in the following passage:

> Father was teaching us that all men are just accumulations dolls stuffed with sawdust swept up from the trash heaps where all previous dolls had been thrown away the sawdust flowing from what wound in what side that

not for me died not. It used to be I thought of death as a man something like Grandfather a friend of his a kind of private and particular friend like we used to think of Grandfather's desk not to touch it not even to talk loud in the room where it was I always thought of them as being together somewhere all the time waiting for old Colonel Sartoris to come down and sit with them waiting on a high place beyond cedar trees Colonel Sartoris was on a still higher place looking out across at something and they were waiting for him to get done looking at it and come down Grandfather wore his uniform and we could hear the murmur of their voices from beyond the cedars they were always talking and Grandfather was always right.

Need I tell anyone that this was a Confederate uniform, that he was always right (justified) because he was in the war, that he and Colonel Sartoris (ironic namesake of young Snopes in "Barn Burning"), together with death, formed a mystic and noble company, which Quentin sees himself able to join only by drowning? With a genetic father whom events have diminished in power and authority (only one of the sawdust dolls of history), paternal resonance tends to be removed into more distant, grandfatherly, partly mythological figures.

A complex dynamic of fatherly availability/unavailability is at work in both earlier and more recent southern poetry as well as prose. It is this distanced relation to a mythologized progenitor-figure, rather than the imperfect accessibility of "an older Southern Scene," that accounts for the "hieratic representations of fathers, mothers, and grandparents" in the James Justus article Dave Smith refers to in his "Snipe Hunt" essay. It works both ways: the unsatisfactory nature of the history-diminished genetic father has cast emphasis on grandfatherly figures; and grandfatherly figures, in their inevitable distance, represent that absence of full human presence implicit in the excessive demands that this quasi-religious southern father-role imposes on any real human being. Even *Lee's* father was distant, as Davidson portrays him:

> *I can hardly remember my father's look, I cannot*
> *Answer his voice as he calls farewell in the misty*
> *Mounting where riders gather at gates* . . . .

Having his father's hand snatched away by history, "a wraith out of blowing mist," Lee made a vow beside his "Lone grave"—the vow that fated him to his heroic, tragic defense of a cause in which he did not believe, for a land that had claimed him by an allegiance too profound and mysterious to bear examination. Much tragedy is encoded, for the South and for the nation, in that allegiance beyond logic, beyond reason—beyond all words but those of certain emotive sacred texts, scriptural and poetic.

Dave Smith sees the conclusion of my earlier essay, a glimpse of southern university campuses among the kudzu, pines, used-car lots, and fundamentalist churches, as a definition of the southern poet: in his words, "a Romantic one." I must protest a misreading here, a distortion of the larger context of my essay. The earlier attempt to formulate a central quality in southern poetry was actually my explanation of the remarkable fit between modernism and the Fugitive group of poets, from Ransom to Jarrell. The management of profoundly irrational subject matter by a highly rationalized technical innovation and formal order is an artistic paradox as applicable to Eliot, Joyce, Picasso, and Stravinsky as to Ransom and Tate. This is why the first great southern poet, Poe, as filtered through the French Symbolists, was an important influence on twentieth-century poetry.

If there was any implicit definition for a continuing southern poetic in my dual vision of vine-tangled landscape and university towers, it was of a continued union between intellectuality of aesthetic approach and the inevitably irrational inheritance of subject and tone. Those are also the components of the modernist synthesis, as I see them. I do not mean to assert that southern poetry should (or will) continue in the earlier modernist stance, however. What *is* important, I think, is to understand what earlier southern modernism was, how it was altered by succeeding generations of poets, and what these changes imply for the current situation. The classically trained, ironic, formally perfect Fugitives make a set of literary fathers about as distant from the current generations of southern writers as General Lee, Colonel Sartoris, and the bodies in the Civil War graveyard were from Davidson, Faulkner, Tate, and their brethren. Yet even as these writers reached across a gulf of difference and oblivion to recapture a pattern of identity essential to their art, so have later southern poets stretched out across the lapse of time and change to incorporate aspects of these literary progenitors and their characteristic themes. The most important of those later writers may be identified in part by their ability to incorporate aspects of the earlier stylistic identities in an individuality specific to their times.

In poetry, aspects of the old, repressed southern romanticism (oh novels by Walter Scott, oh gallant horsemen and warfare) come back after World War Two, transformed, in the work of James Dickey. Dickey's relation to the Fugitive heritage is complex. He studied at Vanderbilt after the war, with, among others, Monroe Spears. His poems are often formal and stanzaic, yet he hardly ever rhymes, and his personae and subjects are dynamic, unqualified by Ransomesque irony. Just as the Confederate hero-image was undercut for the Fugitives by an almost unbridgeable distance of time and circumstance, so was the modernist southern protagonist hampered by a Hamlet-Eliot surplus of thought, of self-consciousness, like that of the narrator of Tate's graveyard ode. The progressive dismemberment of Ransom's Captain Carpenter is in part a trope for this self-dissection by intellectual analysis. But Dickey, who had participated in another big war, and on the winning side, is able to step back over this mock epic diminution to reassume new versions of older southern roles. And Dickey's reanimation of heroic feeling and action is sometimes associated with a successful father-quest.

In "Hunting Civil War Relics at Nimblewill Creek," the protagonist and his brother use a metal detector to bring alive again the intensities of a Civil War battle through the magnetic resonances of shrapnel, bullets, dishes, and other buried fragments. The narrator at the end falls on his knees in a quasi-prayerful posture of digging for a past, an enabling history. He sees himself there,

> *Like a man who renounces war,*
> *Or one who shall lift up the past,*
> *Not breathing "Father,"*
> *At Nimblewill,*
> *But saying, "Fathers! Fathers!"*

Perhaps this ancestral, collective father in part provides solace for the inadequacies of the genetic parent, who in "The Hospital Window," the next poem in *Poems 1957–1967*, is seen as dying. Like the reach back over the merely social father in Peter Taylor's great story "In the Miro District" to a historic grandfather who was actually *in* the Civil War, Dickey goes over the head of the merely living, limited man to a collective image (in "Nimblewill") or to a religious apotheosis (in "The Hospital Window"). The latter poem begins with the divine father-son suggestion of "I have just come down from my father" and ends on the vision of the dying man's face made a kind of saintly icon "in the pale, / Drained, otherworldly, stricken, / Created hue of stained glass." Thus the earlier southern need to stretch out over an almost-unbridgeable gulf to the father continues in Dickey but is subtly modified. The dying man in "The Hospital Window" is *there* as fallible human: weak, propped up, finally waving to his son from the pure edge of the beyond. And in the wonderful poem "The Celebration," the protagonist follows his fully human parents through the midway of a carnival, seeing his father's "dog-eared cane," his mother's wrap "of exhausted weasels." The couple are made both mythic and approachable, as they walk and, finally, ride the Ferris wheel. The speaker understands "the whirling impulse / From which I had been born," the transcendent biological continuity in its decay and yet continuity of possession, as he becomes, on Lakewood Midway, "In five strides a kind of loving, / A mortal, a dutiful son." The carnival wheel is biology, inheritance, and also the biblical "wheel in the middle of the air."

I have narrowed the subject of southern poetry to the theme of place and its past, to partially dispossessed sons and their need of fathers. Thus I have excluded from consideration the great womanly lineage in southern literature, which runs from Caroline Gordon, Katherine Anne Porter, Eudora Welty, Flannery O'Connor, and Elizabeth Spencer through Doris Betts, Lee Smith, Bobbie Ann Mason, and Josephine Humphreys. I have not mentioned the greatness of Zora Neale Hurston and Alice Walker. I have not mentioned Betty Adcock and Ellen Bryant Voight. My exclusions must be forgiven as the price of my focus on an obsessive theme.

I believe that the southern poetry (or any poetry) which gives up too completely its acknowledged dependence on a technical mastery founded in an assimilation of key, progenitor texts is less resonant, less profound, than that which reads as from engraved stones rooted in the multilayered soil of a history

that is enigmatic, sometimes alien and alienating, but essential. This is one reason that Fred Chappell, for example, is finally so much better than poets whom
he may superficially resemble. His own progenitor-quest has led him through
texts from Dante to Goethe to Borges. "Forever Mountain" of *Source*, as it sees
his own father after death on some "Pisgah slope," is a poignant tribute to the
dead parent but also a paradigm of that sense "of obligation, of piety" Dave
Smith finds in southern writing. The following lines would be as true for the
living poet, practicing his art, as for the father after death:

> He is alone, except what voices out of time
> Come to his head like bees to the bee-tree crown,
> The voices of former life indistinct as heat.

For the writer, this "former life" may reside not in personal memory but in
the meanings others of our place and time have lived and inscribed. Chappell's
poems come to me with the force of recollection. He is presently engaged, like
Jim Seay, Dave Smith, Betty Adcock, David Bottoms, and others, in a project
of living over again in language the memorable, unremembered South of our
parents and their parents, pushing toward a freshening originality that incor-
porates and changes old seasons like new rings in tree trunks. David Bottoms
has made a kind of paradigm of this continuing attempt to recover the not-
wholly-recoverable, in his poem "The Desk." He breaks into the old school
building and reenacts, in his violent removal of the carved desktop, the violent
sounds of World War Two battles — "of Savo Sound or Guadalcanal." Finally
he carries home the desktop his father had carved, and many of us must whisper with him, still, "I wonder what it means / to own my father's name."

If we see southern writing, in its earlier greatness, as a response to defeat,
deprivation, inherited racial injustice, and even, in a more specialized sense,
the partial unavailability of fathers to sons, we can hardly wish it simply to continue as before. The later writing that excites me, as I have implied, is that
which continues to encounter and assimilate the wounds of our history. But
this statement must be qualified. These wounds, as partially assimilated by
social development and earlier writing, are changed. Yet surely no one is so
optimistic as to think that they are gone.

The plasticising and pseudo-homogenization of the United States by the
cliché images and disposable products of popular culture may tend to disguise
the continued presence of our past among us, but it is still there. We may be
distracted from it, or made to disbelieve it, but it remains as much a demand-
ing pressure as the crisis in the environment, which we also manage to ignore
or disbelieve. Does anyone really think that the legacy of slavery has disappeared? Does anyone seriously hope that poverty, meanness, fanaticism in
implausible belief, atavistic blood-lineages producing both intense loyalty and
intense hate, paranoias of limited localities, and illiteracy have magically vanished? Some of the southern concerns have escaped into the national arena,
but they are as pressing as ever. Southern blacks, deprived of social and economic opportunity, took flight to northern cities, and now the old repressive

southern politics of race versus the hope for real freedom is played out nationally, in the radical distance between Jesse Helms and Jesse Jackson. Literary discussions of the South and southern poetry or southern writing sometimes say or seem to say things like this: "I think the South exists more in writing than anywhere else": (*Southern Poetry Symposium*, The Academy of American Poets, 1986). This strikes me as very odd.

The grandeur, the moral and spiritual dimension, of Faulkner, Welty, Ransom, and Tate resides in a human coming-to-terms-with-defeat, in moral and material terms: an acknowledgment of having been tragically, heroically *wrong*. Perhaps the nation shared this fall in self-esteem and moral self-conception following Vietnam. Certainly the nation is now sharing in the shame of racial prejudice. And certainly the Reagan-era politics of callousness, insensitivity, hypocrisy, and wishful thinking, together with the national penchant for disguising fearful realities under a wave of pop culture, have contributed to a distancing of the southern writer from her or his deep subject. But though the southern writer is now less isolated within these concerns, which the nation to some extent now shares, and though there are new impediments to a compelling involvement with the old legacies in their new forms, the writer is not therefore absolved of her or his responsibility to encounter again and yet again, in language, those earlier tragedies, inequities, and losses, which urge the further completion of the uncreated conscience of this place.

To specify my own hopes in respect to the theme of the father, let me broaden the paradigm to include what is only an impression of the older father-legacy, but one imprinted over a lifetime in the South. Briefly, the post–Civil War white male, in a position of authority, seemed to feel an almost crushing responsibility. He felt himself partly impotent, hemmed round by partial knowledge and by known or potential foes. He felt he had to protect his land, his family, his community against forces of moral and financial chaos. He became a tyrant, a dispenser of Truth and Order as he saw it. The more aristocratic version of this figure is consummately portrayed by George Carver, the narrator's all-powerful father, in Peter Taylor's *Summons to Memphis*. This powerful male treated women as children, children as dumb animals, and blacks as a separate species. His racism and sexism were automatic, part of a patriarchal stance of responsibility that sought to uphold an intuitive "righteousness," in the image of the Old Testament Father, against a social and even natural order that threatened to return to precreation chaos.

My hope for the future is that this distanced, forbidding father, not given to discussion, more likely to deliver thunderbolt proclamations than helpful concern, may be resocialized, through a progressive understanding founded in the movements for racial and sexual equality and in psychoanalytic theory and practice. This must—and will, I hope—occur in actual relationships and politics, as well as in poetry and fiction. The old quasi-divine, traumatically forbidding father was a crucial feature of earlier southern writing, providing something like the harsh, fierce, primordial fire-principle of Jacob Boehme, an electrical source giving these texts energy and tension. This southern father was most himself in the Civil War, a fiery hell out of which came the South after the Fall. The aboriginal, resisted, yet admired creator-out-of-fire, in all his irrationalism, was needed in order to father forth the design of events. He is still there in the mind of the South, brooding like lightning-potential within a cloud. His love is sharpened by hate; his cherished, sacred causes are surrounded by desecration and defilement. Davidson's General Lee heads a series of fathers forever mythologized beyond direct imitation by their stationing in a frieze of primal events—whether charges, retreats, red banners, defeated heroism, or hunts, epic journeys, endurances—beginning history as the southerner has known it. There fathers have fathered forth wooden, rhetorical, self-mythologizing fathers, and resentful, diminished sons—like Big Daddy and Brick in Tennessee Williams's *Cat on a Hot Tin Roof*. The real-life heir to this lineage carries his Confederate battle flag and rifle still, literally or mentally: opposes equal opportunity, abortion, Communism, any but a literalist reading of the Bible; voted for Reagan and Bush and will vote for Oliver North. The longed-for loving father has become, by the quirks of history, a tyrant within.

It is much to hope for that we should be able to extract from this source, which Boehme calls sour as well as fiery, a principle like his sweet light. But literature needs its ideal goals, and this is mine. I know that tobacco is still being raised, blacks despised, women and children abused, in fields near moccasin-infested pocosins in eastern North Carolina. I know men whose fanatical eyes, still, convince me they would have faced the grapeshot from Cemetery Ridge.

The South has not gone away and is not likely to. Though its fertility has been partly poisoned by pollution, or paved over by shopping centers, nevertheless, a poisonous fecundity sealed away from direct observation, festering underground, was always its characteristic source-principle for the writer. Southern writing is certainly possible still, for the ones given to an excavation below the paved, illusory surface, into the still-violent reservoir of our land's historically conditioned unconsciousness. Greater psychological insight, the conscious, explicit handling of the historically intensified Oedipal tragedy—as in Warren's *All the King's Men*, the poetry of Randall Jarrell (especially *The Lost World*), and, more recently, Peter Taylor's *Summons to Memphis*—seems to me an inevitable, necessary line of development, at least for the white male southern writer. I recognize and admire this direction in the work of Fred Chappell and David Bottoms. I find Dave Smith one of the more powerful of that generation of poets who, born in the South, have escaped the earlier bondage to its obsessions, and who retain as marks of their southern identity only an occasional choice of material, and an intensity of presentation, aural and imagistic, which renders the objects of their attention with hypnotic palpability.

As I imagine the future of southern writing, I see poems, stories, novels, and essays that use a more explicit psychological insight, to come to terms more directly with the region's historic burden and the related legacy of anger. Maybe younger writers will be able to approach their genetic and literary fathers more openly, in hope of a more human contact. The mythologized giants, those like

General Lee and William Faulkner, have become, if not archaic, at least so much a part of legend that to repeat their names and stories now has about it a quaint sense of ritual obligation. As in a religious catechism, we may hear the murmur of the words without attending to the meanings.

Southern writing needs to get beyond the stereotypes to the realities, the motivating causes. Southerners, including southern writers, have been, often still are, very angry people. Their allegiance to the region is in part the bondage of an unassimilated rage. We don't hate the South . . . yet we do, in a sense. And whether we quite realize it or not, it is partly because of this preponderance of the past over the present. The prominence of an enveloping, affect-laden atmosphere in southern writing is, in psychological terms, a projected, unacknowledged love-rage suffusing the vision. The entombments, the claustrophobias, began with Poe. The Gothic houses holding forbidden emotional attachments, buried and unburied corpses—these houses of regressive emotion and incest typify a region unable to escape its traumatic history and therefore unable to progress into a usable present and future. The southern grotesques, the outrageousness, the bondages of feeling, and the harrowing intensities, even the humor, are founded in a trauma of origin buried in the region's mind like the corpse of Miss Emily Grierson's lover. These paradigmatic tropes of southern writing in the past predict a difficulty for the future. The South and its writers can no longer afford to live in the past, but neither can they ignore a still-unassimilated legacy.

It is time for the South to face its history like a patient in analysis. For that to happen, its writers must be clearer-eyed, free of miasma—one form of which is nostalgia. The South needs a healing understanding of its past and a concomitant ability to live on a human scale, without its habitual outrage and violence, whether physical or of rhetorical excess. The male South needs to face its collective Oedipal complex, its arrested emotional state wherein writers elaborate their bondage to resonances of swamp-mist, woodland vapor, and honeysuckle scent of sisterly bodies: those maternal surrogates. It needs to disavow through understanding the hollow lost leaders, those larger-than-life, hieratic fathers who once led it to a crushing defeat disguised as a moral victory. The southern aesthetic, I predict, will replace blind passion and obsession with intelligence and adaptability.

The South's distinctive story won't disappear. But if it is to be useful to the nation, it must be told differently. Southerners on TV and in the movies are still clichés—Dukes of Hazzard and burly state troopers and colonels of fried chicken. This is in part the result of literary perpetuation of southern typology, without an analysis that might permit understanding. But progress has been made. We have seen how African-American eyes saw the tragedy. Writers like Randall Kenan extend the work begun by Zora Neale Hurston and Alice Walker. We are realizing, I think, how the guilt is historic, widely shared, and a continuing stigma only if the originating attitudes and inequities are continued.

Southern males will adopt new role models: intelligent men, thinkers, who don't still *need* defeat and anger. As a poet I feel myself drawn now to

William Wordsworth, William Carlos Williams, and Wallace Stevens. I greatly admire A. R. Ammons, who has escaped his eastern North Carolina farm past and who meditates in Ithaca, New York, blending biology, physics, and impressions of contemporary culture with his occasional flashes of recollections from the tobacco fields of his youth. I think the future of southern writing belongs to those who, like Ammons, can convert hurt to understanding, and who can see the limited space of the southern past as only one peculiar location on this blue planet suspended in space and time. If this location is as charged with venom as poison oak or moccasins, Ammons and others are successfully distilling the poison, transforming it. The understanding that comes out of a cloud and a confusion is worth more, somehow, than any purer meditation not motivated by pain. The pain we have in plenty. I hope that we have begun to understand it—that we can walk out one day into a home field and feel it *new*, breathing easily and seeing accurately through its clear atmosphere.

2

JACK BUTLER

Still Southern after All These Years

The question gets asked a lot. Let me phrase it like this: Is there still such a thing as southern writing, what with the New South and all, and technology? And if there is, what makes it southern?

I'm grateful for the question. The question has become a sort of small industry helping to ease regional unemployment. Answering the question brings in some useful if not life-changing checks, and it doesn't hurt your reputation, either. If you answer the question two or three times, you're an expert. In fact, if you think about it, answering the question is one of the things that infallibly identifies you as a southern writer. In fact, if you think about it some more, the question itself has served as a good way to keep southern writing going, at least as a panel topic. We question our existence, therefore we must exist. That's a nice modern way of addressing the issue, even if it does smack of how we tried to resolve the confusions created by our first philosophy class.

Suppose the answer to the question was no. No, there's not any such thing as southern literature anymore. Would we have to quit having conferences and seminars? Could anybody *make* us quit? Who could? The Jewish writers? Do *they* still exist? If so, they're disqualified from the judging. If anybody's going to make us quit talking about whether or not we exist, it will have to be a group that already for certain doesn't exist. The midwesterners, maybe. Or the minimalists. Or the thirty-something urban trend jockeys.

If we turn out not to exist, will I be forced to pay back the travel expenses I wrote off on my income taxes for going different places to answer the question?

Maybe in 100 to 150 years, someone is going to be raising the question of whether there's anything in American literature any more that can seriously be referred to as Vietnamese writing.

I have a shelf of books I call "the Local Group." The joke is that's what astronomers call Andromeda, the Milky Way, the Clouds of Magellan, and various other assorted objects within a radius of several million light-years. My

Local Group is not determinedly southern, and it is certainly not exhaustive. It is really more nearly those writers I have some strong association with. But scanning the shelf I find, mingling poetry and prose indiscriminately, James Applewhite, Madison Bell, D. C. Berry, Roy Blount, David Bottoms, Larry Brown, Hope Coulter, Harry Crews, Turner Cassity, Fred Chappell, James Dickey, Annie Dillard, R. H. W. Dillard, David Dooley, Ellen Douglas, Clyde Edgerton, Fannie Flagg, Shelby Foote, Richard Ford, Marcus Gandy, Ellen Gilchrist, Barry Hannah, Donald Harington, Bill Harrison, Skip Hays, Beth Henley, Rebecca Hill, Mary Hood, Larry Johnson, Donald Justice, Etheridge Knight. Yosef Komunyakaa, Everette Maddox, Bobbie Ann Mason, Michael McFee, Phil McMath, Willie Morris, Kay Murphy, Lewis Nordan, Gloria Norris, T. R. Pearson, Walker Percy, Reynolds Price, Charles Portis, John Fergus Ryan, Ferrol Sams, Valerie Sayers, Dave Smith, Frank Stanford, Steve Stern, Leon Stokesbury, Alice Walker, Larry Wells, Jim Whitehead, Miller Williams, Johnny Wink, C. D. Wright, and Al Young.

These writers are as different and maybe as distant each from each as the members of the astronomer's Local Group. You and I might argue their relative merits — some are good friends, and so I may be biased — but they are all well published and are all clearly, by some meaningful standard, southern.

I would suppose there are at least ten times as many worthy southern writers as I can produce with a quick glance at a limited library. Considering so great a host, I find it obvious that the real question is not the question of existence. There can be no doubt that there will be, for quite some time to come, a recognizably southern literature. So what is it that we are really talking about?

The real question is the question of description: Will we be able to *discuss* this literature, identify schools, chart developments, demonstrate theses? Or will we gaze upon a realm so vast, so nonhomogenous, so pluralistic that it cannot be usefully distinguished from the messy rest of America? Must we abandon review, criticism, theory, and dissertation, all those strategies by means of which the foolishness of a life spent scribbling can be at least partially and meagerly made to produce income and a social niche, however inglorious? What summaries can we make, oh what conclusions draw?

This question has a different value for writers than it has for scholars and critics. The scholars map the coastline. The writers *are* the coastline, which continually changes shape, and on closer resolution shows finer and crazier variation. The map says *something*, the map is useful, but the place where the sea comes battering in is always beyond the map.

Metaphors, too, are maps, and this one threatens to turn sodden and come apart in my hands. The coastline, after all, doesn't study the map of the coastline, but writers do pay attention to discussions of literature, to charts of literary movements, and to theses based on perceived regional similarities. Therein lies a danger: The descriptive question, so vital to scholars and critics, can be preemptive for writers.

The best to be hoped for when a writer asks herself such a question is that he will gain a sense of perspective, of scope, of relation: a needed, if fragile awareness of community. The danger is the danger of internalizing the definitions, of allowing generalizations into the place from which the live particulars must come. It seems to me that all writing is a negotiation between what you have to write and what you are able to write. Assuming you have the ability, the trick is finding out what you need to write, which is often very different from what you think you ought to write. Write too much of what you think you ought to write, and you could wind up committing Art.

What is southern writing? Am I a southern writer? What kind of things should a southern writer write? Such thinking can amount to a sort of obnoxious feedback in the writer's mind, producing loud squeals and rips of meaningless sound, obscuring any clear and original message. Still, bring human, we continue to quiz ourselves in such ways, and to act on the answers we give.

Seeing ourselves as southern, we attempt to incorporate the old familiar definitions. We refer to Faulkner's Nobel assertion, the indomitability of the human spirit, as if that was more what his work was about than the comic and preposterous and horrible performances that call into question the very existence of such a spirit. Why didn't Uncle Bill talk about that side of his work? I guess you don't crack jokes to a bunch of people dressed like penguins and walking like them too, not when they have just elevated you above the mortal realm forever.

We refer, dammit, to Faulkner. To Flannery O'Connor. To Eudora Welty, still going strong. To Tennessee Ernie Ford. Sorry, I mean Williams. Of course what they did still counts as much as ever. Literature isn't science, we don't progress by irrefutable experiment, and old views are not invalidated. We can realize all that and still feel the modern imperative—don't repeat. Sure, we're modern. We're southern, but we're modern. Pursuing that modernity, it becomes easy to confuse the necessary novelty of being a new person with a brand-new voice, and the presumed novelty required to render the New New South.

In all the authors of our grand canon, we think of five things: We think of a place; we think of the darkness and splendor of families; we think of a way of talking; we think of the Bible; and we think of black and white locked into a mutual if inharmonious fate. These five elements made one, a recognizable world, a single defined realm against which we could distinguish human motivation with remarkable clarity. To use, even though literature isn't science, a couple of scientific metaphors, being a southern writer was like having some very clean and well-stained slides to put under your microscope; it was like receiving a radio signal with very little noise. The slides aren't clean anymore, and the background radiation of the rest of the universe seems to have gotten louder.

The essential character of the old definition, the force that bound its elements together, was its powerful association of locale and behavior. The locales still exist, though they are now dotted with satellite dishes and traversed by small Japanese or Korean four-wheel-drive pickups. The behavior still hovers recognizably near the old locales, and in recognizable relation to the old behaviors. Nobody in a shotgun shack in the Delta, the day after we took a giant leap for mankind, woke up suddenly free of old habits, old presumptions. If there is such a thing as history, it doesn't work that way. The future doesn't erase the past; it colonizes it. The day after that July day in 1969, Annabelle Latine Thomas shuffled out to hoe the tomatoes, and she said "Yessum Miz Cahter" when the woman she was weeding them for asked her to water the chickens too. It may have been that Latine and Mrs. Carter discussed those television images, comfortably and momentarily agreeing that the whole thing was a fraud and a fake, filmed right here on earth: Jesus don't want people walking on the moon. It's his, and he put it where we can't get to it. So must be the government and the TV people made it all up. They have sold themselves to the devil, and you can see it because of all this pornography and free love.

I do not see how we can afford to forget that there are murderers who have never come to trial walking the streets of the New South, some of them wearing old badges still.

The question for writers is how we are to observe these things, with what manner of awareness. An old fact that survives into a new context is a new fact. It can't be dismissed as irrelevant, it must not be handled as cliché. If the old locales and behaviors still exist, they are beginning to decouple. And further, the rate of the disassociation is increasing. But whenever writers get together to talk about the fate of southern writing, the rhetoric I hear still has largely to do with roots, the importance of place, and the story-telling tradition. As much as I like this sort of chat, as true as it may in some sense be, I must say that it is beginning to sound more and more like chamber-of-commerce releases.

(Not to be unfair to the chambers of commerce, some of whom are now smart enough to make literature a municipal resource: More and more writers are making luncheon speeches, declaiming *See, Oh See!* to the COC's.)

Place? It isn't that we don't *have* roots any more. There is still a unique continuity to the southern experience, and the least interesting fiction of all to me is that sort of fiction that seems to have as its sole purpose the exposing of the essential meaninglessness and vapidity of life. Oh, we have roots, all right. But what sort of roots? We have to go where the jobs are, just like anybody else. A lot of us grew up on farms, but we don't live on them now. They aren't there to live on, even if we wanted to, even if we could stand going back to a universe in which back issues of *Progressive Farmer* and the SBC's *Sunday School Magazine* filled the lacquered reading tables. And then there are the divorces: She moved to Atlanta and went into real estate, putting the kids in Montessori. You gave up and became a staff writer for the senator, moving to D.C., where you developed a real fondness for Ethiopian cuisine. We have roots, yes, but we have become like those plants that send rootlets out into the air: a sense of *places*, not a sense of place.

And so much for families, too. Our children are city kids. Christmas reunions are sequential—negotiated conferences of various feuding groups. A semester or so in drug rehabilitation isn't that strange an event in any family now. How gradually we welcome the partner in a new marriage, with what uncertainty that they will stay, that we will be seeing that same face ten years from now. Latine's granddaughter may be working on her doctorate in astrophysics, though if she is she has had to beat the educational odds. Does she come home to visit Meemaw? If she does, is she ashamed or proud? Do they argue? Does the granddaughter bring her live-in lover with her when she comes?

A way of talking? Listen to your television. Bad southern accents are everywhere. Once we could localize them to a few containable manifestations. Now the good old boys pick up expressions from *Designing Women*. The whole United States is talking more southern. Everybody's an expert, just as all stand-up comedians are born certain of their Yiddish. Even if it meant something to be able to identify a pure tone, who would be able to hear that tone? And suppose you were subtle enough and good enough to somehow get the very cadence of the corruption itself in your use of a corrupted dialect—who would be able to hear *that*?

The Bible. Somewhere between ten and fifteen years ago I realized that southern college freshmen no longer knew the Bible. If I spoke of bloodiness even in the wise, and instanced Solomon sending Benai, his priest-assassin, after his brother Adonijah, it was all news to them. I had done battle all my life with minds destroyed, as I saw it, by the narrow-gauge application of the scriptures, and suddenly here I was mourning those same scriptures. I might go so far as to say this has been the single most important change in southern culture, this loss of a standard fund of stories, a standard style of language. Our children have not learned science, as the slightest review of their academic records will demonstrate, but they exhibit all of the worst side effects of living in an age that considers itself scientific, including the comfortable assumption, with regard to our predecessors, that they wasn't as advanced as we are, and its parallel default, the sense that we're just too modern to need all those old Bible tales. The heck with Greco-Faulknerian mythology, we're losing our *own* myth. Babel is upon us, and the kids I say that to don't even know what I'm talking about.

What about race? Black and white do not exist in harmony now anywhere in the South, or anywhere else, for that matter. *America is Mississippi now*, Marcus Gandy says. *You don't think it is? You wrong.* There is as much hatred as ever, maybe more, since the infection is now systemic, like syphilis—outbreaks of horrible chancres everywhere. All this country needs is a severe depression and a couple of slick bad politicians to convincingly blame some minority group for said depression, and we could put the German death camps to shame. Any progress we have made toward equal justice we owe to law and not to basic human nature, except insofar as we come to accept what we see on television. But even there, has Bill Cosby made television black, or has television made Bill Cosby white?

In all of these areas, in terms of the new science of chaos, a critical limit has been passed, and a smooth flow has suddenly become turbulent. If we use locale and behavior as our phase-space coordinates, suddenly the graph is all over the place. Instead of a regular cycle, the so-called pendulum of society, we have a strange attractor indeed. Several strange attractors. Southern behavior owes less to any one locale, and more to all of them, and even more to the feedback I spoke of above: It picks up its own signals and amplifies itself. It, like the racial enmity that is so deeply a part of it, is spreading out. Mountains and croplands, West and South are blurring together. Hillbilly and redneck and cowboy grow more and more similar, goat-ropers all, all needing love too.

The fact that I see the processes described by a new science like chaos as a good metaphor for what is happening to southern culture is in itself probably a strong indicator of some of the things that are happening to southern culture. When the scientists say chaos, of course, they don't mean *chaos* chaos. They mean the study of structure of turbulence, of mixing. It may come as a surprise to us to think that turbulence has a structure. What is happening everywhere, and also in the South, is a very rapid mixing. Not that detail is lost, but the level of detail shows an increasingly fine grain.

One of the things this means to writers is that larger and larger amounts of energy are going to be required to establish background and character. Before, you had a lot of givens in the culture. You could shorthand some of the information and still get 3-D effects. It isn't that Flannery O'Connor didn't use supremely good details. But her details had the whole culture backing them up. The assumed society was the sounding chamber for her implications. If you try that now, the detail may seem antiquated or worse, clichéd. Write how some people still actually speak, and see if it doesn't make you groan and think of *Tobacco Road* or Elizabeth Taylor in *Cat on a Hot Tin Roof*. There's still a lot of sheriffs out there with cowboy hats, big fat bellies, and mirror shades, but try getting away with using one as a character. James Dickey was the last serious writer able to do that, and he probably only succeeded because he had so much temperamentally in common with the type. A southern author now must provide not only character but also the context in which that character is credible. The shopping malls, the trailer houses, the corporate offices, the frozen yogurt shops, the video racks in the country groceries. Before, a writer was measured by the fidelity of his rendering. Now she is measured by her ability to accumulate real-world details. There is a difference. The first is a gestural technique, instinct with movement. The second is additive. What is gained is perhaps a sort of freshness and vividness in the portrait. What is lost, perhaps the hardest loss of all, is resonance. Yes, I know that lately that word, overused, has gone out of fashion—see what I mean?—and I promise to use it only one or two more times in the entire rest of this essay.

So where are we, then? In all this welter of disassociation, are there patterns? In closing, I identify, for what it's worth, and with no motive more serious than whimsy, four strategies that modern southern writers use. Although there are no writers who fall completely and cleanly into any one of the categories implied by these strategies, there are a few who seem to illustrate them rather clearly. In one way or another, we seem to me to be conservators, updaters, deniers, and futurists.

The conservators want to hold onto the old resonance, the old clarity. Typically, they set their stories in the past, or they restrict the field of view sufficiently to minimize the effects of recent history, which usually means they choose small and somewhat isolated societies. If this sounds negative, I don't mean it that way. It's the depth you get to that counts, not how state-of-the-art your locales are. We are a long way from finishing the mining of our mutual past. Reynolds Price is something of a conservator, with perhaps an admixture of updating. A writer who seems to me to be among the giants of the conservators is Donald Harington, who, in novels like *The Architecture of the Arkansas Ozarks* and the recently released *The Cockroaches of Stay More*, has saved nearly an entire region, in speech, in manner, and in value. The conservators are not practicing ignorance of the modern world: In fact, they allow plenty of play between the present and the past they mostly write about. They aren't writing about the past as if they were still in it. Fred Chappell is a fine example, in poetry, of a conservator. Wendell Berry is a conservator so far gone he is almost off the scale, almost futuristic.

Bobbie Ann Mason is clearly an updater, and so are people like Clyde Edgerton and T. R. Pearson. For that matter, so is John Fergus Ryan. So is Larry Brown in *Facing the Music* and *Dirty Work*—so far, though lately he's making noises like a futurist. The updaters move us visibly forward from the old recognizable patterns into newer generations, trying to suggest why we have created the kind of New South we have, trying to show the almost genetic continuance of the tradition. Some of them perhaps regret the inadequacy of our current mythical resources, the way we have to struggle for significance, or simply enjoy the comedy of what we make of what we are. Many southern poets are updaters—Bottoms, Henry Taylor, Whitehead.

Richard Ford is our great denier. Although his first two books borrowed pretty heavily from southern types and southern speech, he has been steadily purifying himself away from influences, toward a sort of dispassion that Hemingway could only preach about and would doubtless envy. Richard will tell you flatly that he's not a southern writer. You get the feeling that he doesn't believe that there is any such thing as a southern writer. He doesn't much believe in characters, either, at least not in that mythopoetic way in which we declare how real our characters are, how we wept to see them suffer and die. Again, the term I've chosen may sound negative, but I don't mean it that way. The deniers are after something fundamental. They have to use the societies they know to get at it, but the societies themselves are not necessarily the point. Madison Bell, an updater in his most recent book, *Soldier's Joy*, was more nearly a denier in *Straight Cut* and *Zero Db*.

Barry Hannah is a futurist. So is Leon Stokesbury. I don't mean that they write science fiction. I mean that they live for style, for the scintillating edge of what a sentence can do. They do not seem to be worried so much about monitoring social change in the new world as about making certain that the instrument of perception always stays bright and clean. They are modern because they create never-before-seen relations. And yet I find both of them inescapably southern. Lewis Nordan, in his two splendid collections of short fiction, *Welcome to the Arrow-Catcher Fair* and *The All-Girl Football Team*, is the wildest futurist of all. I will take him as my final example, a happy way to conclude: Even when he appears to be rendering the small-town or backwoods Mississippi of decades ago, the boundaries of his creations waver like the edges of the *Twilight Zone*—strange music rises, things go invisibly surreal. In his hilarious and haunting stories, Nordan writes what many of us must now learn to try. He writes the Mississippi of the mind, not of the map.

3

RODGER CUNNINGHAM

Writing on the Cusp

Double Alterity and Minority
Discourse in Appalachia

In a very bad review of a very good book of short stories from West Virginia, Diane McWhorter of Birmingham, Alabama, wrote in the *New York Times Book Review*:

> [Pinckney] Benedict's characters are the new lost generation from the border states. Working the not-long-sodded subdivisions, his literary elders . . . gave us the first wave, a postrural sub-bourgeoisie. . . . Mr. Benedict's people are the skulls they see in their Sears mirrors; his turf is the dismal sludge underneath the cartoon strokes of Al Capp's Dogpatch. . . .
>
> On the cusp of two vital American cultures—the northerly one devoted to the making of money, the other to the making of myth—the border country has little of either. (13)

As I said in a letter in reply to this review:

> Come now. Can any group in this country other than Appalachian mountain people be subjected to this sort of ethnic slur by a national magazine in 1987?
>
> To be sure, you've laudably tried to have the book reviewed by a native of the same region. Alas—with the Steinberg map behind your eyelids, you've handed it over to a Deep Southerner who proceeds to air all her region's standard prejudices against what she self-revealingly calls "the border country." . . .
>
> The sad thing is that while "two vital American cultures" join hands over the presumably moribund form of "moonshine America" whenever something like this comes along to confirm their interlocking prejudices, the "national" literary world remains nearly unaware of the burgeoning of writing within the region in the past generation. There is an enormous amount of first-rate poetry and fiction by native Appalachians of all backgrounds which fits neither century-old convention—pastoral idyll or

degrading stereotype—but seldom is it reviewed in "national" publications unless . . . it lends itself to misunderstanding in stereotypical terms.[1]

McWhorter's review and my reply to it only scratch the surface of a complex and important phenomenon. It is a commonplace by now that the American South is defined by the North, or by "America" in general, as its Other. Indeed, North and South constitute themselves as each other's Other in a set of shared dichotomies with reversed valuations. There is, however, within America another Other—indeed, an Other's Other—a region marked by a double otherness that complicates its very sense of its own being and yet, by that very fact, opens up unusual possibilities for a self-articulation of being. This essay will explore both the dimensions of that otherness and some of the literary realizations of those possibilities.

To begin with, the editorial contexting of McWhorter's review also rewards a close look. In her opening paragraph, she writes: "Pinckney Benedict has screeched off the pastoral path of many young writers going back (not so terribly far) in mock innocence and is taking the reader on a hell ride across the hindmost gullies and hooch-sodden hills of an American inferno" (13). The first-page copywriter turns this all into: "Pinckney Benedict's turf is the dark side of Al Capp's Dogpatch. In 'Town Smokes,' the 23-year-old West Virginian goes screeching off the pastoral path of standard coming-of-age tales and takes the reader on a hell ride across the hooch-sodden hills of another America." One notes the use of an allusion to a classic book on poverty in order to establish Appalachia explicitly as an Other within America. Finally, this squib has been titled "Moonshine America," with a sketch of a dismal-looking man whose bib overalls are made from an American flag. Thus at each stage of condensation (and of condescension) the image becomes more stereotypical—and more paradoxically identified with "America."

In all this we see a distinct pattern that goes far beyond the collusion of one southern writer and one "national" magazine. The "border country" of Appalachia is defined by "America" in general and the South in particular in terms of a negativity, an area in which dichotomies overlap and therefore cancel each other out—are perceived as a blankness. As the Africa of Christopher Miller's *Blank Darkness* stands to the Orient of Edward Said's *Orientalism* in the eyes of the West, so Appalachia stands to the South in the eyes of America. As Miller says:

> The two interlocking profiles of Europe and the Orient leave no room for a third element, endowed with a positive shape of its own; as on a sheet of paper, both of whose sides have been claimed, the third either tends to be associated with one side or the other or to be nullified by the lack of an available slot in our intellectual apparatus. It is Africa that was always labeled the "third part of the world," and Africanist discourse reads as a struggle with the problems inherent in that figure. (16)

And in the New World as in the Old, "there is more than one 'they' to be analyzed, more than one discourse of otherness to be extricated from its elaborate guise of realism" (Miller 15). As Africa is the third part of the world, so the "border country" of Appalachia is the third part of America. The South stands to "America" as "a fully constituted nonself" (Miller 15) — indeed, North and South stand thusly to each other — but Appalachia is marked by a negativity conditioned by an overlap of these alterities, an overlap perceived as a gap. The defining social fact of the Appalachian South is that, as a whole, it was never part of the slave/plantation economy, whence most of its other differences from the Deep South. As a traditionalist, land-rooted society without sharp status divisions, Appalachia has been both quintessentially southern in its basic nature and very non-"southern" in its voice. But only in recent times has that voice been articulated and heard by the "outside" world.

This situation has a long history, which I would like to summarize as briefly as possible. As Miller begins with the vexed etymology of "Africa," so we can begin with the paradoxical etymology of "Appalachia." The word, strangely, means "by the sea," for the Appalachee Indians lived around the mouth of the Apalachicola or Chattahoochee River. What happened was that the Spanish, who after DeSoto's disastrous reconnaissance largely confined their attentions to the coasts, used the word "Apalache" to refer to the entire Chattahoochee basin, then to the mountains in which the river rose. Later, when coastal areas received new names, the name "Apalache" remained attached to the mountains — a native word that the natives had never used for them, a name sucked into a gap in knowledge across a map made slippery by forgetfulness and indifference.[2]

The name "Appalachia," then, is am embodiment of blankness, "a privileged locus of lags, breaches, delays, and failures in understanding and knowledge," as Miller says of Africa (20). And the mountain themselves, too, as well as their inhabitants, have been marked by such an ambiguity. I have shown elsewhere how even in pre-European days they were a zone of transition between North and South and also between East and West (Cunningham, *Apples* 80–84, 88–90); and how the people whose descendants were largely to populate that land have been characterized by a double otherness that has repeated itself in changing terms for eight centuries. The anglicized Celts of the Scottish lowlands had found themselves not only geographically but in many other ways caught between English and Celtic cultures and societies, seen by each as a version of the other in the most derogatory sense. In the Ulster Plantation, they had reprised this role between English and Celt in Ireland as the terms of the distinction became ideologized into an opposition of civilization and savagery; later, they had reproduced their ambiguous relation to *this* opposition on the frontier of America. Here, though, they and their neighbors seemed to escape this condition precisely by settling in the mountains, which had been defined from both sides as a ridge instead of a region, a barrier without an interior. Here, not so much for physical reasons as for reasons of "intellectual apparatus," they fell out of the conceptual slots of "two vital American cultures" and escaped the destructive attentions of "America" until war broke out between their neighboring regions and the overlapping and ambiguous character of their land and people once more asserted itself to their disadvantage, literally on all sides. From the North, armies ravaged their land; and, as an eyewitness said, "when the best Union men in the country make appeals to the soldiers, they are heartlessly cursed as rebels."[3] But if many northerners were aware only of Appalachia's otherness from the North, the South was perfectly aware of its otherness from the rest of the South, and the racist and antipopulist backlash that followed Reconstruction came down on mountaineers as well as blacks.

Meanwhile, the region was attracting large-scale attention from outside writers (and outside capital) for the first time. The preserved and tightened unity of the Republic was already perceived as accompanying a growing uniformity of American life, and literature turned to "local color"—both celebrating the diversity of American life and implying by this metaphor that local differences were a "color" laid on a blank background of underlying sameness. Significantly, the local color writers of Appalachia were outsiders; the most important, Mary N. Murfree ("Charles Egbert Craddock") and John Fox Jr., were drawn from the upper class of the bluegrass areas (of Tennessee and Kentucky, respectively) immediately to the west of the mountains, and they had first become acquainted with the mountains via tourism and industry respectively.

Later, northern writers took up the stereotype of "the border country" elaborated by these elite lowland southerners (whom the northerners perceived as native observers). As the Jim Crow laws of the late nineteenth century separated northern missionaries from the objects of their philanthropy, these missionaries turned their attention to the South's other subject nation. In the same epoch, the final subjugation of the Indian and the overseas expansion of the American empire led to a perception of Appalachia in the same terms that were being applied to the other "people without history." The keynote of all this was struck when W. G. Frost, president of Berea College, called Appalachians "our contemporary ancestors" (Frost 311). This "mysterious realm," this "*terra incognita*" (Kephart 13), "a land about which, perhaps, more things are known that are not true than of any part of our country" (Campbell xxi), could only be known by being filled with a version of oneself, and a version deprived of a relation to time—like Africa, "persistently depicted as *stuck* in time" (Miller 170). The rhetoric survives to this day in the talk of "yesterday's people" (cf. Weller) and in the whole "development" ethos, in whose terms Appalachians cannot have any valid perception of what is in front of them in the present, but instead exist only as a timeless blank to have being conferred on it by whatever intrusion is necessary.[4]

Not only does this situation endure to the present, but also, after the migrations that brought Appalachians along with blacks to northern industrial cities, another dimension has been added to it: a further overlap and a further gap, that between "WASP" and "ethnic." The close relation between Appalachians and "Americans" acts to the former's disadvantage, as "Americans" are constrained by their "intellectual apparatus" to perceive Appalachians only as a kind of brand-X version of themselves, a "subculture" whose differences are nothing but shortcomings, failures—in short, absences. This "curious inner division of the WASP identity" (Snyder 130) leads to much more severe blindnesses and more destructive relations than if it were a relation between two identities clearly perceived as distinct. Only this can explain the persistence of the full panoply of ethnic prejudice toward Appalachians among many "enlightened" people long after it has become unrespectable with regard to more obviously "marked" groups. "The invisible minority" (cf. Philliber and McCoy) have all the disadvantages of (other) ethnics, and studies have shown that in this regard they are second only to blacks and in some ways surpass them; but their status as such in terms of benefits and the like is steadfastly denied by those in power, to whom it is "nullified by the lack of an available slot in [their] intellectual apparatus." During the heyday of ethnic assertiveness in the 1970s, Ernie Mynatt, a prominent Appalachian activist in Cincinnati (where Appalachians make up 40 percent of the population), used to suggest with tongue in cheek that his people imitate their ancient ancestors by painting themselves blue, thereby making themselves "visible" (as "people of color"?) and countering the tendency of local liberals to mistake Appalachian self-help groups for "white power" organizations ("heartlessly cursed as rebels" indeed). The joke carried the bite of an exasperated desire to inscribe one's blankness, to make oneself seen so that one could be heard.[5] The desire and the exasperation persist today, as even in the academic world Appalachian scholars strive largely in vain to break into the anti-Establishment Establishment's rigid canon of noncanonical groups—to combat an attitude which seems to be, "When the hillbillies produce a García Márquez, *we* shall read him."[6]

Thus Appalachia exists in a blank created by a double otherness—a *doubly* double otherness. For the region is not only an internal Other to the South as the South is the internal Other of America, but it is also the occupier of a simultaneous gap and overlap *between* North and South. But this gap in discourse opens up a space for dialogue, and for counter-discourse *from within.* As Africanist discourse is "an unhappy Orientalism" (Miller 23), so the discourse about Appalachia is an unhappy southernism—an unhappy version of the southernism of both North and South—that "will call into question the terms and conditions of the discourse that created it" (Miller 23). "Third World" and "minority" models have been applied to Appalachia for over twenty years in economic and political terms, but only recently have they been expressed in terms that emphasized not only the forms of power but also the power of forms, of ways of speaking and writing, of sign and symbol. Hence, as the terms of the problem have much to do with the discourse *about* minorities and the Third World, so the terms of the solution can learn much from the discourses *of* minorities and the Third World.

In thus finding its own voice, Appalachia must negotiate a complex relation to the voices of both "vital American cultures," because these voices themselves are complex and indeed contradictory. Contrary to the received wisdom in both North and South, throughout much of the colonial period it was the South that was the bustling commercial society and New England the rural, idealistic back-water (cf. Kearney 299–302). The growth of new trade patterns, augmented by the Industrial Revolution and subsequent history, reversed the relation. Since then, the self-definition of both regions has been marked by a complex duality. On one side stands a southern "agrarianism" that rails against northern indus-trialism but is embedded in an aristocratic romanticism about the "folk"—a romanticism that is conditioned by its own forms of oppression, especially slav-ery and its aftermath.[7] On the other side stands a North whose concern for jus-tice is conditioned by the Puritan/Yankee duality, a combination of self-right-eously moralistic rhetoric with ruthlessly self-seeking activity, which has manifested itself since before the Civil War but is especially evident in the con-trast between the words of that conflict and the deeds of 1877. (In later times, too, the duality shows itself not only in its capitalist form but perhaps even more in its orthodox Marxist form—in either case, a missionary attitude combining an explicit will toward "uplift" with an implicit urge toward the expansion of elite metropolitan power and rationalization.) And in the middle, "the border country," neither aristocratic nor metropolitan—with neither myth nor money, in McWhorter's words—once more, in short, a blankness in the language in which the nation's "two vital cultures" have agreed to define themselves in rela-tion to each other, the language of double discourses each of them strengthened in its own false premises by its valid critique of the other one's.[8]

But a blankness can be a clean sheet on which to start. The unsupported nature of the position preserves, by that very fact, a critical potentiality for a self-defining, self-asserting voice on the part of "an object that refuses to conform to the demands placed on it" (Miller 16). More and more, we Appalachian writers are en(cou)raged to fill in the blanks ourselves—to construct, out of inner necessity, a radical critique of both master-discourses. On the one hand, the task is to recover the valid aspects of agrarianism-with-a-small-*a*, while sort-ing these out from the closed, elitist rhetoric in which the Agrarian school embedded them. On the other, the task is to find paths to liberation while see-ing (through) much standard "radicalism" as being as trapped in the ideology of the modern as any coal-company apologist. The task, in short, is to displace the categories of domination in both directions and thereby to push open not a vacuum but a creative space; not an interlocking structure of necessity but an expanding framework of possibilities.

To some this language will sound "humanistic," a word that any number of my colleagues use in much the same tone (and with much the same preci-sion) as Pat Robertson. Perhaps this is one reason that southern and Appala-chian writers have been shy of jumping on the anti-"humanist" bandwagon. But more importantly, this project of deconstruction originates in a project of recovery of what, for lack of a better name, we call "the human" in contrast with those alternatives to it which have been so richly illustrated in Appala-chia's history and present life. A pure textualism is no more an option for Appalachian writers than for any (other) Third World and minority intellectu-als, to whom contemporary theories have "provided tools . . . for an increasingly sophisticated sociocriticism" rather than, as in the Western metropole, "for the production of . . . exercises that make literature ever more self-referential and solipsistic" (Laguardia 276). This descriptive statement by Gari Laguardia is given a theoretical dimension by Kumkum Sangari:

> The problems of meaning and representation that beset the "Third World" are very different from the slippage of meaning and of the "real" which currently confronts *academic* discourses of Europe and America. To say this is not to claim the possibility of arriving at some essential indigenous truth by a more tortuous route, but to insist that the epistemological problem is *itself* a historical one. . . . For us, the difficulty of arriving at "fact" through the historical and political conjunctions that so powerfully shape and mediate it leads not to dismember finally either the status or the existence of fact. Rather, it tends to assert another *level* of factuality, to cast and resolve the issues of meaning on another, more dialectical plane, a plane on which the notion of knowledge as provisional and of truth as historically circumscribed is not only *necessary* for understanding, but can in turn be made to *work* from positions of engagement with the local and contemporary. (161)

The question that presents itself, that is, is not "What is reality?" but "What is *our* reality?" What have we been separated from, not by some inherent fall into existence or language but by mystifications and falsifications of existence and language that originate in domination—by an alienation that resounds with the etymological meaning of the word: "robbery"? As Nancy Hartsock says, "Rather than getting rid of subjectivity or notions of the subject, we need to engage in the historical and political and theoretical process of constituting ourselves as subjects as well as objects of history" (204). And if there is nothing outside the text, there is plenty between the lines to be read and recovered.

I have overgeneralized, no doubt; but these are not just the projections of an armchair theoretician/rhetorician. They are not only prescriptive but also descriptive of the burgeoning of first-rate Appalachian writing of which I spoke to the condescending ears of New York and Birmingham. I should like to conclude this essay by briefly examining in this context a work by one of Appalachia's best contemporary writers, Lee Smith.

Oral History, Lee Smith's best-known novel, has received much acclaim; demurrals have been few but significant. One native Appalachian reviewer expressed surprise at its enthusiastic reception and called it a pastiche of every kind of stereotypical writing about Appalachia in the past hundred years. And indeed it is; but pastiche (especially multiple pastiche) is an important technique in postmodern fiction, and by foregrounding language itself as a plainly nontransparent medium between form and content, it can say as much about the one as about the other, as much about language itself as about "reality," and especially much about the relation between the two. Being as much about the *subject* as about the *object* of discourse, it problematizes the relation between the two and lays the groundwork for that reappropriation of which Hartsock speaks.

Oral History is indeed, as its title implies, a pastiche of different voices — so different that we eventually suspect that none is reliable. And as soon as we do so, we begin to hear the whispers of the authentic voice underneath, a voice present by erasure — a blankness made articulate. As Sangari says of García Márquez's *Autumn of the Patriarch*, "[T]here is a polyphony of voices . . . which are to be deciphered on the dialogic and representative level. . . . No place in the narrative is exempt from scrutiny" (166). The *pastiche* is made up of *pastings-on* of two-dimensional discourse, underneath which, in its irregularities, can be glimpsed the contours and movements of a real dialogic life in three dimensions, Frantz Fanon's "hidden life" beneath the "outer garments" of culture, "teeming and perpetually in motion" (223–24). It is a living and authentic existence calling into question all its two-dimensional simulacra — an existence, as the title implies, embedded in history, speaking it and speaking through it.

The book is framed by a section set in the present, printed in italics and written in a spare, "objective," omniscient authorial voice. Here we meet the present-day inhabitants of Hoot Owl Holler with their Amway sales and Foxy Lady T-shirts; and here we meet Jennifer, who is working on an oral history project with her supposed grandparents (neither of whom, it transpires, is actually related to her by blood). The first other voice we encounter is hers in her notebook, in which she writes romantically condescending prose about her relatives in a delightfully excruciating style bespeaking Smith's extensive experience with freshman writing. The entire rest of the book is inserted in a break in this episode — a break occurring at the moment of dusk, reminding us of the *Sandyabhasa* or "twilight language" of Hindu magic, "encoded so that several levels of meaning can be invoked at once" (Versluis 43), like the shapes of things at twilight. And in that twilight we have already been introduced, at second hand, to the ghost that haunts Hoot Owl Holler and the novel.

Soon we are involved in the midwife Granny Younger's story of the first Almarine Cantrell and his doomed turn-of-the-century love affair with the witch Red Emmy, whose supposed curse when he rejects her sets in motion the tragic train of events throughout most of the next century. It is her ghost that supposedly haunts the district. In narrative "fact," however, Smith has revealed, Red Emmy is not a witch at all but a psychotic, sexually abused in her childhood by a preacher and his wife (Smith in Smith and Hill 27). Almarine is not really bewitched, then, as he thinks; his longing for this strange beauty has simply intersected and colluded/collided with her longing to be a normal human being and induced in him an acute state of anima possession, and it is his cultural training and her own embedding it in that lead him to project this state upon her as bewitchment. But as the text stands, we see this episode — including the "signs" preceding the couple's first meeting — only from Almarine's much later viewpoint as filtered through Granny Younger, who tells Almarine he is bewitched and must reject Red Emmy to save his life.[9]

Smith had written an entire episode from Red Emmy's viewpoint, but her editor had her delete it (27).[10] Thus the reality of Red Emmy's personal tragedy is literally present by erasure, pointing to what is muted—namely, a voice silenced by traditional Appalachian culture itself in the persons of Granny Younger and Almarine Cantrell. Thus *Oral History* does not idealize that culture, as some have said, but rather presents its mechanical "folk"-solidarity as the first of the master-discourses that obscure the facts of domination. Granny Younger is not a repository of timeless folk-wisdom, as she has often been called in praise; instead, she is the first of the voices of that history against which the human souls of the characters are locked in struggle. And Red Emmy's real "curse" is one that she does not pronounce but rather exemplifies—that few if any of the characters are able to call into question the forms of power and the power of forms in which they are embedded, and therefore to become able to live their own existences in authentic ways. The ghost that haunts Hoot Owl Holler is the trace of the lives that none of its inhabitants are able to live fully. And this is only the novel's first instance of tragically crossed perceptions as two people see each other as a magical Other who can fill in all one's own lacks.

Next the book's voice shifts drastically from that of traditional Appalachia to that of upper-class Richmond in the person of young Richard Burlage, who goes to Hoot Owl Holler in 1923. He has been hired to teach, but first and foremost he is on a personal search for meaning: "a pilgrimage back through time, a pilgrimage to a simpler era, back—dare I hope it—to the very roots of consciousness and belief" (Smith 97). Just so, Miller notes of Conrad's *Heart of Darkness* that in it, "[t]he temporal and the spatial are conflated in such a way that physical travel will take 'one "back to the earliest beginnings of the world"'" (172). Elsewhere I have quoted this sentence with regard to John Fox Jr.'s *Trail of the Lonesome Pine* (Cunningham, "Signs" 25); and Richard Burlage's narrative can be described—indeed, may well be intended—as a *Trail of the Lonesome Pine* minus the sublimation and the wishful ending. Burlage's affair with Almarine's daughter Dory leaves her with two daughters and a permanent discontent with her narrow life, which eventually leads her to commit suicide under the wheels of the train that now carries the coal out of Hoot Owl Holler.[11] But before this happens, Burlage returns to the area, eleven years after his first visit, this time as a collector of Appalachian photographs (another kind of extractive industry)[12] and glimpses her one last time. His irruptions into the holler are central to the book in more senses than one. The exact central line of the book is a line of exclamation points conveying his masturbation subsequent to an early visit by Dory. And, indeed, his whole account is the trace left by a deliriously excited self-absorption, fed by the self-alienation that leads him to seek "meaning" as he does. Just such a compulsion, too, destroys his and Dory's daughter Pearl, Jennifer's mother, in her affair in the 1960s with a student of hers—an affair that is a mirror image of the one that produced her.

The only main character in the book who finally attains some center of authenticity—and that at a price—is Pearl's half-sister Sally. The key to her success, and to that of the novel, is her statement, "Life is a mystery and that's a fact" (275). This sentence, with its placing of "fact" and "mystery" on different meta-levels, subverts the dichotomy between the factual and the marvelous better than pages of theorizing on marvelous realism. For *Oral History* is Appalachia's nearest equivalent to García Márquez's *One Hundred Years of Solitude*, and this affinity is nowhere more apparent than at the end of the book, after Jennifer has gone back to school and married her Miami Yankee teacher Bernie Ripman (who gave her the oral history assignment and whose name is nearly Richard Burlage's backward). The second Almarine (Wade), step-grandnephew to the first, flees the burden of the family "curse" embodied in his name by becoming a gimlet-eyed entrepreneur; he makes a killing in Amway and invests his earnings in converting his land into a theme park called Ghostland. Thus he updates Richard Burlage's exploitative image-making by turning the land itself into a commodity and the spirit of the mountains into a spectral fixed image, a simulacrum as dim and distorted as Burlage's last picture of the stooped and careworn Dory Cantrell.[13]

And yet this is, literally, not the whole story. In the novel's final passage,

> the old homeplace still stands, smack in the middle of Ghostland, untouched. . . . It's surrounded by a chain link fence, fronted by the observation deck with redwood benches which fill up every summer night at sunset with those who have paid the extra $4.50 . . . to be here when dark comes and the wind and the laughter start, to see it with their own eyes when that rocking chair starts rocking and rocks like crazy the whole night long. (286)

On the narrative level, this is presumably a mechanical trick, another piece of image-manipulation; and it is significant that it is another Almarine who thus manipulates the image of witchery, just as the first Almarine became victim and victimizer of such an image. But the passage is hauntingly (no pun intended) equivocal. Whatever it "really" is, the last voice in the novel (within the author's narration—not an irrelevant point) is that of Red Emmy, returning like the repressed, rising "like crazy" out of the depths of time and madness to mock those, "insider" and "outsider" alike, who continue to misunderstand and to remain ignorant of the falsity of their perceptions and their lives. Smith has succeeded in the project that Michael Taussig cites from Frederick Karl on Conrad—"to penetrate the veil while retaining its hallucinatory quality" as "a twofold movement of interpretation in a combined act of reduction *and* revelation" (Taussig 10); to discover, in Sangari's words, "a figurative discourse that produces a knowledge inseparable from its performance in language, image, and metaphor and that can be understood in its total configuration but not necessarily explained" (163).

Thus Lee Smith's *Oral History* illustrates the applicability to Appalachian life and literature of contemporary models of otherness and domination, and it exemplifies the burgeoning of writing that is being stimulated by realization, confrontation, and negotiation with these conditions in Appalachia, as it is in Latin America, Africa, and other peripheralized areas of the world. There are many more such examples; I might have written of the poetry and essays of Jim Wayne Miller, which grapple in an exemplary manner with the challenge of creating a mode of perception for modern Appalachia "which is neither of the West [etc.] nor of the past" (Dirlik 19); of the novels of Denise Giardina, which explore the past century's invasions of the region multivocally from the inside of both the culture and the soul; or even of the social-comedy mysteries of Sharyn McCrumb, which play deliciously with crossed perceptions and fixed images. In any case, it is inevitable that as a vital American culture has sought its own voice and its own power in a time when thinkers have been concerned to the point of obsession with voice and its relation to power, the region has produced, and is producing, voices of great power in the quest for the path "from self-consciousness to self-possession" (Snyder 132).

Notes

1. *New York Times Book Review* (September 27, 1987): 54. McWhorter's reply to this letter was brief and flippantly dismissive. A more recent example of this phenomenon is the Pulitzer Prize awarded to the egregious Robert Schenkkan.

2. My account is based on my own study of maps, mainly in Johnson, and differs somewhat from that given by Walls.

3. *The War of the Rebellion: A Compilation of the Official Records of the Union and Confederate Armies* (Washington: Government Printing Office, 1880–1901), series 1, vol. 31, pt. 3, pp. 507–8; cited in McKinney 133. The Union loyalty of many mountaineers, especially the more rural and traditional element, is well known. Less well known is the fact that this pattern tends to be reversed in the northern parts of the region (Waller 30–31). In both cases, the mountaineers' motivation was that of "defending their autonomy" (Waller 31) against the nearest dominant culture.

4. Some years ago a national cable weather program employed several regional maps, including the South, the Midwest, and the Northeast. West Virginia was on none of them. At the same time, West Virginia was being targeted as a leading candidate for toxic and radioactive waste dumping from neighboring industrial states. It should be evident by now that these facts are not unconnected.

5. Cincinnati is now the only city in the United States which officially bans discrimination against persons of Appalachian ancestry.

6. For an extended example of this phenomenon, see Branam. As I remarked to Branam, New Presbyter is but Old Priest writ large.

7. As Joel Kovel points out, southerners who criticized the effects of the factory system on the human spirit simply "attacked the North for pushing wider what [southerners themselves] had already pushed deeper" (190).

8. McWhorter's dismissive evocation of "the border country" may also be read ironically through Raymond Williams's use of the concept.

9. The "curse" story was really spread by the near-psychotic Rose Hibbits, and is presented as clearly her invention. Later it is fostered by the envious Ludie Davenport. Thus from beginning to end, Red Emmy is caught in a web woven by women to trap women.

10. Some readers may doubt the legitimacy of using deleted material to explicate a novel's intentions. But the deletion was editorial, prompted by a desire to leave a "mys-

tery" at the heart of the novel (27). Though Smith acceded to the deletion and claims to agree with it, I suspect that under the pressure of metropolitan discourses about Appalachia, she has here stepped over the line between mystery and mystification.

11. The role of June Tolliver in Fox's novel is here split between Dory and her younger brother Jink (whose name follows the J— pattern of June and of all the other main protagonists of Fox's novel). Both idealize Burlage, but it is Jink whom Burlage singles out for his intelligence; whose language, like June's, contains anxious "corrections" of his own English and many other signs of his incipient cultural alienation; and who eventually uses his male mobility to leave Hoot Owl Holler for parts unknown. The orange which Burlage gives him and which he saves without eating embodies his own ideal of Otherness clung to as a fixed and withering image.

12. Space forbids an examination of how Burlage's own description of his photographic activity is made a vehicle for devastating commentary on the production of Appalachia as image.

13. Cf. the fantasy of returning Lonesome Cove to "nature" at the end of *The Trail of the Lonesome Pine*. One is as unreal as the other—better, as artificial a construct for consumption without regard to history (cf. Cunningham, "Signs" 40–43).

Works Cited

Branam, Harold. "For Appalachian Literature, No Room at the MLA." Paper presented at the Appalachian Studies Conference, Blacksburg, VA, March 1994.

Campbell, John C. *The Southern Highlander and His Homeland*. 1921. Lexington: UP of Kentucky, 1969.

Cunningham, Rodger. *Apples on the Flood: The Southern Mountain Experience*. Knoxville: U of Tennessee P, 1987.

———. "Signs of Civilization: *The Trail of the Lonesome Pine* as Colonial Narrative." *Journal of the Appalachian Studies Association* 2 (1990): 21–46.

Dirlik, Arif. "Culturalism as Hegemonic Ideology and Liberating Practice." *Cultural Critique* 6 (Spring 1987): 13–50.

Fanon, Frantz. *The Wretched of the Earth*. 1961. Tr. Constance Farrington. New York: Grove, 1968.

Frost, William Goodell. "Our Contemporary Ancestors in the Southern Mountains." *Atlantic Monthly* 83 (1899): 311–19.

Hartsock, Nancy. "Rethinking Modernism: Minority vs. Majority Theories." *Cultural Critique* 7 (Fall 1987): 187–206.

Johnson, Adrian. *America Explored: A Cartographical History of the Exploration of North America*. New York: Viking, 1974.

Kearney, Hugh. "The Problem of Perspective in the History of Colonial America." K. R. Andrews, N. P. Canny, and P. E. H. Hair, eds., *The Westward Enterprise: English Activities in Ireland, the Atlantic, and America 1580–1650*. Detroit: Wayne State UP, 1979. 290–302.

Kephart, Horace. *Our Southern Highlanders: A Narrative of Adventure in the Southern Appalachians and a Study of Life among the Mountaineers*. 1913. 2d ed. 1922. Knoxville: U of Tennessee P, 1976.

Kovel, Joel. *White Racism: A Psychohistory*. 2d ed. 1970. New York: Columbia UP, 1984.

Laguardia, Gari. "Introduction" to "Perspectives on Literary Criticism." Bell Gale Chevigny and Gari Laguardia, eds., *Reinventing the Americas: Comparative*

Studies of Literature of the United States and Spanish America. Cambridge: Cambridge UP, 1986. 271–77.

McKinney, Gordon B. "Industrialization and Violence in Appalachia in the 1890s." J. W. Williamson, ed., *Appalachian Symposium*, 131–44.

McWhorter, Diane. "Cigarettes Rolled from the Bible." [Review of Pinckney Benedict, *Town Smokes*.] *New York Times Book Review* (July 12, 1987): 13–14.

Miller, Christopher L. *Blank Darkness: Africanist Discourse in French*. Chicago: U of Chicago P, 1985.

Philliber, William W., and Clyde B. McCoy, eds. *The Invisible Minority: Urban Appalachians*. Lexington: UP of Kentucky, 1981.

Sangari, Kumkum. "The Politics of the Possible." *Cultural Critique* 7 (Fall 1987): 157–86.

Smith, Lee. *Oral History*. New York: Putnam, 1983.

Smith, Lee, and Dorothy Hill. "'Every Kind of Ritual': A Conversation." *Iron Mountain Review* 3, no. 1 (Winter 1986): 25–27.

Snyder, Robert. "Image and Identity in Appalachia." *Appalachian Journal* 9 (1982): 124–33.

Taussig, Michael T. *Shamanism, Colonialism, and the Wild Man: A Study in Terror and Healing*. Chicago: U of Chicago P, 1987.

Versluis, Arthur. *The Philosophy of Magic*. Boston: Routledge, 1986.

Waller, Altina L. *Feud: Hatfields, McCoys, and Social Change in Appalachia, 1860–1900*. Chapel Hill: U of North Carolina P, 1988.

Walls, David S. "On the Naming of Appalachia." J. W. Williamson, ed., *Appalachian Symposium*, 56–76.

Weller, Jack E. *Yesterday's People: Life in Contemporary Appalachia*. Lexington: U of Kentucky P, 1966.

Williamson, J. W., ed. *An Appalachian Symposium: Essays Written in Honor of Cratis D. Williams*. Boone, N.C.: Appalachian State UP, 1977.

4

FRED CHAPPELL

The Shape of Appalachian Literature to Come

An Interview with Wil Hickson

Wil Hickson was born in Madison County, North Carolina, in 1975. He attended the University of North Carolina at Chapel Hill as an undergraduate and received a Master of Fine Arts degree in creative writing from the University of Arkansas in 1998. His first publications were in poetry, and he was a prominent member of the movement called the Hellbillies Group, poets who pursued Appalachian themes in their work and advanced Appalachian concerns in a variety of ways. His first volume of verse, Galax Galaxy, *was published by O'Possum Books while he was still an undergraduate and was followed by* The Wind's Wil *(1995) and* Television Creek *(1997). He is probably best known for his fiction; the book of short stories,* Grab You a Handful, *was designed, he says, as a companion to his second book of poems. His two novels,* A Bitter Thirst *(1998) and* The Slaking *(2000), are the first of a projected six-volume series telling the story of two families, the Carltons and the Haneys, who inhabit a cove in Hickson's native mountains.*

Though he is only twenty-six years old, Wil Hickson seems mature and wise beyond his years. A shy person, he is capable of passionate outburst when provoked by a question or a subject, but he more often maintains an amiable humor that seems somewhat at variance with the lyric intensity of his work. He lives with his wife, Brenda, and their sons, Jason and Louis, in a roomy and comfortable cabin not four miles from the farm where he was reared.

This interview took place September 6–7, 2001, mostly on the porch of the Hickson cabin.

Question: This is a fine porch you've got here, with a lovely view down into the valley. Do you ever write any of your books out here?

Wil Hickson: Sometimes I do, if the weather's good. I find that I can write poetry out here, or lyric poetry anyhow, because you spend a lot of time just musing when you do that. But with fiction you kinda have to get on with it, so then I write in my study. It's easier to write out here than to read, though. If I try to read, I'll just laze away the whole afternoon.

Q. You don't write, then, as Wordsworth suggests, with your eye on the object?

WH. Like a painter with his sketchbook, you mean? Nah, never like that. I mean, what if I was working on a sex scene in a novel? "Excuse me, honey, hold it right there till I get this down—" *(Laughs.)*

Q. But you stated in a previous interview that you were interested above all in getting on paper "the immediacy of experience."

WH. Yeah, I said that. But you don't get it done by writing while you're doing something else. When you're writing you'd better be thinking about writing.

Q. Well, let's go back to the beginning. How did you get started as a writer? Was yours a literary family?

WH. Not as far as I know. As long as we can recall, we've mostly been farmers, though some of my uncles are in the military. I got started as a writer by reading books. I didn't pay much attention to books when I was real young, but when I was sixteen I ran across a novel that opened my eyes and made me want to try to see if I could write.

Q. I was going to ask about literary influences. What was the novel you read?

WH. *River of Earth*, by James Still. It was a real old book, but it was new to me. The thing about it was that I could tell that every word of it was true, I could test it against my own experience and *see* that it was true, and that was important. All the stuff I'd read in books up till then seemed just made-up, but I could tell that Still knew what he was talking about. So then I began to read seriously.

Q. What other writers would you list as influences?

WH. Well, Elizabeth Madox Roberts made almost the same impression on me that Still did. *The Time of Man* is maybe a great book, I don't know. And it wasn't just what these writers wrote about, but also the way they used language, Still and Roberts. The electricity they got into the sentences. The jolt.

Q. Did you read Cormac McCarthy?

WH. Yeah, later on I did. I was too young for him in high school, but when I read *Child of God* in college, it was just like finding Still all over again. I felt the same way about a writer named William Goyen who is not an Appalachian writer.

Q. Do you think it's important for contemporary Appalachian writers to read the earlier ones?

WH. Well, a lot of them you have to read because they make you do it in school. That's how most of us come to read poets like Jim Wayne Miller and Jeff Daniel Marion and Robert Morgan. Because when you're a kid you usually don't go around reading books of poetry. I'm glad I read them, but I might not have done it on my own.

That's always a problem. Some writers get to be "official" and then they're not so attractive. Maybe Thomas Wolfe and Jesse Stuart are terrific, but they were schoolwork assignments, and that takes all the fun out of it. I mean, it's a real obstacle sometimes. For instance, in high school we had to read a story by Lee Smith called "Cakewalk." But we didn't have enough sense of history for that one, so a lot of people still think of her as a writer who has to be explained to you. When I read her novel *Oral History* last year, it was a real revelation to me. It's easy to see now that this one novel is probably the seminal work for current Appalachian fiction. It's where we all come from now, whether we know it or not. She's the mother of us all. *(Laughs.)*

Q. What makes *Oral History* so important?

WH. Its urbanity and its ironies and the complexity of its vision. It covers a long period of time in an extremely economic and resonant fashion. It is full of ironies about what we call nowadays the "inside-outside" theme, that is, the difference between how Appalachian experience is seen by outsiders and how we folks who were born here experience it from the inside. The language is not so lyrical as in Still or Roberts, but it's so accurate that it comes out as a different *kind* of lyricism.

And Smith is not sentimental, and that's enormously important. She's very clear-eyed, sharp. Sentimentality has been the curse of Appalachian writing ever since the beginning. Back in the 1970s and '80s they thought they were getting rid of it, but it's easy to see now that the work of Fred Chappell, for instance, is just as sentimental in its own way as that of John Fox, Jr. Especially in Chappell's novels about the Kirkman family. . . . Wilma Dykeman's work too is sentimental, but in her best books she exhibits a big ragged mythic quality that takes the curse off. . . . I could go on all day and night listing Appalachian writers whom sentimentality has undermined.

Q. Why do you consider sentimentality a special danger for Appalachian writers?

WH. Again, it's the inside-outside theme. The real insiders, the writers who were born and raised in the mountains and lived their lives there, are rarely sentimental. But writers who were more or less tourists, or writers who moved away and looked back nostalgically—that's where you get your gooiest sentimentality, people writing about their childhood in the hills. James Still wrote about childhood but managed to avoid that trap.

Q. What about Thomas Wolfe?

WH. He may be a great writer, but in this respect he's the very worst offender. . . .

In poetry, the man who struck the killing blow against sentimentality was Robert Morgan. The modesty of his designs and his commitment to precision set him apart from the very start in a little book called *Zirconia Poems*. His later work—*Land Diving*, for example, and *Groundwork* and *At the Edge of the Orchard Country*—shows advanced technique and deepened sensibility, but the essence of his poetic was there from the beginning. I've heard other poets of that generation, Jeff Daniel Marion and Rodney Jones, for example, speak of the excitement with which they first encountered Morgan's poetry. . . . And when you pick it up today, it's just as fresh as it must have been then. Now, though, we read it as being heavily programmatic, while during Morgan's heyday it was seen as being "pure," as nonprogrammatic.

Q. How is Morgan's poetry programmatic?

WH. You have to remember that during the '70s and '80s Appal Lit was neatly divided into the political and the pastoral, according to Jim Wayne Miller's formulation. An Appalachian work was either a celebration of rural virtues and ideals or it described and protested the horrors of strip mining or water pollution or some other trashy disaster. Morgan's poems were purely pastoral because he almost never interjected commentary into them. Now in our time, in the twenty-*first* century, the pastoralism itself seems political, more powerfully political than the more propagandistic works back then.

Of course, it was the breakdown of Miller's description that freed the work of my generation of writers.

Q. I think you probably need to explain that.

WH. Well, after a while the Hellbillies Group broke up because we got tired of propagandizing and politicking. We weren't really doing politics anyhow, not running for office or supporting slates of candidates—we were just heckling politicians of every stripe. Disrupting rallies, jamming the telephone switchboards of candidates' headquarters, putting out satiric broadsides. . . . All that has been written up in the journals, people pretty well know all about the Hellbillies. . . .

We said that we were establishing a new agenda, but the truth is that we were burned out. Takes too much time and energy to do what we called "antipolitics." It's probably even harder work than doing legitimate politics. It certainly leaves you with no time to write.

So we decided to turn our backs on both the pastoral *and* the political modes. We decided to put purely artistic aims first and foremost, to make works of art and leave the messages to the television evangelists. We formed the Aga Group then and published the manifesto, but we didn't stick together as a group. Everyone went off separately to do his own thing.

Q. Maybe you could say something about the Aga Group.

WH. Not much to tell, because it didn't last six months. This was Jim Burward, Kermit Kerry, Alicia Wylie, Ralph Exxum, and myself, and we invited Stephen Marion to join but he wasn't interested. At first we were going to call ourselves the Mountain Lions because we took our motto from the MGM movie logo with the lion roaring. That's what Aga stands for—A-G-A, Ars Gratia Artis. Some folks thought we must be fancy classical scholars, but we just got it off the old videotapes.

Anyhow, we published our manifesto, "A Hard Gemlike Flame," and said that from here on out we were neither pastoral nor political but were espousing the high ideals of Baudelaire and Flaubert and Proust and—who else was it? I can't remember.

Q. Rilke.

WH. Oh yeah, Rilke. If you want to sound impressive you mention Rilke. We said that it was time that Appal Lit was recognized not only along with southern literature or even with American literature but with world literature, that it should be recognized in the way that a national literature is recognized. We pointed to the fact that in geographical area Appalachia is larger than a lot of European countries with recognized literatures. We tried to show that the separatist history that Appal Lit has claimed for itself is specious and that it derives straightforwardly from European romantic tradition. We proposed Washington Irving as the progenitor of us all. He makes an interesting partner for Lee Smith, don't you think? *(Laughs.)* I think a lot of people didn't even know till then that the Catskills are part of the Appalachian system.

Q. That manifesto, "A Hard Gemlike Flame," caused some stir in southern literary circles.

WH. We were attacked by *everybody*. Especially by the academics who have so much invested in the old view of the history of Appal Lit. It's easy to see why they were so damn defensive. Appalachian Literature was just a little tiny bit of a thing, with only Thomas Wolfe and Harriette Arnow as nationally ranked reputations, and here it was nestled like a toadstool beside a rotting log against southern literature, which may still be the proudest literary tradition in the United States. And Wolfe had always been listed as a southern author rather than as an Appalachian writer, and he's probably still thought of that way. The scholar Hugh Holman once went so far as to deny that Wolfe had any connection with Appalachian literature.

So the Appal Lit scholars were trying to make sure that their good stuff wasn't confused with Grit Lit, with southern literature. But in setting it so far apart from its nearest neighbor, they also set it apart from *all* literature. They were making it seem that Appalachian literature was connected to no other literature in the world, that it was an absolutely independent tradition. Written by Martians.

We only stood this attitude on its head to say that Appal Lit was connected to all other literatures in the same way that any legitimate regional literature, whether ethnic, nationalist, or subnationalist, is connected to every other literature. It wasn't hard to point out the similarity of themes in Appal Lit to themes in novels and poems and dramas in Estonian and Latvian and Albanian and Peruvian and Korean literature. That part was easy, since traditional themes, as themes, are the same everywhere. To tell the truth, we simply went to the Stith Thompson Folk Motif Index and brought that classification to bear on written literature.

Q. You talk as if you no longer believe that was a legitimate critical method.

WH. I don't know whether it was legitimate or not. But I can tell you that we weren't serious about it; we just wanted to stir up discussion, to muddy the waters a little bit. We were surprised when the critics and some of the teachers took it seriously.

Q. You must have had a good laugh over it.

WH. We did sorta grin a little bit, but then on the other point where we *were* serious, no one paid us any mind.

Q. How was that?

WH. We proposed that the dominant theme of Appal Lit, the impact of industrialism on an agriculturally based society, was the dominant theme of world literature after 1950 — and that Appal Lit had produced, during the time of its whole existence, the most memorable, searching, and durable treatments of the subject. We advanced the notion that in some very important respects Appalachian Literature was in the avant garde of world literature and that the world was none too swift in catching up with us.

Q. But this must have been a popular view among Appalachian Literature specialists.

WH. You'd think so, wouldn't you? What we heard instead were howls of outrage. Even the oldest and most faithful partisans, the ones who had fought to get courses in Appalachian Literature taught in the universities and high schools, the ones who had worked so hard to publish anthologies and text-books, were upset. They thought we were trying to make the stuff *too* important. They thought that we were being sarcastic or ironic or just snotty. But we weren't. We were pretty straightforward about it.

Q. But not *completely* straightforward.

WH. We weren't *completely* straightforward about *anything.* . . . We had an idea that we'd be accused of exaggerating, but we didn't expect that kind of reaction from our friends. Of course, we were exaggerating a little, but we were experienced writers and critics, after all, and we realized that in order to get attention you have to make outrageous claims.

Q. But your plan didn't work.

WH. We found out for the first time — or at least I did — that the canon of modern literature is already carved in stone as far as the colleges and the crit-ics go. They have established a pecking order of immortals that goes something like this: the great European writers like Joyce, Mann, and Valéry are at the top; then come the lesser European writers, like Italo Svevo, Ivo Andrič, and Hermann Broch; then come the writers in other literatures, like Kobo Abe, Octavio Paz, and Wole Soyinka; then come the great American authors like William Faulkner and Raymond Carver and Ann Beattie — and then after that all the writers, American and foreign, who are studied in a kind of sociologi-cal way, as specimens of regional fauna or as symptoms of some disease of mod-ern times or as classic examples of various neuroses.

When we tried to name Appal Lit as one of the shining elements of mod-ern world lit, it was like we had spray-painted the temple. I got a letter from one professor who said that she would believe our notion when she saw a six-part series on Appalachian literature in the *New Yorker*. And I got at least a dozen comments to the effect that *PMLA* had never published articles on the subject, so we had to be guilty of a hoax. And letters and telephone calls all saying, in effect, "Do you mean to tell me that you put Denise Giardina on the same level as William Golding?" We never made any rankings like that, but it's perfectly clear to me that she's a better writer than Golding, and I even told one caller that I thought so. And he said, "Don't you know that William Golding won the *Nobel Prize?*" And I said, "So did Johannes V. Jensen." And he said, "Well, Jensen deserved the Nobel Prize." "For those poems?" I said. "They're great poems," he said, "whether *you* like them or not." So I hung up on him. As far as I know, Jensen never wrote any poems, and it was clear this guy had never heard the name before.

It's wonderful how upset people get when you disturb the petty little order of their priorities.

Q. You made your point, though. What do you see for the future?

WH. Appal Lit will keep on rolling along. New poets and writers will be broaching new themes and treating traditional themes in new ways. But the emphasis on style and high artistic finish will continue for a good while, I think. That's what sets my generation apart from our predecessors. To paraphrase the old poem by Ezra Pound, "They broke the wood, Now is a time for carving." I think we'll be able to do some carving to be proud of.

Q. I'm sure you will, and we all wish you every success.

WH. Thank you.

5

KATE DANIELS

Porch-Sitting and Southern Poetry

Back in the 1950s, before the advent of the present interstate highway system, U.S. 1 swept through Richmond, Virginia, like a dusty garden snake—slow, harmless, and yet, in spite of itself, tantalizing, a messenger from another, more exotic world. The Pike (as we called it, short for Petersburg Pike) meandered southward from Washington, D.C., through the elegant outskirts of Richmond, the nineteenth-century grandeur of downtown, and then across the graceful Lee Bridge, which forded the James River and was, during the period, the primary conduit between Southside Richmond, where my family lived, and the main part of the city. On our side of town, the Pike picked up the flurry of poor folks' commerce at its intersection with Hull Street, where, as my mother always recalled with horror, black Richmonders had danced for nickels and dimes on the street corners on Saturday nights in 1947, when she had come to the city as a British war bride. Then it straightened out into its longest and most memorable portion—a four-lane section of road periodically interrupted by stoplights and populated by a curious mixture of private homes, boardinghouses, restaurants, roadhouses, trailer parks, factories, and all kinds of small, privately owned businesses, like Bleacher's Store, where we charged penny candy on a running account.

During these years, I spent much of my time at my paternal grandmother's home, a small, scrupulously tended white frame house at 2512 Royal Avenue, only one house in from the Pike, separated from its more or less constant rush of traffic by a narrow alley of sharp, black cinders and a tumbledown shack of a house that embarrassed my family. The front of my grandmother's house was distinguished by a broad-eaved porch with wide cement steps, painted over in shiny gray enamel, leading up to it. Either side was shaded by American Beauty red roses trained up a white trellis. A long metal glider took up most of the space on one end.

When I recall these years, I see that porch where we sat on warm evenings from May to September of each year eating homemade ice cream and sometimes singing oldtime Baptist hymns to my grandmother's awkward accompaniment on a beat-up guitar. I can recall, without any effort at all, her voice, always midpoint in one of her long and psychologically fascinating family narratives. She was an uneducated person, having only gone through the eighth grade, but her language—marked by an endless digressiveness and a deep, "country" accent—was the one that first introduced me to the possibilities of verbal expression. Her home was all but bookless. There was a Bible, its broken spike sewn clumsily together with coarse cotton thread; a dictionary she used to do the crossword puzzles published in the paper; and a twelfth-grade English grammar that her youngest son, my Uncle Henry, had never returned to the local high school.

In spite of this pronounced absence of literature, stories lived all around my grandmother—if not in the pages of books, then in the tales she told of our family; of her early life on a farm in Tidewater Virginia; of the peddlers and salesmen who regularly rapped on the porch steps before venturing up them; of the conditions of life during the depression, which remained vivid in her mind; and, of course, of the neighbors. As she gave me her versions of the lives that surrounded us on Royal Avenue, the xenophobic egoism of early childhood was punctured pleasantly for me, and I became aware that life itself is ultimately a kind of story. The people whose lives she recounted to me—the Thompsons, who lived in a secretive and possibly violent world in their large, unpainted house three doors away; the sad and beaten-down Jonseses, who had lost their only son, Sparky, my father's best friend, in the Korean War; the Reverend Holloway, a Christian Science minister, and his family, who lived across the street and seemed very provincial to us, with their plain clothes, their flat and tidy hairdos, and the fact that they didn't own a television set— all these exercised an endless and perambulating fascination on my growing mind and fancy.

My grandmother related these stories in the summer evenings as we sat together in the metal glider, pushing it back and forth with our feet, its rusty creak more companionable than annoying, and watching the Pike traffic pass, near enough to smell and hear, but psychologically distant. We watched, too, our neighbors concluding the day. Across the street, the Holloways lurked in the secrecy of their screened front porch, discussing things we could not even imagine or holding a family prayer meeting. Beside them, my grandmother's elderly friends Mr. and Mrs. Cleary sat on their porch in yellow metal chairs with latticework on the back. They emanated a profoundly antique dignity that was composed of his gold watch chain and wooden walking cane, her seamed stockings and starched lace collar, their iron posture and pleasant nods to all who passed. In the disreputable house across the alley, the Hammonds crouched on their broken back steps.

On every porch, stories *lived*, and, occasionally, when a neighbor would walk up the broad stairs onto our porch, or we would cross the street to one of theirs, I don't recall anything beyond the most preliminary of polite conversation before the stories would begin. The innocent inquiry "How are you feeling today, Lucille?" would lead into a long, many-branched story about the condition of the kitchen garden, how hot it was today bending over the baking biscuits, my uncle away at boot camp in the coolness of Dutch Gap, and crop conditions down in Charles City County, where my grandmother's much-loved nieces and nephews lived on a large farm. Somehow it would all be knit together, a present tied up neatly, no loose ends, no unexplained plot lines, no unresolved conclusions. And then in response would come another narrative from the visitor, and so it would go—slow story after slow story, all up and down the neighborhood.

The background to all of this was the Pike traffic: the refrigerator trucks rushing southern fruits and vegetables northward, the tank trucks of oil and milk and gas, the vacationers driving south to Florida and the Outer Banks, the southerners who had packed it in heading north, their belongings tied to the top of the car and towed along behind in homemade trailers. The Pike was progress and modernity and speed. It was escape, adventure. We could join it if we wanted, and most of us, at one time or another, would or had. But on those summer evenings as I grew into literature and moved toward consciousness, it was not the Pike but the porch-sitting that moved me, and even more than that, the story-poems that came of porch-sitting. Now, of course, at the end of the twentieth-century, as we keep inside our air-conditioned houses, eyes focused on the VCR, porch-sitting is hardly more than a metaphor. In the middle of the century, though, it was real: a vehicle for *conversation*, that most important resource of the southern writer, whereby the region's peculiar language is validated, reinvigorated, and, ultimately, preserved. Still, regardless how much the realities of our lives have changed in response to technology, the metaphor remains pervasive in southern poetry, I believe. And the characteristics of those porch-sitting poems—the slowness, the civility, the absolute confidence in closure, the strength of the native materials—continue to identify and inform the work of contemporary southern poets.

In a marvelous little book called *The Language of the American South* (1985), Cleanth Brooks speaks of the southern writer's historical "dependence upon the spoken language" (37), and he asserts that "a Southern language veritably exists and constitutes a rich resource for the writers of the South" (52). Like many writers, I suppose, I never questioned the fact of a uniquely southern language until I found myself outside the region for an extended period of time. In New York City, attending graduate school at Columbia University, I heard myself for the first time in the context of another English language: louder than mine, abrupt, impatient to get to the point. I said cē'-ment and pē'-cân and pe-ōn'-y instead of ce-ment', pecän', pē'-ôn-y. I left words open at the end whenever I could and took a long time to get them out. They closed them down, bit them off, and rushed on to devour the next one like a marauding tribe of linguistic carnivores.

At the 92nd Street Y, I sat in the second row listening to Robert Penn Warren read from his poetry and felt homesick for the first time in two years. The
elongated vowels, the ornate syllabification, the quiet and mannerly presentation brought to consciousness a thirst, unrecognized until then, that was satis-
fied, simply, by the sound of the poet's voice. Settling deeper into my seat, eyes
closed, I heard Mr. Warren becoming not just himself but a *place* speaking to
me, a whole community of people sharing a curious and deeply emotional
attachment to their language. Outside, on the broad city street, the spell was
broken when a fellow student and native New Yorker asked grumpily, "What
the hell was he saying, anyway?" He had not understood, he claimed, any more
than 10 percent of the words that rolled so gloriously from the poet's mouth.

When critics discuss the phenomenon known as "southern poetry," what they
agree on most often is this: that it is and has been characterized by the need for
story, thus lending it a distinctively narrative impulse; that it has addressed itself
to the largest of the philosophical abstractions (Time and Death and History);
that it has exhibited a consistent fascination with its own distinctively southern character; and that it has not arisen from the lives of southerners as often
as fiction, a genre perhaps more accommodating, in our time, to conventional
narrative needs. This is, of course, immediately obvious in the work of those
poets whose work has come most vividly to represent twentieth-century southern poetry: the Fugitive poets John Crowe Ransom, Robert Penn Warren, and
Allen Tate.

As the millennium approaches, I find myself thinking more and more
often of these poets and of some of the politics and personal values they shared.
Reacting fifty years ago against the early century's rapid acceleration of industrialization, which threatened the integrity of the rural, primarily agrarian
southern lifestyle, they sought a rare and daring compromise with modernity.
Recognizing the urgent necessity for the economic rehabilitation of the region,
they pondered ways to achieve this without laying waste to a lifestyle that was
already becoming unique—if not anachronistic—in its belief in the individual
grandeur of human beings and in the stabilizing value of domestic ceremony
and social responsibility. Poetically, this translated into an attempt to utilize the
new techniques and internationalist spirit of modernism in the service of a literary vision that focused on a region, a people, a historical lifestyle whose practices and values often conflicted destructively with the mad rush forward of
modernism, which would eventually culminate in technologizing, nuclear
weaponry, and the despairing postmodernist philosophies of literature and art.

What the Fugitives sought is, perhaps, precisely what the porch-sitting
metaphor represents in our own time, in our *New* South: a need among certain southern poets *not* to be so brief, so contained, so fragmented as much of
twentieth-century literature has been. Might not this need actually work
against the adamantly lyric impulse that has beat at the heart of twentieth-century poetry? Perhaps it is exactly this regionally and culturally determined need
for more *space* and more *time* in the *telling* that has accounted for some of the

interesting experiments in narrative that recent southern poets have made: Robert Penn Warren's *Audubon: A Vision*, for example, or Fred Chappell's tetralogical novel-in-verse, *Midquest*. I am not hesitant to proceed farther along these lines to suggest that the exploration of psychic and social fragmentation and the willful descent into chaos that have been characteristics of some postmodernist literature are also urges that just might exist in opposition to the cultural and political mandates of the southern region. However well-integrated into the body of the country the South is becoming, it is still struggling, psychically, to *recover* from the chaos and fragmentation of secession, the Civil War, and, more recently, the civil rights movement, which resulted in much vaster social realignments in the South than in other parts of the country. The struggle of much recent southern literature has been to overcome that fragmentation—rather than to mirror it—and to forge a new vision of wholeness that will reflect the changes the twentieth century has brought to bear on the region. A number of younger southern poets, black and white, have dealt with this issue directly in their work. Bin Ramke, for example, in "The Birthplace of Joel Chandler Harris," struggles with the painful question of regional identity for the contemporary white writer in the South.

> *Without it I would have no memory*
> *of that summer, the top-down drive*
> *from Athens between trees*
> *themselves exuding heat even in shade*
> *and the later long arrow-shot*
> *to Savannah. A sign on the highway*
> *reminiscent of See Rock City*
> *but cheaper and smaller announced*
> *the greatest southern writer*
> *with no apologies to Faulkner,*
> *O'Connor, Welty, McCullers.*
> *And in that miniature house,*
> *that cube of shade with a woman*
> *collecting quarters, and two*
> *bored children from Michigan,*
> *I believed it.*
>
> *I cannot remember which Atlanta paper*
> *covers Dixie like the dew,*
> *but he wrote there. I remember*
> *Br'er Rabbit, and Bear, and the skin*
> *showing through the holes*
> *in the clothes of children walking*
> *past our house to the bayou.*
> *I wondered if they hated us, assumed*
> *they did, then watched without awe*
> *or anger the sixties smoke and burn*

around us. How many hands
stuck to that Tar Baby in the end;
some of my best friends were blackened.

A more indirect approach is taken by Henry Taylor in "Landscape with Tractor." A (presumably white) farmer discovers that what he originally thought was a "clothing-store dummy" is actually the body of a "well-dressed black woman" with "two bullet holes / in the breast" at the edge of a field he is plowing. Without ever abandoning the porch-sitting narrative style that led into his poem, Taylor creates a harrowing metaphor of those issues that have haunted twentieth-century southern literature: memory, guilt, collective responsibility.

Weeks pass. You hear at the post office
that no one comes forward to say who she was.
Brought out from the city, they guess, and dumped
like a bag of beer cans. She was someone

and now is no one, buried or burned
or dissected; but gone. And I ask you
again, how would it be? To go on with your life,
putting gas in the tractor, keeping down thistles,

and seeing, each time you pass that spot,
the form in the grass, the bright yellow skirt,
black shoes, the thing not quite like a face
whose gaze blasted past you at nothing

when the doctors heaved her over? To wonder,
from now on, what dope deal, betrayal,
or innocent refusal, brought her here,
and to know she will stay in that field till you die?

The easy-going way in which both these poems begin—as if the poet had no more ambition than to relate a nostalgic or arresting memory—strikes me as a perfect example of what I have called the porch-sitting mentality. The reader is lulled into the poem by the promise of a good, long story. Before long, however, it is obvious that the poem is far more than a diverting story offered up on a hot night. Each poem is speaking to issues that are right at the heart of contemporary southern life: the civil rights movement, the continuing invisibility of black citizens, the profound shame and sadness that southern whites of conscience experience about the region's racial history. What is interesting about the direction of much contemporary southern poetry is this desire to maintain a traditional narrative style even while introducing radically new subject matter.

What I see when I read the southern poets of my own generation and those of the generation preceding mine is an old and very familiar voice: garrulous and leisurely, narrative, many-branched, constantly harking back to the conditions of the earth itself, possessed of an inveterate sense of place and an implacable confidence in closure. This is not new; what *is* new is the shared desire to *reinvent* the South—to invent, poetically if you will, the New South—in the face of the momentous social and political changes that have occurred in the region. This somewhat divided impulse—to address the new without changing one's narrative style—reminds me very much of the Fugitives' similarly dualistic mission: to utilize an internationalist aesthetic in the service of a regional mentality.

Dave Smith is probably the best-known southern poet of his generation, and his work has always transcended a purely regional characterization; he has achieved a success similar to that of his Fugitive literary predecessors in invigorating the genre with a new subject matter without abandoning its historical narrative style. Such an endeavor is not without risks, but Smith has never been afraid to take them. Consequently, his work can be difficult for some readers who seek, perhaps, less ambivalence and more certainty in literature than actually exist in life. As a younger poet searching for southern literary mentors, I worried over his work for years. While it was easy to accept (and love) the work of the much older Robert Penn Warren, Smith's work was more problematic for me as a young writer struggling with the issue of poetic identity. I could accept Warren's outdated ideas about race relations and his tendency to mythologize (often tenderly) black characters in his work as a valid response to his early life in the 1910s and 1920s in rural Kentucky. After all, the South that he was born into and that was so important in the formation of his character was not, it seemed to me, my South at all. I was free to love the grand voice of his poetry, his constant investigation of the implication of the southern past within the southern present, and a quintessentially fulfilling storytelling impulse that informed all he wrote. Dave Smith, however, presented a problem. Born only eleven years before me, he was a product of the same time and space, more or less, as I was. (It is probably a significant difference, though, that I attended legally integrated schools for most of my education; he would not have.) The oracular rhetorical style (particularly of some of his earlier work) and his emphasis on traditional and familial values—both of which called to mind his southern literary mentors (like Warren)—irritated me, a decade ago, for reasons I could not then identify. Despite this, however, I could never stay away from his work, and I found myself drawn back to examine it again and again, always with deeply ambivalent feelings. There was one poem in particular that drove me wild with feelings I could not then articulate. It was a poem called "Night Fishing for Blues," from his third collection, *Cumberland Station*. The poem relates, through a first-person narrator, an incident that occurs during the annual running of the blues in the Chesapeake Bay. Alone, the narrator baits his hook and casts. Suddenly, he is "not alone": "three Negroes plump down in lawn chairs" beside him to claim their own share of the bay's bounty. One of the newcomers is an elderly black woman, "a grandmotherly obelisk" who chews tobacco and "hollers *I ain't doing so bad / for an old queen.*" In the course of the excitement over the running fish, the narrator accidentally lands his hook in the woman's cheek, not realizing for a moment what has occurred:

> *Incredibly it happens: I feel*
> *the hook hammer and shake and throw my entire weight*
> *to dragging, as if I have caught the goddamndest*
>   *Blue in the Atlantic. She screams: Oh my God!*
> *Four of us fumbling in beamed headlight and blue*
> *arc light cut the hook from her face. Gnats butterfly,*
> *nag us: I put it deep and it must be gouged out*
> *like a cyst.*

After her cheek is patched up, the woman goes back to fishing. Immediately, her line becomes entwined with the narrator's:

> *our lines leap rigid as daquerreotypes; we have*
> *caught each other but we go on for the blue blood of*
> *ghosts that thrash in the brain's empty room.*
> *We pull at shadows until we see there is nothing, then*
> *sit on the shaky pier like prisoners. Coil after coil*
> *we trace the path of Bluefish-knots backward,*
>   *unlooping, feeling for holes, giving, testing,*
> *slapping the gnats from our skins. Harried, unbound,*
> *we leap to be fishers.*

The poem ends with the woman instructing the narrator in how to pack his fish on ice "to keep them cold and sweet." Then the two of them "drink beer like family." The poem concludes,

> *All the way home thousands of Blues fall from my head,*
> *falling with the gray Atlantic, and a pale veiny light*
> *fills the road with sea-shadows that drift in figure*
>   *eights, knot and snarl and draw me forward.*

For years I found myself agonizing over what I considered to be the poem's cavalier attitude toward the damage inflicted on the black woman, the (presumably) white narrator's apparent indifference to it. What did it mean, I asked myself, that the injured woman wanted "nothing but to fish," that she seemed to "forgive" the careless fisherman so easily? Was this the New South's way of forgiving itself its racial history? A fantasy that the victims have forgiven the perpetrators? This social vision of the contemporary South, which labeled both blacks and whites "prisoners" of a shared destiny, both perplexed and embarrassed me for a long while as I sought to put aside disturbing parts of my personal history: the racism of my own family; my memories of life in Richmond before integration, when blacks rode in the backs of the buses and never came to the front door of my grandmother's house. My solution to this was to simply cut it out of my consciousness—a simple task as long as I was living out of the South, in California, New York, Massachusetts.

It is interesting to me that this poem did not make itself available to me until I had returned voluntarily to the South—to the Deep South, no less—after years of expatriation. The decision to leave New England for Louisiana was preceded by months of painful deliberation. I found myself remembering in great detail my early life and questioning the character that had been formed by those years in that place. Ultimately, the decision to return to the South—which I now consciously identified to myself as *home*—included the willingness to struggle again with the difficult issues that are specific to life in the region: a specious history of racial discrimination against blacks, political conservatism, and sexism that continues to masquerade as Old South chivalry. I found that I was finally willing to take these issues up again in exchange for a lifestyle that I had been unable to attain in other parts of the country: more value-oriented, less secular, conscientiously holistic in its integration of work, family, and pleasure. I wanted, too, more porch-sitting: time to sit with friends and family and *talk*, to tell stories, and to experience a kind of closure as I sat on the porch swing with my own son. This urgent need for closure, for circularity, this *demand* for resolution is so endemic to my southern consciousness that it took me years to identify it as such.

Then and only then the real meaning of "Night Fishing for Blues" became apparent to me. Although the line "We drink beer like family" may still be—is, in fact—a fantasy, it is *not* the fantasy of the Old South, where the "family" of black and white was one predicated on the subjugation and dependence of one and the institutionalized authority and debilitating paternalism of the other. This new family toward which Smith aspires in the poem is one in which the destinies of each are as entwined as twisted fishing lines, and however painful this proximity has been, the future will not be served by the propogation of old attitudes, nor by breast-beating or paralyzing guilt. Real people await real lives, real opportunities, real work; and so, in Smith's poem, both black and white accept the place to which they have been born by a painful past, and they find themselves "knot[ted] and snarl[ed] and draw[n] forward" into the future, where hopefully they will be transformed into the liberated "fishers" they now merely "leap to be."

This bring us, then, to the unspoken question on which this volume of essays is predicated. What *is* the future of southern letters? Is there one at all? It must be obvious that I would think so. Porch-sitting—real and metaphorical—persists, and will persist, I suspect, as long as there are stories to tell, people to relate them, and others to glory in the hearing. The positive human values I see reflected in contemporary southern poetry (in writers like Dave Smith, David Bottoms, Fred Chappell, T. R. Hummer, Alice Walker, Charles Wright, Cleopatra Mathis, James Applewhite, Brenda Marie Osbey, Margaret Gibson, Yusef Komunyakaa, and Betty Adcock)—however much they militate against the prevailing poetic spirit of our age—encourage me to imagine a rich future for southern letters in the twenty-first century. Beyond this, the intellectual ambitiousness and political conscience I see in poets like Bin Ramke and Dave Smith, who struggle with the most difficult questions of life in the contemporary South, are an indication that this genre, at least, is alive and well—invigorated rather than defeated by the challenges.

Southern poetry continues to invite the reader *in* with the promise of a story, which is, poetically, to insist on the importance of audience in the literary experience. This makes it a dynamic experience, energized by the participation of reader *and* writer, and enriched by the contributions of both. I find southern poetry, on the whole, to be resolutely antisolipsistic. The consciousness, then, that I have called "porch-sitting" is not an escapist or retrograde one, as some might suggest, however unfashionably it may compare to the work of *au courant* groups like the Language Poets, or even the so-called Neo-Formalists. The terror of the century, so well documented in the work of American poets, has not passed by unobserved or been less present in the lives of southern writers. Nevertheless, it is true that work by southerners has consistently exercised a more positive hope for the future and placed its faith in traditional, often religious values. Perhaps the terror has simply been more *bearable* for southern writers, who continue to experience their links with the past not only through their literary imaginations but also through the history-laden rituals of their daily lives. Southern writers rarely find it possible to escape intimate encounters with history, whether that history is a personal or public one. Charles Wright, for instance, hardly a southern writer if one considers the imaginary terrain over which his work has ranged, remains, to my mind, indubitably southern with regard to his obsessive poetic returns to his early life in Tennessee and his questioning of the role that memory plays in defining history. He has, perhaps, made the ultimate poetic comment on the porch-sitting mentality in the ending of his long poem "The Southern Cross," where he confides that he'll stop trying to remember and make a story out of his memories one day—the day he's dead:

> It's what we forget that defines us, and stays in the same place,
> And waits to be rediscovered.
> Somewhere in all that network of rivers and roads and silt hills,
> A city I'll never remember,
>   its walls the color of pure light,
> Lies in the August heat of 1935,
> In Tennessee, the bottom land slowly becoming a lake.
> It lies in a landscape that keeps my imprint
> Forever,
>   and stays unchanged, and waits to be filled back in.
> Someday I'll find it out
> And enter my old outline as though for the 1st time,
> And lie down, and tell no one.

Is this the kind of poetry that will fade away or languish, unnourished, by appreciative readers? I think not. The emotive connotations of our regional language are far too strong, connect us much too intimately to a place, to a *feeling* of *being* in a place, to disappear without a fight. While other poets quarrel over whether or not words mean anything and the return to strict form, southern poets remain where they've almost always been: sitting on the porch, listening, talking, and making poems out of a shared history and an imagined future. And that, after all, is the work of poets.

Sources

Brooks, Cleanth. *The Language of the American South*. Athens: University of Georgia Press, 1985.

Ramke, Bin. *The Language Student*. Baton Rouge: Louisiana State University Press, 1986.

Smith, Dave. *Cumberland Station*. Urbana: University of Illinois Press, 1976.

Taylor, Henry. *The Flying Change Poems*. Baton Rouge: Louisiana State University Press, 1985.

Wright, Charles. *The Southern Cross*. New York: Random House, 1981.

6

FRED HOBSON

Of Canons and Cultural Wars

Southern Literature and Literary
Scholarship after Midcentury

A couple of decades ago, the boundaries of southern literature—and south-ern literary scholarship—appeared to be rather fixed and unchallenged. Simply stated, the major southern writers of this century were William Faulkner, Thomas Wolfe, Robert Penn Warren, Allen Tate, Eudora Welty, and perhaps Flannery O'Connor. The contemporary novelists to be reckoned with—besides Welty—were William Styron, Walker Percy, and perhaps John Barth. (One observed as well a number of southerners trying to write like Faulkner; they were said to be "in his shadow.") The reigning interpreters and critics of southern literature—it is little exaggeration to say the founders of southern literature as a modern academic discipline—were such figures as Louis D. Rubin Jr., Lewis P. Simpson, C. Hugh Holman, and Thomas Daniel Young, with certain other scholars, such as Walter Sullivan, making occasional brilliant forays into the field. The genres worth pursuing academically were the novel, the short story, poetry, and perhaps—in the case of Tennessee Williams—drama. Those who did the pursuing were professors of English, and although Professors Rubin, Simpson, Holman, and certain others operated from a literary method that was also keenly aware of history, in general the scholarly approach to southern literature—or literature in general—was a sort of literary formalism inherited largely from the New Critics. The centers of publishing for southern literary scholarship were Chapel Hill and Baton Rouge; but the only places southern writers of fiction and poetry could be pub-lished were in New York or, occasionally, Boston. *All* creative writers from the hinterlands, south or west, were published in New York and Boston.

All that was in, say, 1970, even 1975, and some of what was true then remains true. Faulkner, Warren, and Welty—if not Wolfe—are still considered the major southern writers (although Ralph Ellison would now likely be included). Styron and Percy are still major figures as well, and Chapel Hill and Baton Rouge are still the centers for publication of works on southern thought and writing. Professors Rubin and Simpson are still, twenty years later, perhaps the most distinguished figures in southern literary studies, indeed in the whole realm of southern cultural history. But in other respects, much has changed. To begin with, it seems to me—as an editor who saw a couple of thousand short story manuscripts come across his desk in the mid- and late 1980s—that many southern writers now operate not under the shadow of Faulkner but under that of O'Connor and Welty, their respective brands of southern humor perhaps *seeming* easier to imitate than Faulkner's cosmic drama. As for those writers who find success, they often find it now in places other than New York. Not only are university presses below the Potomac and Ohio publishing some of the finest southern fiction and poetry, but a commercial venture, Algonquin Books of Chapel Hill, publishes some of the most distinguished southern writing.

Nor are those who write about southern letters any longer exclusively English professors. Some of the most stimulating recent work about southern writers and writing has come from such historians as David Donald, Bertram Wyatt-Brown, Michael O'Brien, Richard King, and Daniel Singal. (C. Vann Woodward arrived long ago.) And for most of those English professors who treat southern fiction, neither the New Criticism nor the old historicism is the method of choice. I will leave it to others in this volume to discuss the contributions of contemporary literary theory to the understanding of southern letters; suffice it to say that in most quarters the old method of literary formalism has lost favor (although I would add that, in some respects, the old New Criticism and the new critical approaches have more in common than either camp has acknowledged). Neither are the poem, novel, short story— and, occasionally, drama—any longer the sole provinces of the American and southern literary scholar. Autobiography, biography, memoir, diary, the essay of cultural reflection, "literary journalism," oral history, even the sort of subjective history Wilbur Cash wrote: All of them are—and should be—the province of the literary scholar as well. If the journalistic essays of Addison and Steele, the history of Gibbon, the *Life of Johnson*, the writings of Burke (and, in the following century, the histories of Carlyle and Macaulay, the criticism of Ruskin, and the essays of Arnold on the condition of England) are to be studied in literature courses, as certainly they should be, so in twentieth-century American literature should be the essays of Mencken and Edmund Wilson and those several histories, biographies, memoirs, diaries, and so forth that have achieved genuine literary distinction. The finest works in these genres should not have to be a century or two in the past and across the ocean to qualify as "literature."

What we have seen in the past two decades, then—and it has been said so often it has become a cliché—is an expansion of the American literary canon and, for our purposes, the southern canon. The canon has expanded for two reasons, one literary, the other extraliterary, although the two can hardly be separated. The former I have already mentioned: It has become clear that the tools of the literary scholar might be applied to forms of nineteenth- and twentieth-century American writing other than fiction, poetry, and drama. Through this means, various southern works—James Agee's *Let Us Now Praise Famous Men*, William Alexander Percy's *Lanterns on the Levee*, the Southern Agrarians' *I'll Take My Stand*, even Cash's *Mind of the South*—that once were read, if at all, in social and intellectual history classes have been deemed worthy of study in southern literature courses. And not only those works but, more important in a social and cultural sense, the narratives of Frederick Douglass, Harriet Jacobs, Zora Neale Hurston, Lillian Smith, and others. The expansion of the canon, then, came as well for extraliterary reasons: Literature responded to the needs of, the changes reflected in, society. The civil rights revolution of the 1960s, the women's movement, the questioning of "official truth" during the Vietnam War era: The academy—broadly speaking, and with exceptions— responded to all three creatively, imaginatively. What has taken place in the past twenty-five years might be described as the second wave in the democratizing of American literature in our century. The first wave occurred in the century's earliest years as Mencken and Dreiser—Mencken with conscious intent, Dreiser simply writing what he knew—led a charge against the Genteel Tradition, the exclusively *English* cultural tradition in America, and demanded that other writers, writers of German and Eastern European origins, be included in American literature as well. That battle was won by the 1920s, but the second battle—for the inclusion of slave narratives, documents of liberation for blacks and women, other forms of African-American literature, Native American literature, Chicano literature, and so forth—had to wait until the 1970s and 1980s. This time members of the academy—again, broadly speaking, since one finds exceptions—assumed a somewhat different role in the battle. In the early twentieth century, academicians—the "doktor-professors," Mencken called them—were the guardians of the Genteel Tradition. A notable English professor, Stuart Sherman, decried the "barbaric naturalism" of Theodore Dreiser, and Sherman rather accurately represented his brethren. But if, in the early twentieth century, the literary academy was an exclusive, conservative institution—the target for Mencken and the iconoclasts—it has become, late in the century (as reflected, say, in the MLA), a leading proponent for something close to inclusiveness in American letters.

I do not state a universally held opinion when I say that this has also been the case in southern literary scholarship, although at a pace somewhat slower than in other parts of the country. That slow pace was particularly noticeable in one respect: Southern blacks were incorporated into the canon far too slowly, although for reasons (to be explored later) more complicated than simply white racism. In the twentieth century, southern women—white women, a certain *kind* of white women—were never really excluded, as evidenced by the central roles of Welty, O'Connor, Katherine Anne Porter, Caroline Gordon, and Carson McCullers in modern southern letters. One might argue that these women were accepted because, except perhaps for McCullers, they did not truly challenge the patriarchal southern system—and it is true that they did not, or were not perceived to at the time, in any substantial way. The reception accorded a southern woman who did challenge the racial and sexual status quo—say, Lillian Smith—was quite different. Not only certain of the Agrarians found fault with her, as might be expected, but leading male white liberals as well, Ralph McGill and Hodding Carter among them. It is important to point out, however, that Lillian Smith *as a writer of fiction* was accorded a lesser position than Welty, O'Connor, Gordon, and Porter not so much because she was an integrationist and a feminist but because, as a novelist, she was far less skilled than they at her craft. She simply did not write fiction as well. She did write autobiography and cultural commentary brilliantly and creatively, and the primary reason for the exclusion of Lillian Smith from the southern literary canon was not her positions on race and gender but rather that her best writing belongs to genres that were not considered appropriate for literary courses. *Killers of the Dream* and *The Journey*—not her novel *Strange Fruit*—were her masterpieces, and they are southern classics. On the subject of racial and sexual roles, Smith was the boldest, most original white southern thinker of her day, a truly radical analyst of southern society. But what she wrote was not universally considered to be "literature."

I.

It may be clear, from these opening remarks, that I should like to undertake a rather freewheeling consideration of the state of southern literature (or the imaginative writing done by southerners) and of southern literary scholarship (the writing done about the writing) in our time, although perhaps reversing the natural order and looking at the scholarship first. For southern literary scholarship, at least as a systematic body of writing, is a rather recent phenomenon and, given such past efforts, a noteworthy one. There were, to be sure, earlier attempts to "study" southern letters—first by William P. Trent and William Malone Baskervill in the 1890s, continued in some fashion by John Spencer Bassett and Edwin Mims in the early years of the twentieth century, and executed most successfully by Jay B. Hubbell in *The South in American Literature* in 1954. Yet Hubbell's book extended only to 1900, and as any sophomore survey student knows, it is the southern literature written since that time that counts most.

It seems to me that we find the origins of modern southern literature as an academic discipline in a volume published in Baltimore in 1953: *Southern Renascence*, edited by Louis D. Rubin Jr. and Robert D. Jacobs. The book (and its paperback edition, published thirteen years later) has been used by scores of teachers and students of southern letters, yet its importance in establishing a field of southern literature has perhaps never been fully acknowledged. Its publication was in its own way an event as momentous (though it would hardly have seemed so at the time) as the publication in 1930 of *I'll Take My Stand* or that in 1941 of *The Mind of the South* or, in 1951, of C. Vann Woodward's *Origins of the New South*. For what *Southern Renascence* did was to define and open up a field of study—the literature of the post-1920 South, as distinct from the southern writing that had gone before—presenting critical essays on the works of William Faulkner, Thomas Wolfe, Robert Penn Warren, and some dozen other writers, as well as general essays on southern literature and the southern mind. "The Mind of the South" as set forth in the first three essays, by Robert Heilman, Richard Weaver, and Andrew Lytle, was portrayed as an essentially conservative mind, but the volume also included essays by liberals Woodward and Howard W. Odum and essays about (besides Wolfe) Erskine Caldwell, Ellen Glasgow, and James Branch Cabell, none of whom could be called a southern traditionalist. The 1953 volume, then, was a largely representative book (with one major exception, which we shall consider later), but most of all it was a book bringing order to the brilliant but somewhat disconnected outpouring of fiction and poetry from the South of the previous three decades. And it affixed a name, "Southern Renascence" (a term that had been used, on occasion, before by Tate and others), to that period of southern literature between 1925 and 1950, a name that took hold even more firmly than, say, F. O. Matthiessen's "American Renaissance" or Van Wyck Brooks's "Flowering of New England." It also might have suggested to the alert reader—although the editors did not so state specifically—that what had happened in the southern states in the preceding quarter century was comparable to what had happened in New England exactly a century before and in the Middle West a half century earlier—the rise of a great regional literature that was far more than regional—and perhaps for something of the same reasons as New England and the Midwest in their flowerings: the challenge to the old agrarian society by the new industrial order, and a "backward glance" (as Allen Tate put it) as the South slipped from one world into the next.

Thus in one respect it might be contended that—by defining, by identifying—Rubin and Jacobs, nearly as much as Faulkner and Tate and Warren, were "responsible" for the "Southern Renascence," that is, for a period of literary history bearing that name. They also played a great part in establishing a canon—Faulkner, Wolfe, Warren, Welty, Tate, O'Connor, Caroline Gordon, and so forth—which, if one considers the task, is not an easy thing to do in the midst of a literature being written. Consider an equivalent task—drawing up in the mid-1990s a list of those southern writers and those works since 1965 that are worthy of study and will continue to be well into the twenty-first century—and one will have some idea of the difficulty of the undertaking. Certainly there were omissions from the writers under discussion—most notably, black southerners (a reflection of the thinking of even the "advanced" white South in 1953, a time when liberals such as Odum and Ralph McGill still doubted the wisdom of school integration). But the undertaking and the vision it required was remarkable and accounts in large part for the origins of what Lewis P. Simpson has called "the Rubin Generation" in southern literary scholarship. That the generation might in fact perhaps be called "the Rubin-Simpson Generation" (Cleanth Brooks once called the two men the pillars of the southern literary establishment) does not change the point. It is no exaggeration to say that Rubin, Simpson, C. Hugh Holman, and their generation did in southern literary scholarship what Faulkner did in southern fiction: They brought it, and more consciously than Faulkner (and, they would say, operating in a less imaginative realm), into a new age. They too cast a long shadow, and just as novelists found it difficult for a good while to escape Faulkner's shadow, southern literary scholars have found it difficult to escape theirs.

This brings us, without too much of a leap, to the present, or at least to the recent past, and perhaps the most significant event of the past decade in southern literary scholarship is the publication in 1985 of *The History of Southern Literature*, a work for which Rubin served as general editor and Simpson, Blyden Jackson, Rayburn Moore, and Thomas Daniel Young—that is, the leading figures of the Rubin-Simpson generation—as section editors. *The History of Southern Literature* received widespread praise, but it also stirred minor controversy. I think in particular of an essay titled "Southern Literature: Consensus and Dissensus," by Michael Kreyling, published in *American Literature* in March 1988. It is Kreyling's thesis that the *History* is inadequate in many ways, that it grants the South "the privilege of icon, sacred rather than historical"; that the volume and the approach to southern letters it represents is "sequestered in consensus" in an age of dissensus; that it does not give sufficient attention to contemporary literary theory; and that it owes a "heavy debt to the conservative consensus of the renascence," a consensus with its origins in Southern Agrarianism.

I should say at the outset that I think more highly of *The History of Southern Literature* than Kreyling does, and I think it is important to examine certain of his contentions. Much of what he says has merit: The volume does not give sufficient attention to contemporary theory (although to do so might be difficult in a work of this scope), and there has always been a tendency to make the southern tradition, including the literary tradition, essentially a conservative tradition—although I should point out that this tendency is less characteristic of the *History* than of its predecessors, and that in this volume, that tendency has far more to do with the nature of much modern southern writing than with the politics of the editors.

But the larger point—independent of *The History of Southern Literature*—requires discussion. The "southern tradition" is certainly not exclusively a conservative tradition: sociologists such as Odum and Rupert Vance are just as much a part of it as Donald Davidson, Thomas Wolfe as much as Andrew Lytle, Wilbur Cash as much as William Alexander Percy—and Richard Wright and Zora Neale Hurston as much as any of them. I have argued elsewhere that those "aspects of the Southern Philosophy" identified and celebrated by the Agrarians and by neo-Agrarians such as Richard Weaver are open to great debate: that those qualities stemming from the Civil War and its aftermath—a tragic sense, a greater attention to the past, an acceptance of man's finiteness and his penchant for failure—probably *are* more characteristic of the southerner than of other Americans, but that other qualities pronounced distinctively southern—a religious sense, a closeness to nature, a greater attention to and affection for place, a preference for the concrete and a rage against abstraction—are in fact rather characteristic of any rural people who have lived in a traditional society in a single area for a great number of years: upper New England, for example, or even parts of the eastern Middle West. In fact, one might contend that the southern mind, despite its stated abhorrence of abstraction from the 1840s on, has been in certain respects the most abstract of minds. What else was racial segregation but a monstrous abstraction, what else the identifying and categorizing (and thus restricting) of any individuals—including women—by group?

So Kreyling is justified in raising the broad issue—in questioning whether we have too readily accepted the Agrarian definition of the South and the southerner, and thus the Agrarian definition of southern literature—but I believe he is excessive in presuming a conservative bias on the part of the editors of *The History of Southern Literature*, or, in other particulars, making them overly responsible for the sins of some of their contributors. Kreyling focuses, for example, on an ill-considered remark by M. Thomas Inge in an appendix that serves as a survey of southern literary scholarship. In considering Richard H. King's *Southern Renaissance* (1980), Inge charges that King "moves beyond history and sociology into cultural anthropology and psychoanalysis, which in conjunction with the sympathy for the liberal tradition makes a balanced treatment of the literature impossible." This is hardly the case: King's book, in fact, adds much to the discussion of twentieth-century southern letters—partly *because* of his use of psychology and his "sympathy for the liberal tradition"— and Kreyling is right to contest Inge's evaluation. But he also seems to suggest that Inge speaks for the editors and the general philosophy of *The History of Southern Literature*. Kreyling writes:

> This is a clear warning: the study of southern literature shall be reserved
> for the community of the faithful who believe in the South as icon above
> and beyond history and intellect, who eschew literary approaches through
> alien territory occupied by the tribes of Levi-Strauss and Freud, and who
> espouse a conservative tradition as far to the right as T. S. Eliot.

I would doubt, in fact, that the editors and most of the contributors to *The History of Southern Literature* "believe in the South as icon above and beyond history and intellect," that they reject Freud (Lévi-Strauss may be another matter), that they position themselves "as far to the right as T. S. Eliot." The editors of the *History* are hardly guilty of an act of "literary secession"; they are not afflicted with "literary-historical amnesia that, by design or not, has overtaken the study of southern literature."

One other issue that Kreyling raises needs to be addressed: liberalism and conservatism and their relation to southern letters. It is a subject that was often discussed in the 1930s, with the Agrarians in Nashville and the liberals in Chapel Hill taking their stands and representing two distinctly different schools of southern thought. Politics indeed got into literature: Donald Davidson, for example, charged that Howard Odum's liberalism had ruined a number of writers who attended Chapel Hill—including Thomas Wolfe, who

Davidson felt was particularly tainted by Odum's liberal "social program." (That Odum did not arrive in Chapel Hill until the year after Wolfe graduated, Davidson did not consider.) Wolfe, Davidson contended, would have been a vastly different and better writer if he had turned west to Nashville, not east to Chapel Hill.

Davidson was wrong about that, and in fact he was falling into the same sociological trap—the assumption that environment explains all—that he warned others to avoid. Thomas Wolfe can no more be explained by social and cultural environment than can William Faulkner, who emerged in the 1920s in Mississippi, the least likely state in which genius could appear, according to all the sociological indexes. But Davidson *was* right when he maintained that the Vanderbilt conservatives talked more about literary values than the Chapel Hill liberals. That was understandable: the most prominent of the North Carolina thinkers was Odum, a sociologist, and the writers associated with the Chapel Hill "school"—belletrists such as Paul Green and literary critics such as Addison Hibbard—were as concerned with reforming the South as with producing great literature. Given the condition of the South in the 1920s and 1930s, theirs was perhaps the higher calling. But the point is that they ceded the field of literary criticism, of serious discussion of literature as art, to the Vanderbilt writers, and the most prominent of the Fugitive-Agrarians became the highly influential New Critics. Ransom and Tate, Warren and Brooks were brilliant students of literature, and regardless of the supposed purity of the New Criticism, it was impossible that their remarks on writing not also reflect their social philosophy. Ransom, Tate, and Warren were not only brilliant critics; they were also the finest of southern poets and—in Warren's case and, briefly, Tate's—excellent writers of fiction as well. As literary artists, what were the southern liberals—T. S. Stribling, Paul Green, Frances Newman, Erskine Caldwell, even Thomas Wolfe after *Look Homeward, Angel*—compared to Ransom, Tate, and Warren, as well as Gordon, Porter, O'Connor, Lytle, and other conservative writers? Certainly not as social philosophers but as writers, the conservatives simply won the day.

I say this as one whose natural sympathies lie with southern liberalism, as one who came of age believing that Frank Porter Graham was the nearest thing to a saint the twentieth-century white South has produced and that those who vilified Graham (such as young Jesse Helms as a campaign worker for Willis Smith in the 1950 North Carolina senate race) were the worst the South had produced. I am still of that general persuasion. But Donald Davidson had been right in contending that a "social program" did not lead to the making of a great southern literature. The writer concerned more with reform than with storytelling—more with the plight of a region than with the individual drama at hand—with the story as an illustration of social ills to be exposed and corrected—is not likely to be, all other things being equal, as skillful a literary craftsman. He is not as likely to have his eye on the work of art. That alone hardly explains why William Faulkner was a better writer than T. S. Stribling or Paul Green, but it does, among other things, explain why the Agrarians won the literary battle. (It is perhaps significant that the most important book to come out of the North Carolina school of the 1920s and 1930s was not a work of fiction at all—save perhaps *Look Homeward, Angel*—but rather a creative and powerful work of analysis, *The Mind of the South*.) And to the winners of the literary battle went the right to be the interpreters, the arbiters, of southern literature. Just as surely as the North, after the Civil War, seized the opportunity to write American history, so the Agrarians and other conservatives seemed to have won the right not only to interpret but also to define southern literature. Thus Tate, Ransom, Warren, and Davidson in a number of essays in the 1930s and, in Davidson's case, the 1940s seemed to cast liberal or iconoclastic figures who in earlier years had been highly touted—Wolfe, Green, Cabell, Caldwell, Newman, and Stribling (a paragraph in the history of critical realism, Warren said)—out of southern literature. As it turned out, they were right about Stribling and partly right about the others. But more deserving writers of the 1930s and 1940s—Richard Wright, Zora Neale Hurston, James Agee, Lillian Smith—were also excluded, disqualified largely by race or, in Smith's case, not so much gender as genre.

What does this oversimplified summary of southern literary history have to do with the state of southern literary scholarship at present? Simply that those who have written best about southern letters for the past four decades naturally have been drawn to those novelists and poets—and critics—whose literary skills were most refined, whose imaginative vision resulted in greater works of literature, and that means Faulkner, Tate, Warren, Welty, and O'Connor, not Stribling, Green, Newman, and Caldwell. It isn't that one shares the conservative views of Tate, and the early Ransom and Warren, when one values their literary work, just as one does not necessarily accept T. S. Eliot's politics when one is drawn to his poetry. Scholars go where the good writing is, to works rich and full and suggestive, works that most fully engage their minds. In the South of the past thirty or forty years that has meant, primarily, William Styron, Ralph Ellison, and Walker Percy, writers who have been (certainly in a southern context) political liberals. But when one deals with the literature of the pre-1950 Southern Renaissance, one finds largely conservatives.

We must make another distinction: To be a political (or, in the 1960s, racial) liberal, particularly in the American South, is not the same as to be a cultural liberal (as Walker Percy, among others, illustrates), and this, I believe, is responsible for part of the confusion over whether southern literary scholarship has had a conservative agenda or not. Certainly many of the Agrarians, though hardly all, were cultural *and* political conservatives: One thinks of Davidson resisting any racial change in southern society. But I would venture that many of the most notable scholars of southern literature of the Rubin-Simpson generation and beyond might fall into a category labeled "political liberal and cultural conservative." Such a combination might be unlikely, say, in England, but hardly so in the American South, which presents to the mind and to the senses a variety of phenomena that might drive one, at one and the same time, *into* political liberalism and at least a partial cultural conservatism.

Such a cultural conservatism is dangerous only when it slides into a social conservatism that excludes—because the history of the South, which means a history of southern literature as well, has been a history of exclusion. This leads me to the greatest shortcoming of southern literary scholarship, one I have referred to but not focused on in this essay—its reluctance to accept black southern writers as part of the southern canon. That, it should be noted, is not a problem with *The History of Southern Literature*: black contributors are abundant, black writers are discussed in detail, the black contribution to southern letters is certainly acknowledged. This is but one of many ways in which the editors depart from a "conservative" agenda. Far from abiding by an Agrarian exclusionary policy, the editors include discussions of writers whom Davidson and Tate would never have admitted into a southern canon.

But inclusion of black writers was hardly the case in many quarters of southern literary study as recently as twenty-five years ago, and for reasons, as I suggested earlier, that were more complicated than, simply, white racism. It may seem incredible, but as late as the 1960s it apparently did not occur to some white scholars (many of whom had good credentials as racial integrationists) that black southern writing was exactly a part of *southern* literature, to be taught in southern literature courses. There was the Southern Renascence, and there was the Harlem Renaissance. There were southern writers, there were African-American writers, there were Jewish writers, there were northern suburban WASP writers (Cheever and Updike). And so on. It was not, at least in most quarters, a judgment of literary or personal worth; it was just—so the reasoning would have gone—that black writers seemed to fall into a different category of American literature. Even many of those white scholars who were certainly aware that black southerners were very much a part of southern literature, who taught black writers in their southern literature courses, tended to perpetuate the separation by the way they chose to write southern literary history.

I offer a personal example. In the mid-1970s, I began a book—eventually entitled *Tell About the South*—that endeavored to explore the southern rage to "explain" the South to outsiders and southerners alike. I was concerned with two traditions of white southern "explaining": that of conservatives or apologists (which I called the school or party of remembrance) and that of liberals or critics (the party of shame and guilt). By conscious decision I dealt only with white writers, although I pointed out in the introduction that if any southerner possessed a right, and a rage, to tell about the South, it was the black southerner. But I felt I could not deal adequately with the black rage to explain in that particular book for two reasons: In a practical sense, the book as planned was already long and ambitious enough (it became four hundred pages in print); but, more important, black southerners could not fit into either of the two southern traditions I was interested in exploring. Certainly they could not belong to the party of remembrance and defense, that tradition of Edmund Ruffin, Donald Davidson, and William Alexander Percy; but neither did blacks belong in the southern school of shame and guilt (white liberal guilt). Blacks—

through slavery, segregation, abuse—were at the *center* of that guilt, but, being victims of the abuse, not its dispensers, black southerners could hardly express remorse for it. As I concluded in the introduction, the story of the black southerner's rage to explain was a book in itself, and most reviewers of the book, North and South, accepted that *Tell About the South*, because of the particular dialectic involved, had to be as it was. But one reviewer challenged the dialectic. Although she made several kind remarks, the reviewer also held that the book (as well as similar studies by Michael O'Brien, Daniel Singal, and Richard King) was only partially successful because, whatever the reasons, it did not include black writers. I started to write the reviewer to explain why I did not feel that blacks fit into the categories, the system, of this particular book. But that sounded too much like apologies I had heard before. So I did not write, and have wondered since whether the reviewer was perhaps right: If black writers did not fit my categories, perhaps I should have changed my categories. Would that have been shaping one's scholarship just for the sake of inclusion? I wasn't certain. But I was well aware of the history of southern exclusion—the pretense of separate but equal—that prompted the objection.

II.

What began as preface to this essay has nearly become the essay itself, and what was intended as the essay—on the state of contemporary southern writing—will become an extended postscript, although one sharing many concerns with what has preceded it. As regards, then, the condition of imaginative writing, particularly fiction, in the contemporary South: It seems to me, except for one particular, to be as healthy as it has ever been. I would probably not have held that opinion twenty years ago. Although one then found excellent writers, both established and emerging, it appeared that southern literature, like the South itself, was, to borrow Arnold's lines, "wandering between two worlds, one dead, / the other powerless to be born." If that was indeed the case, that birth has now taken place. Or rebirth. Nascence and renascence, birth and rebirth, have always been very much on the mind of the southern literary scholar. Was the Renascence of the 1920s and 1930s a renascence at all, or was it rather a nascence—the birth of a truly distinguished southern literature—since relatively little of distinction, at least in the way of *high* culture, had come before? And if that was the nascence, would the writing of the past fifteen or twenty years—not only because of its vitality but because of somewhat different assumptions among southern writers—be more accurately a renascence?

The distinction isn't worth pursuing. But it does seem to me that something has happened to southern literature, to southern fiction in particular, in the past twenty years that makes it significantly different from southern writing as recent as the late 1960s. The decade of the 1960s, in fact, might be seen as pivotal in southern life and letters in much the same way the 1920s was: it was a time of great intellectual ferment, of notable attention from without (Donald Davidson, as he did for the 1920s, would have called it neo-abolitionism), of great social change. The scenes this time were Birmingham and Selma and Philadelphia, Mississippi—not Dayton, Tennessee, and Gastonia—but the effect was the same: southern barbarities were exposed, southern traditions and mores were challenged, the South changed (though more decisively this time), a watershed in southern thought resulted—and, in some ways, a new literature emerged. The new set of assumptions had something to do with the fact that after the 1960s, it appeared that the South had endured its crisis, had triumphed over itself, had in fact come through. It had—so said the self-congratulators—thrown off the old albatross of racism, and with that gone the South was no longer what it long had been: defeated, failed, poor, guilt-ridden, tragic. What that change did to the southern writer is intriguing. Faulkner and the great writers of the Renascence had written with the assumption that the South *was* the defeated, guilt-ridden, backward-looking, tragic part of America; much of the power of their fiction came from that assumption. What was the writer to do with what seemed to be a suddenly superior South—optimistic, forward-looking, more virtuous, and now threatening to become more prosperous than the rest of the country? Success would require a new voice—and less reliance on the models of the past.

But that voice did not emerge all at once, was in fact rarely seen before the 1970s. Most writers through the late 1960s still wrote, it seems to me, with an eye very much on past southern giants. William Styron, one of the two most significant southern novelists of the past forty years, could not seem to escape, did not *want* to escape the influence of Faulkner and Wolfe. In ways too numerous to point out, *Lie Down in Darkness* was *The Sound and the Fury* cast in Tidewater Virginia. One also had to be reminded of Faulkner, although less obviously, in *The Confessions of Nat Turner*. And in *Sophie's Choice*, a novel written in the 1970s but belonging very much to the 1950s and 1960s, Styron seemed in many ways to be rewriting Wolfe. Stingo, the autobiographical protagonist of a long, wordy, self-indulgent novel—another young, impressionable, horny WASP up from the North Carolina Piedmont, finding a place in Brooklyn, fascinated by the man-swarm of New York, particularly fascinated by Jewishness and ethnicity, and out to write the Great American Novel—is in many ways the young Thomas Wolfe or Eugene Gant or George Webber. Styron could leave Wolfe behind no more easily than he could leave Faulkner.

Nor could any number of white southern writers, as late as the 1960s, relinquish the southern writer's traditional role in relation to society—an adversary relationship, or more accurately a love-hate relationship seen in numerous earlier writers but exemplified best perhaps by a tortured fictional character, Quentin Compson of *Absalom, Absalom!* Shame, guilt, anger, pride: These were still the feelings pronounced in many southern writers of the 1960s, seen both in novels dealing with race and the civil rights movement and perhaps even more dramatically in a number of non-fiction works of contrition and confession, including Willie Morris's *North Toward Home* and Larry L. King's *Confessions of a White Racist*. These books were very much in the tradition of George W. Cable, Wilbur Cash, Lillian Smith, and James McBride Dabbs, a tradition that required the writer to deeply and painfully probe his relationship to his homeland. But something seemed to be missing in these latter-day confessionals. They are interesting and eloquent—*North toward Home* has become, deservedly, something of a southern classic—but one wonders if their authors really *meant* it as deeply as Cable and Cash and Smith had, if they were risking all in their truth-telling as their predecessors had. Or were they merely writing in a particular southern mode, writing the obligatory love-hate-pride-shame memoir more out of custom and habit—and the realization that they had a good story to tell—than out of true rage, fear, indignation, love, hate, or anything else? In the South of the late 1960s, positive thinking, not contrition, was dominant. Could the writer in *that* South, no longer severely afflicted by an inferiority complex, released from the savage ideal, besieged neither by critics from the North nor in his or her own backyard, write with that same intensity and conviction, even fear and trembling, that drove Cable and Smith and Cash—or, on the other side, Edmund Ruffin or Donald Davidson? Had what was once natural become stylized, what once was deeply and painfully experienced become ritualized? Had the passion disappeared, leaving behind only the form?

To a great degree perhaps it had, but one quality that much of the writing through the early 1970s did share with the writing that had gone before was an acute self-consciousness, an intense awareness of *being* southern, as well as preoccupation with old themes, old settings, and truisms. The white southern writer, generally speaking, still thought he had a love-hate relationship with the South whether he did or not, and he or she had to write the obligatory work coming to terms with his or her homeland.

I do not believe that is the case with most white southern writers who have begun to publish in the past twenty years. Those writers—again, broadly speaking—seem hardly to have the need to join the battle, to wrestle with racial sin and guilt. What one does find in novelists such as Bobbie Ann Mason and Anne Tyler is a relative *lack* of southern self-consciousness. That is not to say that the *voice* often isn't southern—with writers such as Clyde Edgerton and Lee Smith it most assuredly is—or that those old preoccupations of the southern writer, the family and the past, are any less in evidence. Neither is it to contend that black southern writers—one thinks of Ernest Gaines, Alice Walker, and James Alan McPherson—have forgotten the pain and suffering in the South before 1965 and some of the pain that endures. Nor, finally, can one contend that, among white writers, the earlier Savage South of fiction—what Gerald W. Johnson after reading Faulkner and Caldwell in 1935 called Raw-Head-and-Bloody-Bones school of southern fiction —has been left behind completely. Cormac McCarthy, Harry Crews, and Barry Hannah, among other novelists, have written a sort of neo–Southern Gothic. McCarthy's *Child of God* (1973), a tale of murder and necrophilia more lurid than anything Faulkner or Caldwell ever invented—or, in a more contemporary vein, Hannah's *Ray* (1980)—assure us that a savage South still lives in imaginative literature. The problem for neo-Gothic novelists is that southern social reality, broad and representative reality, no longer so dramatically supports their fiction.

What we have, then, is a larger number of truly talented southern writers of fiction than we have had at any one time before, and it would serve no purpose to indulge in an old southern habit and list two or three dozen contemporary southern writers who, *this* time, truly are worthy of stacking up against the best anywhere. It seems that many southerners have at last realized that elusive quality—and in a way Donald Davidson could not have imagined—that Davidson in the 1920s called the "autochthonous ideal": that condition in which the literary artist is in a certain harmony with his environment, is not overwhelmingly concerned with regional interpretation or reform (although he is sometimes still a local colorist), and thus is free simply to tell his story without a regional self-consciousness. (One of the two most notable contemporary southern-born poets, A. R. Ammons, is so devoid of southern self-consciousness, in fact, that his literary ancestors are more nearly the New England Transcendentalists than the Agrarians or any other southern poets.) If one has any concern about the state of contemporary southern fiction, it might be that one finds—despite an abundance of literary skill, verisimilitude, charm, picturesqueness, and humor—a certain want of *power*, a power that often had its origins in or at least was related to—in Warren, Styron, and part of Faulkner—a southern self-consciousness; a power that in Warren and Styron stemmed in part from a philosophical, even mildly didactic intent; a power, finally, that was grounded in the tragic sense. If Styron was the successor to Faulkner—not only did he aspire to be, but I believe in many respects he was—I find no successors to Styron. I find no novel by a young southerner that attempts so much as *The Confessions of Nat Turner, Sophie's Choice*, Ellison's *Invisible Man*, or a more recent work by a non-southerner, Toni Morrison's *Song of Solomon*. The minimalist fiction of Mason and others, no matter how well done it is, does not lend itself to that kind of force, and neither does the new, largely comic southern novel of manners. I say this while realizing that I am perhaps looking for a particular *kind* of power, a particular sort of "ambitious novel." The work of Mason, Clyde Edgerton, Lee Smith, and numerous other writers has the power of observation, the energy and vitality of life as lived, the power of telling the truth, and that is no small accomplishment.

One hesitates to venture prophecies about the future of southern fiction. If one had attempted such a prophecy in 1925, say, one would likely have foreseen social realism of the sort T. S. Stribling was writing, not the mythic and poetic kind of novels William Faulkner was to write. This much appears probable: the promise of southern fiction lies in a direction different from that in which Faulkner, Wolfe, Warren, and Styron took it—the *big* novel—and if young writers still feel the need for models, they can find an exemplar in Walker Percy—well aware of what has gone before but closely observing the here and now, keenly attuned to contemporary science, religion, language, trendiness, false gods of various sorts, and modernity in general. Southern writers must observe *their* contemporary South, not Faulkner's or O'Connor's or Richard Wright's, and that is what the new writer is doing well indeed. But as well as observing keenly, these writers, like Styron, must not be afraid to tackle the big subject, take the big chance.

7

JIM WAYNE MILLER

. . . And Ladies of the Club

"What is that you're a-zaminin so clost?" Sut said as he entered Capehart's Bar and Baitshop, where I sat reading *The History of Southern Literature*, edited by Professors Louis D. Rubin Jr., Blyden Jackson, Rayburn S. Moore, Lewis Simpson, and Thomas Daniel Young, and recently published by Louisiana State University Press (of Baton Rouge and London). "A-squinchin up your eyes and a-holdin your mouf like somebody tryin to bait a treble-hook wif a nightcrawler."

"Sut Lovingood! I've just been thinking about you. This is a new history of southern literature, and you're mentioned in it, Sut."

"I be dodrabbited."

"I'm reviewing the book, and this is what I've said so far: Reading *The History of Southern Literature*, I feel a lot like Sut Lovingood at Mrs. Yardley's quilting party. These seventy-plus essays are attractive and well-made, like the fine quilts hanging on clothes lines stretched to every post and tree at Mrs. Yardley's. Just as Sut has the urge to bolt a horse at the scene (which gets a quilt over its head, wheels, runs wild, tearing down the whole display), I feel like scattering these essays up and down the road and along the creek-bank and starting all over. Or in the words of Melville's Queequeg: *Us cannibals have to help those Christians.*"

"You shore know how to ladle out words," Sut said. "But seem like hit's a power of trouble to go to."

"That's not the half of it, Sut. In fact, it's only the first paragraph." I went on: "*The History of Southern Literature* presents a view of the South not essentially different from that held by the southerners who contributed to *I'll Take My Stand* back in 1930, still smarting apparently from Mencken's characteri-

"... And Ladies of the Club" was first published in the *Appalachian Journal*, fall 1986.

zation of the South as the 'Sahara of the Bozart.' The editors have inherited the mantle of Stark Young & Co.: self-appointed official guardians of the South's literary reputation, which accounts for the (perhaps unconscious) desire to banish poor cousins to the outhouse and put out the best uncracked china for company."

"Yas, hoss, you do go on," Sut said.

If this isn't literary history as defensiveness, it is certainly literary history as defined by English departments: polite, decorous knitting societies convinced of their own superiority. We are all familiar with English department disdain for the populace that surrounds it, combined with high-minded love for the embodiment of that populace as can be read in litter-a-tour. The result: the inability of the professoriate to recognize as litter-a-tour anything that hasn't already been anthologized and taught to them in their graduate seminars."

"I couldn't say edzackly how I know it," Sut said, "but I get the impresshun you ain't too tooken wif that book."

"Right. Now I get to the part about you, buddy. — Maybe there has been some movement — however glacial — from the high-collared disdain Stark Young, taking his stand in the heart of Dixie, had for the tree-dwelling he associated with the raucous and bawdy literary tradition of the mountain South, the height of Dixie. Young might have agreed heartily with Edmund Wilson that George Washington Harris's *Sut Lovingood Yarns* was 'the most repellent book of any real literary merit in American literature.' But Mary Ann Wimsatt and Robert L. Phillips, writing on antebellum humor in this volume, call Harris 'a genius . . . the most gifted of the antebellum humorists.' His *Sut Lovingood: Yarns Spun by a 'Nat'ral Born Durn'd Fool'* they call 'a triumphant, astonishing achievement.'"

"Thas real smoof," Sut said. At first I thought he was commenting on my review, but I saw he was screwing the top back on a half-pint of Jim Beam. I forged ahead:

"*The History of Southern Literature* has not neglected to deal with other figures associated with the literature of the mountain South, such as Hardin E. Taliaferro, Mary Murfree, and John Fox Jr. Herschel Gower, in an essay titled 'Regions and Rebels,' presents James Still, Jesse Stuart, Harriette Arnow, and others as writers whose 'emphasis upon the peculiarities and uniqueness of specific locales . . . does not come at the expense of wholeness and depth of characterization, the willingness to look long and hard at human nature at its least attractive as well as its best, or a subordination of life to landscape.' These writers 'learned to avoid many of the excesses' of the local colorists who were their predecessors.

"So the first native voices from the Appalachian South are noticed and dealt with. The editors and contributors aren't blind, either, to a younger generation of writers whose work is associated with southern Appalachia — Fred Chappell, Mary Lee Settle, Robert Morgan, Lisa Alther, Lee Smith, Jim Wayne Miller."

"There's one, that Jim Wayne Miller, that's a damned easy spared person," Sut said.

"But it's progress, too, Sut." I told Sut about an old lady who once said you could draw a line from Yanceyville to Pittsboro, then down to Laurinburg and the South Carolina border, and west of that line there was *nothing* literary worth knowing about.

Sut pooched out his mouth. "I've larned the hard way, hoss, you take a old 'oman ahine a par of shiney specks—a old 'oman of either sex—you'd better keep your eye skinned. 'Cause they are dang'rus in the extreme. Thar's jis' no knowin what they'll do.—Twenty-five-year-old widders, now, is another animal. More like a smoof pacin mare."

"*The History of Southern Literature*," I continued, "is also reliable where matters of fact are concerned, although it does, inevitably, perpetuate inaccuracies that exist in sources used by the contributing essayists. Jesse Stuart's birth date is incorrectly given as 1907; but then Stuart allowed this error to be perpetuated until his biographer, H. Edward Richardson, established the correct date as 1906. A more serious error is the statement attributed to Stuart's contemporary, James Still, about Stuart: 'We can't know how good a writer is unless we can forget how great he keeps telling us he is.' Still maintains he never made this mean-spirited observation about Stuart; rather, Dean Cadle composed the remark and published it in an essay about Still, justifying himself with the explanation, when Still objected: 'That's what you would have said.'

"But reading these essays, watching their authors bob and bow to one another from Chapel Hill, I feel no real sense of place or of the life the writing comes from. I feel as if I'm in some holy sanctuary, some hallowed, high-priestly place. So it's more than a little ironic to come across Sut Lovingood enshrined here, like a black bear at high tea."

"I believe you flew the track somewheres back there—if you ever was on it," Sut said. "What's wrong with this book?"

"I get to that right here.—*The History of Southern Literature* is flawed in at least two important ways. The first flaw is the result of editorial procedure. According to general editor Louis Rubin, in an interview with the editors of *The Chronicle of Higher Education* published 19 February 1986, the professors asked 'good scholars to write accounts of good writers, and to trust the common concerns and emphases of the time and place to provide most of the congruence.' This strategy has not proved particularly successful, especially in tandem with Rubin's definition of the South, embedded in another statement quoted by the *Chronicle of Higher Education*: 'Southern literature is very much the product and image of something which is geographically and historically and culturally a kind of homogeneous unit.'

"This assumption of a homogeneous South, rather than recognition of the South's diversity, is the reason why the Appalachian South (and other subregions) fail to come into sharp focus in this volume, despite the attention given to individual writers. There are references to the South's 'various subregions and localities,' but the book's organization and emphases do not permit the 'many Souths' to emerge. Emphasis is on 'one South' assumed to be much the same everywhere.

"As a consequence, the South that emerges in these essays is a place of light and shadow. Missouri's Mark Twain and Maryland's H. L. Mencken are brightly lit, but it is hard to make out Mary Lee Settle's West Virginia. And what is literature in this context? Novels, short stories, poems—yes. But what about the books of theologians, journalists, or scholars? William C. Harvard provides an overview of historian C. Vann Woodward's work in 'The Search for Identity,' but Jonathan Daniels and Hodding Carter are mentioned only in passing in this volume. If Howard Odum, W. J. Cash, Frank Owsley, Henry Grady, Gerald W. Johnson, and George Brown Tindall are included, by what criterion are Rupert Vance, V. O. Key, Thomas Clark, James McBride Dabbs, Robert Coles, Harry Ashmore, Ralph McGill, and John Egerton excluded?

"And why in God's name is William Gilmore Simms, a mediocre writer of the old school, given so much space? His index entries are more than double those of Faulkner and Warren.—What do you think so far, Sut?"

"I think perfessers is like const'ibils and suckit-riders—damned easy spared persons."

"There's more."

"I figgered."

"There's an overemphasis on the Fugitive/Agrarians. *I'll Take My Stand* is important, but it would seem that Lillian Smith's *Killers of the Dream*, James McBride Dabbs's *The Southern Heritage*, or Wilma Dykeman and James Stokely's *Seeds of Southern Change* would deserve some consideration.

"The editors and contributors have anticipated criticism for omission of particular authors and titles. In the general introduction Rubin writes: 'In such a work as this one, especially for the later chapters, it has been necessary to make judgmental choices about inclusions. Our choices will not satisfy everyone entirely.' And Donald R. Noble, in 'The Future of Southern Writing,' says: "there are many writers not considered here who might very well have been (to name some would only compound the error).'

"Let's name some anyway (in addition to those already mentioned). We acknowledge the passing mention given to Wilma Dykeman (lumped in a paragraph with Mildred Haun) and to William Price Fox, Lillian Smith, Harry Crews, Jeff Daniel Marion, and others. But we must also note the entire omission of many southern writers of fiction and nonfiction who should have been treated. Here is a partial list: A. B. Guthrie, Janet Holt Giles, Charles Edward Eaton, Willie Morris, Robert Drake, Thomas Merton, Ellen Gilchrist, Bobbie Ann Mason, Borden Deal, William Bradford Huie, May Justus, Archibald Rutledge, Jose Yglesias, Pat Conroy, Richard Marius, Harnett Kane, Robert K. Massie, Paul Hemphill, Grantland Rice, Harry Golden, Eugenia Price, John Howard Griffin—and no doubt others.

"Simply to acknowledge omissions does not relieve one of the responsibility to cover the territory, especially when claims are made about the volume's depth and scope. The omission of so many southern writers from the volume results in a depicted South significantly different from what it would otherwise be. I am not sure that this volume, which has a place for Alice Hegan Rice's *Mrs. Wiggs of the Cabbage Patch* but none for Harry Caudill's *Night Comes to the Cumberlands* nor for John Ehle's *The Journey of August King* or *The Winter People* nor for Gurney Norman's *Divine Right's Trip* and *Kinfolks*, can claim to be 'thorough and reasonably objective.'—How does it sound so far, Sut?"

"Hit sounds to me like the book is a perfect catastrophy, and the persons what done it shoulda tooken thought afore they ventured to 'splain mixed questions."

"My thought exactly. These omissions are not separate from the volume's most serious shortcoming, which is a failure to incorporate scholarship representing progress beyond the long-held assumption of a geographically, historically, and culturally homogeneous South. *The History of Southern Literature* is dedicated to C. Hugh Holman, but the implications of Holman's *Three Modes of Southern Fiction* are nowhere in the structure and organization of this history. The volume blurs what Randall Stewart calls 'the age-old distinction between the highlands and the lowlands: between the Shenandoah and the Tidewater, the up-country and the low-country in South Carolina, the Kentucky mountains and the Blue Grass, East Tennessee and Middle Tennessee.' Stewart's distinction, summarized in his essay 'Tidewater and Frontier,' is subtly but significantly different from the approach taken by the editors of *The History of Southern Literature*. Whereas this history assumes diversity in the South but emphasizes a basic unity of geography, history, and culture, Stewart assumes a basic unity while emphasizing a diversity within that unity—a diversity the result of fundamental differences between Tidewater and Frontier traditions. Stewart identifies William Byrd, Ellen Glasgow, James Branch Cabell, Eudora Welty, Stark Young, John Crowe Ransom, and Allen Tate as representatives of the Tidewater tradition, which he associates with good manners, decorum, justice, interest in polite literature, and wit. Longstreet, Hooper, Baldwin, Harris, Thomas Wolfe, and Jesse Stuart he associates with the Frontier tradition, which exhibits roughness and crudeness of manners, uninhibited, rough-and-tumble behavior. Anti-intellectual in attitude, the Frontier tradition stresses straightforwardness instead of irony and subtlety, slapstick instead of wit. While the two traditions have 'flourished side by side' with a few writers—William Faulkner and Robert Penn Warren—successfully combining elements of both, Stewart maintains convincingly that generally there has been 'little truck between the two schools.'—How does that strike you, Sut?"

"Right in the pit of the stumick, hoss, and spreads a ticklin sensashun bof ways." Sut tipped his half-pint of Jim Beam once more before wiping his mouth on his shirt sleeve. "Are you anywheres clost to windin down?" Sut was beginning to look desperate, cutting his eyes toward the door of Capehart's Bar and Baitshop. I knew not even the consolation of Jim Beam would hold him much longer.

"I'm in the short rows right now, Sut.—Holman's and Stewart's distinctions have explanatory power lacking in *The History of Southern Literature*, whose account of the recent South fails to note the literary quickening that has taken place in the upland South since about 1960, when Cratis Williams thought he was 'putting the mountaineer to bed' in his dissertation, *The Southern Mountaineer in Fact and Fiction*. This development could be accounted for not only by Stewart's diverse South but also by Donald Davidson's view of regionalism ('a process of differentiation within geographic limits . . . predestined in the settlement of our continental area'), and by George Brown Tindall's perspective on the recent past, which permits regional awareness to be seen not as a survival from the past but as a result of change ('we learn . . . from the southern past and [from] the history of others that to change is not necessarily to disappear. And we learn from modern psychology that to change is not necessarily to lose one's identity; to change, sometimes, is to find it.')"

I looked up to discover I had been reading—for how long I did not know—to a life-size cardboard cutout of Jim Beam. In my zeal to finish I had not noticed that Sut had silently slipped away. Capehart said Sut had mentioned something about a yard sale and tractor pull being put on by a young widow over in Ozone.

8

JOHN LOWE

An Interview with Brenda Marie Osbey

I first met Brenda Marie Osbey in 1985, when we were both Harvard Fellows; I was lucky enough to be introduced to her poetry and her gumbo in the same evening. Moses Nkondo had insisted I come to what promised to be a memorable reading at Radcliffe: "Brenda Marie is not to be missed, especially by a fellow southerner like you!" Moses was right; Brenda electrified the audience, and I eagerly accepted his offer to introduce us. I was immediately invited to a party that featured the famous gumbo and other delicacies that were delicious and exotic, even to a fellow southerner (my native Georgia, after all, is almost as different from New Orleans as Cambridge). Brenda had somehow made her small apartment an outpost of Louisiana, decorating it with tropical colors and filling its rooms with the aroma of her famous food. Little did I know that later that same year I'd be transplanting myself to Louisiana, where Brenda Marie's cooking—both culinary and poetic—would find compelling visual and sensual equivalents.

Brenda Marie Osbey is a native of New Orleans. Her roots in Creole culture run deep and give her work a haunting sense of place. Surely no one since Walker Percy has made more memorable music out of the names of the city's streets and the people who throng them. Her poetry is much more than a slice of local color, however, for the metropolis she summons up quickly and magically becomes a backdrop for a display of the ambiance of the black feminine mind. Her women lead lives that often erupt in violence and sometimes end with madness. But alongside all this—and often because of it—we find a riveting poignance and soaring beauty.

Despite the central role of New Orleans in her work, there are other obvious influences from her travels and sojourns elsewhere. Osbey attended Dillard

Portions of this interview appeared in *The Southern Review* 30, 4 (1994): 812–23. Used by permission.

University and Université Paul Valéry at Montpellier, France, and received an M.A. from the University of Kentucky. She has taught at Dillard and UCLA, and currently teaches at Loyola University in New Orleans. She has received several awards, including the Academy of American Poets' Loring Williams Prize, an Associated Writing Programs Award, and a National Endowment for the Arts Fellowship. Brenda Marie Osbey has been a fellow of the Fine Arts Work Center at Provincetown, the Kentucky Foundation for Women, the MacDowell Colony, the Millay Colony, and the Bunting Institute of Radcliffe College, Harvard University. She is the author of three published volumes of poetry—Ceremony for Minneconjoux, In These Houses, and Desperate Circumstance, Dangerous Woman—and has just completed a fourth volume, All Saints.

On a typically steamy south Louisiana afternoon in July 1992, I drove from Baton Rouge across the sun-baked bridges of Interstate 10 toward New Orleans and a scheduled visit with my old friend, Brenda Marie Osbey. Idly glancing at the herons dipping in and out of the swamps around me, I wondered if Brenda's new apartment on St. Claude Street, just outside the French Quarter, would be as atmospheric as the other abodes she had created in New Orleans and other cities. Parking carefully on the time-worn but evocative narrow street, I saw I needn't have worried. Her townhouse was part of a recently remodeled building in a changing neighborhood, one still populated mostly by older black families but increasingly becoming home to young professionals. I found her street number and knocked on the tall green louvered door. Brenda greeted me warmly and led the way over the recently redone wide plank floors through the shotgun lower floor, into the cool tiled kitchen. As usual, I saw an espresso machine and a large bowl of fruit—Brenda Marie trademarks. We had had to postpone this meeting several times because the remodeling had become complicated when termite damage had been found in the ancient building. Brenda was in a joyous mood, however, as she fixed me an iced coffee; all the workmen were gone, and her beloved St. Martin de Porres figure was on the mantel, presiding over the sparely furnished but atmospheric domain of New Orleans's resident muse. As we settled in for a long chat, I had to start with a question about the overwhelming presence of this particular city on her life and work. Eventually, however, we drifted into a discussion of the role other factors have played in her remarkable career, tacitly agreeing that we would eventually return to the original question.

JL: Obviously, New Orleans and her cultures have been the most important influences on your work, but I wonder if you could speak briefly about writers who have been particularly useful in helping you in your poetry, especially in terms of the long narrative poems you've written in the last few years.

BMO: Most of them haven't been southern, although some have been. I suppose the poets I feel have had the strongest influence on my own work are those poets who write the long narrative poems—Robert Hayden, Jay Wright, early Gwen Brooks, Gayl Jones (who is a southerner, in fact she's from Kentucky), Sherley Anne Williams, and to a lesser degree, and I suppose more recently, Melvin B. Tolson, and only very recently, in the last two or three—well, maybe a little longer than that—four years, that I've developed any interest in, or respect for, Melvin B. Tolson's *Harlem Gallery*. In fact, I'm trying to do a piece *on* Melvin B. Tolson *(laughs)*.

JL: That's interesting—I was in the LSU library the other day and there's a new book that's just come out by Michael Bérubé—it's on Thomas Pynchon and Melvin B. Tolson.

BMO: *(Laughs.)* That's an interesting combination!

JL: It's quite interesting—and at the end of it, there's an appendix where he's gone through the MLA annual bibliographies and looked at all the articles and books that have been written about both of them, and a lot of other authors too, and there's almost nothing on Tolson, and yet there's something like thirty books on Pynchon, who's really not that accessible, but (perhaps because of that) he's become the darling of the academy; Bérubé's trying to figure out why Tolson, by contrast, has been so ignored. Do you have any ideas about that?

BMO: Well, I think Tolson's sort of one end of the whole scholar-poet spectrum, and I guess Hayden, who's far more accessible, is the other end, someone who has what I call a "problem with history," who sees his poems as a kind of correction of history, an addendum to history. Tolson, on the other hand, initially comes off as someone who's fascinated with his own intellect, and that's a version—a nice version!—of the impression I had of Tolson when I first had to read him in school, and I thought, "This guy is crazy, he's just showing off his vocabulary; but in fact, what he has done is to try to reveal a very complex set of myths and mythologies, and he was looking at relationships among different levels of black society, and had a very keen vision, and a very keen ear for the language of black folk at different levels—different social and economic, cultural and intellectual levels, and was trying to create a *literal gallery* of black life. There are so many allusions that what we really need is to have someone go through and create a glossary. In order to read Melvin B. Tolson, you have to have a very clear understanding of African American history; you have to have a very clear understanding of world history in the period between the two wars; you have to know black culture; it also helps if you know something about the visual arts, and it helps if you speak or read languages other than English. Someone counted and found that he'd used several hundred words from many languages. But the other thing I have noticed is that Melvin B. Tolson has a very weird sense of humor—but you have to get all the other stuff before you can get the joke! It's like trying to read Umberto Eco's *The Name of the Rose* without knowing any Latin; if you don't know Latin, you don't get the jokes *(laughs)*, and there're some really great jokes in *The Name of the Rose*! Also a number of little problems and puzzles, and all sorts of things—but you have to have this whole set of background knowledge before you can get to them, and I think that's really the main reason for the neglect [of Tolson]. And I'd like to have been able to see what would have happened had he been able to finish the whole *Harlem Gallery*.

JL: Let me see if I can connect this with your work—if I can play the detective. Do you think your work is similar to his in some specifically southern ways, or New Orleans ways, because I know that in the past you had glosses *(laughs)* to your works to words that we use in New Orleans that other people don't know, such as the word "banquette" for sidewalks. In fact, I wondered when you mentioned the title *Harlem Gallery* if you didn't, as a New Orleans native, associate the word "gallery" with balcony *(laughs)* as we do here in New Orleans. Do you see your work as being most productively read by people who share its vocabulary—is that really important in your work?

BMO: It varies. I think my ideal listening or reading audience is probably black, New Orleans, and working-class, because many of my characters are exactly that; many of the characters I write about are working-class black people who lived anytime, say, before 1950. So I think that to those people I don't have to explain that language. When those people look at the glossary at the back, they're pleased that I've gotten the meanings right; and when I haven't gotten them quite right, or when there's some shade of meaning that I've ignored, they let me know that. They'll say, "Well now, it means that, but it means this other thing over here too, and maybe you'll want to put that in there next time." So those are my most *critical* readers *(laughs)*, those are my favorite readers, because they're the hardest on me. But they're also my favorites because I don't have to explain anything to them. On the other hand, I think that once you have the glosses, it doesn't really matter how much you know about New Orleans; I think you need to know that it's different, that it's its own little country. The specifics aren't necessarily that important, because the stories themselves, the stories that I try to tell in these poems, are not that important. They don't have importance in and of themselves. They're important because they're told by certain characters, or they're important because of the way they're told. But you almost never get an accurate accounting of any series of events in an orderly fashion, beginning, middle, and end. What you get is a way of speaking, a way of thinking, and the story isn't all that valuable; but all the things that go into *making* the story are really what count. And I certainly wouldn't presume to say that my work is anywhere near as difficult as the work of someone like Melvin Tolson, or Jay Wright, or Robert Hayden. I think in fact that my work is fairly accessible. What happens, though, is that what I am doing tends to be unexpected. People look at the poems— people come to your first book partly—because they went to high school with your mother, or because *(laughs)* they taught you Sunday school! Or they used to sit next to you in third grade, or they used to be a friend or a lover or something. They're not really interested in your poetry—they're just going to be nice, because they're happy to know somebody who wrote a book that got published. But once you start to read—and once *they* start to read—they come away and say, "This isn't really what I think of when I think of poetry, and I kind of like it because it *isn't* what I think of poetry, and also because I think I know these people." And I pride myself in the fact that I write about people. That's something—I look for characters that are clear, and strong, very visible and very visual, so that people can begin to put faces on the characters I'm writing about.

JL: And of course your characters are New Orleans figures.

BMO: I don't think they could live anyplace else.

JL: I remember talking to you when you were teaching at UCLA, and you were so homesick . . .

BMO: Ummmmmmmm.

JL: You hated LA, and I was kind of surprised, because I thought you'd like LA. But it wasn't your favorite place, and why is that? Is it because you were so homesick for New Orleans, or is it that LA is just so different from New Orleans? Because you've been happy in other places.

BMO: Yeah, I have been happy in other places, that's true; when I first got to Provincetown I was amazed at how unhappy so many of the other fellows at the Fine Arts Work Center were, 'cause I thought Provincetown was just a great little place. I didn't like Boston proper, but I liked and still like Cambridge.

JL: Yeah, I felt that way too.

BMO: I liked parts of Virginia, I liked parts of France, there're all sorts of places that I've liked. Los Angeles I didn't like, because it really isn't a place. There is no longer a city of Los Angeles. There's Los Angeles County and all of its attachments, and there are freeways and malls, and there are filling stations, and there's the university and there's Hollywood and Bel-Air, and whatever else there is. I read somewhere a long time ago that LA was the city of the future, and ever since living in LA I pray that that's not true! *(Laughs.)* There's no center to LA, there's no real downtown anymore; there doesn't seem to be that much of a cultural life away from the university; there are these chain bookstores everywhere. I did manage to find some little dinky used bookstores in West LA, and I loved to go there, because they reminded me of New Orleans! *(Laughs.)* So I haunted the dinky little used bookstores. My favorite, I think, was a store called Vagabond Books, and I went there, I think, every Saturday. I'd sit there on the steps and read. Los Angeles isn't a place; no one that you meet is *from* Los Angeles. Of course that's true in all of southern California—I think I've met *one* person who's descended from the "original inhabitants." Everyone you meet is from someplace else; no one can give you directions; everyone carries a map around in the back seat of their car. There's almost no black cultural life in LA, except for the theater, and I was really amazed by that. People in LA really support black theater, and there is a *lively* black theater. And I don't know anything about theater, but I went regularly so that I could see other black people. Another thing about LA that I hated, I guess, more than anything else, besides the pollution and the smog, was the beaches. *(Laughs.)* I mean, beaches full of naked people, bodies all crammed together. It's sort of *not* my idea of the beach. But the other thing is that LA is probably the most assimilationist place I've ever seen in this country. *Everyone* in LA is a white person. Black people are white persons, Asian Americans are white persons, Latinos are white persons, white persons are white persons—*everyone* in Los Angeles is white. People would always explain to you why their parents were ethnics, but they are not. And they describe themselves as non-black, non-Asian, non-Latino, and that kind of self-denial and that kind of assimilation is really, really disturbing to me. We're not talking about people "passing" like in mid-nineteenth-century Louisiana; we're talking about people who look like James Brown explaining to you why they're not black people. And that's really disturbing. Another thing was that I was returning to teaching; I hadn't taught since 1981. In 1988 I took a summer teaching job at Dillard University in New Orleans and it was really hard. And then I went out to Los Angeles and I had classes where I had 120 to 150 students. Because I was teaching African American literature I had students who were constantly complaining that it was depressing them because they didn't want to read Zora Neale Hurston; they didn't want to read Alice Walker. They found this oppressive.

JL: I'm assuming that all these things that you say Los Angeles didn't—doesn't have, you do feel New Orleans has.

BMO: Yes.

JL: For instance, there's definitely a sense of a city; there's a core, and not only is there a core, there's a core within a core where we're sitting now, right on the margin of the French Quarter.

BMO: Yes—there's an old city, and you can see how the rest of the city has grown out around you out of the French Quarter and the downtown area. The other thing is that New Orleans is very ethnic; people cling to their ethnicity, and even flaunt it!

JL: And not only in the black community.

BMO: Exactly. Exactly. And people have a sense of comfort with themselves, even when they have nothing to be comfortable about. You can find the poorest person, I think, in New Orleans, and that person will identify himself or herself as a New Orleanian. And that person will claim this place as her place or as his place. So people here have a sense of belonging, and I think that that's one of the reasons people come here, because it is a place that you can belong to. The place seems to define the people, rather than the people defining the place. In LA you have a culture of change; everything's changing all the time. Here, you have a place where almost *nothing* changes! *(Laughs.)* We're always whining about how nothing ever changes here.

JL: The more things change here, the more they stay the same?

BMO: Exactly.

JL: I wonder, too, about your comment about history and Los Angeles. Of course Los Angeles is a very old place too; it was settled centuries ago by the Spanish, but the displacement of the Hispanic communities means that people who live there now, even the Hispanics, by and large, are not connected to that history; the opposite is true.

BMO: Yes, and all the physical evidence of their presence has been destroyed. There's almost nothing that would identify it except in one area of West LA, where you see Spanish colonial architecture. There's no visible evidence of the place ever having been inhabited by anyone other than twentieth-century people. And there's no appreciation of that historic architectural style;

everyone likes glass and steel beams there. There's a complete lack of appreciation for anything old. The whole culture focuses on youthfulness. Whereas here, the whole culture focuses on age; we appreciate things because they are old. In fact, we have a tendency to enshrine any and everything simply because it's old and it's always been here. But yeah, yeah, I think that's one of the differences, that here we have all of the evidence of the oldness of the place, and we cling to the oldness of the place and refuse to give any of it up, or to change it, and again, that's what draws people to the place. It's old, and you can see it.

JL: Do you think that's true of much of the rest of the South? I'm thinking now of Atlanta—I know you've been there—and there's a wonderful, vibrant black community there, and yet Atlanta seems, more than any city in the South, intent on tearing down anything more than ten years old.

BMO: Yeah—do you know, Charles Rowell is always joking that they're always burning Atlanta—that the war didn't end the process! *(Laughs.)* And that's one of the things about Atlanta that I both like and dislike. I go to Atlanta and I don't see anything very old—you're right, they think that "old" is ten years old—but it *is* a burgeoning black metropolis—it's always growing, it's prosperous, it's upbeat, it's the southern city of the young black professionals. It's nice to get away from New Orleans and go to Atlanta, but I always want to go to Atlanta and then come back. I've gone to the National Black Arts Festival there, which is great. But Atlanta is part of the fabric of the South. When you look at the South what you get is a kind of patchwork quilt; there are certain commonalities that all southerners have, and yet each place you go to is very different. I went to school in Kentucky and I lived in Virginia for some time; Kentucky and Virginia are neighbors, and yet they're completely different, even the landscape. The land is very, very different. In Mississippi they have rolling hills, and down here we have flat land; it snows right next door to us, but it doesn't snow here. So you get this strange kind of patchwork in the South; you get a variety of landscapes. People look and talk and think and feel and eat and worship and do everything differently, and yet, there are these commonalities that keep cropping up over and over again. There is an insistence on tradition and on the making of traditions. There is a certain kind of religiosity about the South. People, I suppose like myself, grow up in very religious families and then move away from religion. I, at least, am always able to detect something religious, however, in the makeup of southerners. There's something there that's always there, whether you're talking about people who are Baptists, or a whole state like Louisiana, which is mostly Catholic. There's an aura of religiosity and there's a concern with religion. There is a concern, and perhaps an obsession, with death, and with loss. There is an intense love for the land; one of the things that southerners, and especially southern men, do that identity them as southerners, is to identify themselves personally with a piece of ground. Men, very often in the South, identify themselves through the landholdings of their families, and I don't mean in a classist way. When people talk about their childhoods, when they talk about their pasts, when they talk about what's good in their lives, that is more often than not associated with a place and with a piece of ground. Whenever my grandmother talked about her mother, she always talked about her mother's land. She talked about how her mother forbade all her daughters to live anyplace where they couldn't have a garden. My grandmother always had a rose garden; she had fruit trees growing in the backyard. She felt that she was not a woman if she wasn't growing something. If she couldn't make something grow, if we couldn't tend a piece of ground, then there was something spiritually wrong with us somehow, and so we always had something growing. Men define themselves that way too; I think the South is the only place that I know of where most of the men know most growing things. One of the ways that southern men win women is to talk about trees, flowers, and growing things. You go to other places and ask, "Oh, what kind of tree is that?" And people say, "What? I don't know, it's a TREE!" *(Laughs.)* Here we all identify with growing things.

JL: That must be one of the reasons you were attracted to this apartment, the peach tree and the banana trees in the back patio.

BMO: Yeah, it reminded me of my grandmother's when I walked out back. When I saw the floor and the gaping hole that my landlord promised to repair I was really disheartened, but then I saw the peach tree in the backyard and I just gave it all up! And that's one of the things I like about being downtown. People down here always have had gardens. That's one of my most pleasant memories—always growing things. My father always lived on farms—he says that until he was fourteen or fifteen he never ate anything that his family didn't raise or grow. And that association with the land—I think that's one of the things that people from other places—the North—hold against us, that relationship to the land. What we see as wholesome and life-giving about ourselves is often criticized as "country" and "backward." One of the worst things you could say to somebody, at least to someone in my generation, was, "You're country." That was like an indictment of everything that they stood for. There was no way you could deny being country. If you were country everybody knew it. *(Laughs.)*

JL: There's that wonderful song that Carla Thomas and Otis Redding sang, "Tramp," where she said, "Otis, you're country—you're straight from the Georgia woods!" and he'd say, "That's good!"

BMO: (Laughs.) Exactly!

JL: Let me follow up on this idea of spirituality: do you think New Orleans is preeminently a spiritual city? I've noticed in your own work and in your remarks today that you often use the word "aura"; I'm constantly struck by this kind of magical aura that emanates from your work; it's not just from any one element, it's the whole tone and atmosphere that everything in the poem creates. And you also said a moment ago that you're not particularly interested in narrative per se, but in the things that a narrative can do. Is that "aura" created by elements in the narrative, or it perhaps that New Orleans gives you access to aura better than any other place?

BMO: I think so. New Orleans definitely is the spiritual core of everything that I write; that's really true. It's strange, because often when I'm someplace other than New Orleans, people say things like, "Oh, I'm waiting to read your poems about Virginia or Los Angeles!" *(Laughs.)* It isn't like I go from place to place and I pick up things that I write about from there just because I've been there. I'm always writing about New Orleans; it's the true spiritual core of everything that I do, and I think that that's what this focus on narrative is all about, because narrative both perpetuates and transforms. Every time we tell a story we're perpetuating whatever the essence of that story is. There is some spirit, some tradition, some something, some STORY that we're perpetuating, but at the same time, we're making the story our own, or we're seeing and hearing it differently. And so I like to have characters, several characters, all telling the same story from differing viewpoints, or to have individual characters who each tell the story from *several* of their own many viewpoints. So that one character will be speaking several different versions or in different voices at different levels. New Orleans is a place that gets its identity from its mixture, and we never really bother to take the mixture apart. So sometimes I like to have a character who speaks a narrative or thinks a narrative or *is* a narrative at these different levels, and we get to see then what the components of that mix are. But the stuff that you referred to as magical, I think that's definitely there, and like I've told you before, I spent most of my teens and twenties denying any kind of religiosity in my own nature. Now that I'm in my thirties, I'm willing to accept the fact that at the core, I am a religious person, that I have deep religious feeling, but I probably don't have any mechanism to express it. I can't express it in the religion of my childhood. So I'm looking for ways to understand what it is about New Orleans that makes it what it is. I see New Orleans as a female place, a feminine place, and I'm always trying to understand New Orleans as a woman—not myself, but New Orleans as a woman. And there's something about the river too.

JL: Let me ask you about the fact that so many black New Orleans are also Catholic, and that the city in general is Catholic. I wonder if that extra aspect of Catholicism that tends more to the mystical, that you don't often have in Protestant sects—even some black Protestant sects, which tend to be more mystical than the white Protestant varieties—doesn't have something to do with all this. One of the things I love about Catholicism is its strong visual sense—and maybe this will link up with our idea of New Orleans here, because when you were talking about the idea of beauty, ambience, the look of the city—its topography, its trees, its fruit—I've always thought of New Orleans both as a spiritual place—spiritual in a very wide sense of the word, which is the way I take your statement—but as a place that is also spiritual because of its aura of beauty. Maybe the way we read it is special, because there's a very special kind of Catholic perspective that's practiced here. *(laughs.)*

BMO: There sure is! I was raised Lutheran, which is weird (well, it isn't all that weird, actually—there's a sizable black Lutheran community) but my mother's father was Catholic and converted, and so everybody after him was raised Lutheran. In fact, our family belonged to one of the oldest black Lutheran churches, St. Paul's. But what happens in New Orleans is that Catholicism is pervasive. What also happens is that what everyone else calls "voodoo" and what we call "hoodoo" is even more pervasive than is Catholicism. And then there's a kind of Protestantism that is peculiar to New Orleans as well; we have the early Spiritual Sanctified churches here, which Spiritual and Sanctified people will tell you do not grow out of hoodoo, but all of the evidence is that it did. But the nature of religion in New Orleans is really very bizarre. One of the things that Catholicism does to New Orleans is that it allows for coexistence of all kinds of seeming opposites. So that on the one hand we have churches on every corner, of every possible description, and we have bars in the middle of the block! *(Laughs.)* So that we have the seeming corruption of Bourbon Street near St. Louis Cathedral. Right down the street we have a bar that lets out in the back of one of the oldest churches in the city, but they have a very good relationship; when mass starts, they turn off the music, they unplug the jukebox. They don't go all pouring into the church, but they unplug the jukebox. There's a kind of peaceful coexistence among institutions and among people, and among ideas and among cultures. The other thing is that New Orleans absorbs just about anything and everything and makes it its own. I have friends who are Italian-American, and in New York, they're very Italian, or in the Los Angeles of the '50s, when they grew up, they were very Italian. They come to New Orleans and they say, "Well, these Italians are Italian, but they're not *really* Italian!" and it's because they're New Orleans Italians, and everything gets colored by that kind of Creolism. That Italians eat as Italians, but it's Creolized Italian food. And the same goes for just about everything else. And I think that that's because this place is African. It's predominantly African in terms of its spirit. Anything and everything that comes through New Orleans is black in spirit. And when we look at how traditional African religions colored Catholicism, so that you have a variety of cults of individual saints, so that you have all kinds of seemingly bizarre practices going on in Catholic churches, I think that all that going on points to the strength of our basic Africaneity. The spirituality here is uniquely African in nature. When we look at voodoo, what we're looking at is a series of principles that have primarily to do with balance, that have to do with how the world is structured, and how you keep, or create, or search out, a balance in your personal life and affairs, and how you equate that to the balance that exists in nature. So that you're always looking for harmony, and you're always looking for healing; you're always looking for some opportunity to heal. What that means is that when you've grown up with that strange combination, as I did—Catholicism and Lutheranism and hoodoo—is that you grow up thinking—and not consciously thinking—but you grow up with this idea that almost anything can be healed, almost anything can be righted. So you can always be cleansed, you can always be forgiven, you can always forgive; there are only one or two sins so horrible that they can't be forgiven. The only two that I can think of, and I know there's a third—suicide is unforgiveable, and forgetting. You do not forget to honor the dead; you do not forget to honor the elderly;

you do not forget to honor your parents; you do not forget who you are and what your connections are; you do not break vows. So the two greatest sins I can think of are forgetting and self-denial. If you do those things you live and die in constant turmoil or confusion.

JL: Do you think this idea about not forgetting is something that makes the South in general unique? The whole idea of remembering what happened, to be aware, to be faithful?

BMO: Yes. Remembrance *is* the South. It really is. And people here remember everything. People even remember things that didn't happen! *(Laughs.)* Remember everything, just in case! You don't want to get caught. And I think that's one of the things that definitely connects New Orleans to the South. A lot of other things remove New Orleans from the South and connect it to the Caribbean, or Latin America, or Africa, or any number of other things. But remembrance ties New Orleans to the South, because remembrance carries so much under its wing. There's that relationship with the land, there's always family, there is ancestry. People focus a great deal on ancestry in the South. One of the questions that southerners always ask is who "your people" are. They want to know who you belong to, so they'll have some idea of where to place you in their memories. In the South, you don't meet people just because they do the same things you do; you don't meet people because you work with them; I don't meet other people because they're writers—you sort of fall in with people and you find certain commonalities in your pasts rather than in your presents. "Oh, I grew up in such-and-such a place," or there'll be a cousin in this town that neither of us ever met. The notion of the family and of family obligation, and our obligations to the dead, and our obligations to the past, and codes of behavior—it sounds silly to say that in 1992, I suppose, but there are still codes of behavior. Which is not to say that we don't ever break them—we're always breaking them. But we *know* that they're codes, and we *know* that we're breaking them! *(Laughs.)* But there's a fascination, I think, with structure; we like structure.

JL: Let me see if I can relate this to this very beautiful and traditionally New Orleans apartment we're sitting in. You've already spoken of the courtyard and how its fruit trees remind you of your grandmother. We have whirring ceiling fans over us, and the wall is lined with French doors that open directly to the street. One of the things that I've been thinking about lately in my own work on Zora Neale Hurston is her essay "Characteristics of Negro Expression," where she talks about the relentless need to adorn. For her, this is a key component of African cultures, and of course one of the reasons that is so is that in a spiritual world like Africa—and India is very much like this as well—everything in life becomes spiritual, everything becomes a reflection of spirituality. Nature, your dress, the vernacular architecture—it's all of a piece. New Orleans is like that—it's a world of adornment that's connected, and it is African in that sense—I think you're right about that.

BMO: Yes. Everything is both itself and yet stands for something else, perhaps something in fact very different. This house, for instance, was a chicken restaurant at one time; it was a grocery store at one time. It was built in the 1780s by Claude Tremé, who owned this entire tract of land; he never lived here, of course. He had it built and he sold it to two free black women, Marie Willamine and Nannette Énoul. I think there is something in an area this old—many of the buildings in this area are older than the buildings in the French Quarter—something of the spirit of the people who lived here continues; there's always a connection to the past. The past is always with us, even when we don't recognize it. Our culture, or our cultures, are identifiable, even when we don't know what the signs and the symbols are. They're here. It's on us to decode them, if you're interested, as I am, in decoding, and in understanding how things work together, or against one another. Sometimes, after leaving New Orleans and coming back, I see things that seem to be at war with one another visually. Houses with Italianate architecture laden with heavy cornices; everything seems jumbled together. But when you've been here awhile you begin to see the unity of things. When you grow up with them you tend not to pay any attention to them at all—until they're gone. In a neighborhood like this, where throughout the twentieth century successive blocks and tracts of land have been destroyed, we begin to notice what we're losing. When someone comes along with a bulldozer and knocks it down, just razes an entire area, you notice.

JL: You said that to you, New Orleans is a very feminine city. Does this idea of adornment that we've been discussing have something to do with that?

BMO: I think so. There are people who say that New Orleans is a kind of sprawling whore, a French courtesan; I don't know about that. But the city is definitely a woman, and I think that the adornment comes in layers and layers of visual elements at any given moment in New Orleans. It's like an eighteenth- or nineteenth-century woman wearing layers and layers of clothing; and each layer serves some purpose and, at least in that time, was necessary. That's very much a part of the spirituality too, adornment.

JL: Let me ask you something else in this regard. You mentioned a special feeling for poor New Orleanians. As I was rereading your most recent published work, *Desperate Circumstance, Dangerous Woman*, there's that wonderful scene when one of your heroines is bathing her mother. I kept thinking about Degas's pastels of poor women washing in a tin tub; those pictures, despite their realistic detail, have a special aura of spirituality, not only because of the way he draws them, but because we understand the world that surrounds these women, a French world so specific to its place and locale. There's a kind of spirituality there. Is that an accurate way to describe the feeling one gets about that poem?

BMO: That scene, where Marie bathes her mother before her death, is like that, but I don't think of Marie as a poor woman. When her mother dies she owns the house. But yet, they're definitely caught in a time frame; they're capsuled. It's the kind of thing that I suppose is the most natural thing in the world. Your mother is old, she's infirm, so you bathe her. But it's that kind of thing—so natural and you don't think about it—so maybe it's something that we *ought* to think about. That's a very loving thing to do, to bathe someone, to care for someone in that way. And then Marie's mother dies within moments of her bath, and confers a kind of blessing on her daughter, and that's the end of it. Marie spends the entire poem struggling with memories of her mother, while Percy spends most of the poem struggling with his memories of Marie. They're lovers, they're living in the same house, he's left his wife and children, and yet his primary concern seems to be that she's put a fix on him, that she's hoodooed him. We don't have any evidence that this is true, except of course that she spends an awful lot of time at the hoodoo woman's house. And again, nothing is ever what it seems. She's going to the hoodoo woman because the hoodoo woman was her mother's best friend many years ago. And so she goes to talk, and she almost never talks about Percy, even when she knows that Percy has been to see the hoodoo woman about her. So what you have are two persons struggling with their memories and with their fears of what those memories mean. And you have a man who is obsessed with a woman, who is obsessed with her dead mother. His argument with her—his fight with her—is that he's still alive, that he's there, that he loves her, yet he cannot be a lover to her. And that's not something he should try to do, that's not something he should have to do. But all of that goes in one ear for Marie and out the other, because she is mourning, and she doesn't seem to be able to come out of that mourning until somewhere very near the end of the poem.

JL: Why did you name this character Percy? You've mentioned him as someone who's wounded, someone who's in search of healing and is wandering. Did that have anything to do with the Parsifal legend, or was your selection more specific to the New Orleans scene?

BMO: No, I had some cousins named Elmo, Cuccia, and Percy; they were grown men, and Percy was my favorite; I had a crush on him. He let me believe that I was his girlfriend *(laughs)*. I was just in elementary school, so I guess I was his "pet." I just saw it as one of the nice Negro-gentlemen-of-another-era names. I've always liked the name and always saw it as very black and very southern. But his character, and his relation to mourning, is very different. And that's something that I think is very southern and very New Orleans. This fascination with death. Death is never just death for us; it symbolizes something. It says something about us; it marks us in some way. In New Orleans we have this tendency not just to remember death but to revel in death, to celebrate death. I think that in part we are so afraid of solitude—or rather, I should say, we're afraid of being left alone, we're afraid of being without family, without friends, that that's one of the reasons for the commandment against forgetting. Even when people are dead, we maintain relations with them. We don't want anything to end, and so the dead are always there for us. People we would never love in life suddenly become these god-like figures—"Now that you're dead I could love you" *(laughs)*; "all these years I've been waiting for you to die so I can love you the way I should!" Because you're my mother, because you're my father, because you're so-and-so. There is this reveling in death and in the trappings of death; we have jazz funerals and a city that is constantly surrounded by death: the cemeteries above ground, decaying buildings; everything is a little bit worn in New Orleans, and somewhat irreplaceable. And that's how people in our lives function— irreplaceable. We cannot release them to the grave; we maintain that connection beyond the grave. If anything, we intensify those connections beyond the grave. And that's something that people notice about New Orleans but no one ever really talks about.

JL: It's something a lot of writers have picked up too, even if they're not from New Orleans; for instance, Toni Morrison's *Sula* has a section that's set here, where characters have come down for the burial of the grandmother; it's almost as though New Orleans is the land of death. That song, of course, in the 60s, *The House of the Rising Sun*, is full of images of death. I also think of *A Streetcar Named Desire*, where Williams, who was clearly obsessed with death, seems to pick this up. I think he had a lot of the same feelings about New Orleans that you do. I wonder, in fact, if there are any New Orleans writers you've read, black or white, male or female, whose work you admire who have maybe tangentially influenced your work. We've already discussed the fact that most of your influences have come from other traditions, outside the city and outside the South; but is there anyone whose work you particularly admire, who's also treated New Orleans?

BMO: I can't think of anyone, really. The only thing I can think of is that Williams's plays seem to me to be some of the best representations of New Orleans as a culture. It's very rare, actually, that I see something about New Orleans that seems like New Orleans to me. But I can't think of any New Orleans writers—both my mother and her father, my grandfather, were writers in their youth. My grandmother, of course, was the family storyteller. I never met Marcus Christian, although I did talk with him on the phone. He was a friend of my grandparents, my mother's parents. His brother, Ned Fennimore Christian, was one of my grandfather's very best friends. When I was a high school student, writing poetry and developing an interest in literature, I wrote a letter to him. In fact, I came across that letter in the Marcus Christian Collection! *(Laughs.)* I wrote a letter to him saying that I wanted to meet with him sometime, to talk with him and interview him, reminding him about my grandparents and their friendship with his brother, and so forth. He wrote me back a lovely letter, but I never did get to meet him; he died not long after. My mother had a great deal of admiration for him, and in the years since then I've read some of his work. I would love to see someone bring out an edition of his poems. Marcus Christian did a massive amount of work in a number of different areas, and I don't think it's doing any of us any good to have his life's work just sitting over there in boxes at UNO [University of New Orleans], when we could be looking at it. He also wrote a history of black New Orleans, but it was never published. He self-published some things. I have a fascination with the mind of Marcus Christian; and there are other people like Marcus Christian. There are those French-language writers from the nineteenth century, the Les Cenelles writers, Victor Sejour, and that whole group, Armand Lanusse; Charles Rousseve. There's also the folk historian John Rousseau, who was still living the last I heard.

JL: One of my students is writing a dissertation on the Francophone writers of Louisiana. That's such a rich set of texts—we really need translations. But let me return to the issue of Marcus Christian; some of my students in the seminar I taught this morning, "Redefining Southern Culture," were telling me the histories of their families—particularly my black students. They were talking about a number of situations where a white plantation owner would have a black wife—in one case, four in succession! They would marry them, leave property to them; there are all these extensive stories and narratives that have never been used, never been revealed. Why is that? Does it have something to do with the lack of encouragement of budding black artists?

BMO: I think so, because I think it's really material that has to be treated by black writers. Whenever it's been treated by white writers, it's always come off as offensive, as racist. You always see these tragic mulattas *(laughs)* as the end result—once more that "ounce of black blood."

JL: You mean Fanny Hurst's *Imitation of Life*, the movie *Pinkie*, works like that.

BMO: Yes—and even when black writers have tried to treat this in the past, their models of course were white writers, and they were writing for a white audience. I think that's part of the problem, that black writers haven't expressed too much interest in that material. But also, black writers aren't being especially encouraged to produce; I don't think that anyone is fostering a new generation of southern black writers. That's really a shame. And it's really a long, tiring process to convince young black people to write (I'm thinking about doing a writing seminar next summer). That's part of it; the other thing is a sense of shame that is attached to anything that has to do with the subject of slavery on the part of black people, and that's bizarre to me. I always thought that if anyone should be ashamed about slavery it should be whites. And the other thing is that there's a sense of shame about race-mixing. Black people have worked very hard for a unified identity, and focusing on difference very often gets black people in trouble. I've found myself in troublesome spots by focusing on difference. It's a touchy business.

JL: I want to ask you about the way you see the shape of your work over your career. Could you talk about the ways the books developed, and what led to the changes in the issues you address, and in the ways in which the poetry develops?

BMO: The first book, *Ceremony*, was written while I was a graduate student at the University of Kentucky. I went there specifically to study with Charles Rowell, and he proved to be a very good reader and listener for me, and called me to read poems at all hours of the night. He would call me to read things to me, too. But what happened was, I wrote all those poems during that period, and then I came home to New Orleans and took a teaching job at Dillard, and then did some other things. What I sent him was chosen from a manuscript of maybe forty or fifty poems. From among those James Borders helped me choose something like twenty or twenty-five that might be a workable manuscript. I sent these on to Charles, and he then winnowed down to something like fourteen poems—I'm not sure—a very short number. Yes, there are fourteen poems. So he pulled together those poems that had certain common themes, and the things that he saw were most significant were the poems that focused on New Orleans as a character, and those poems that focused primarily on women—on black women in New Orleans. I was at first disappointed when I saw how few poems there were, and then I was happy when I saw how well they worked together. So the first selection of poems was not really mine, it was Charles's. He was telling me what other professors had told me when I was an undergraduate, that my best topics seemed to be families, women, and New Orleans. So that's how the first book came into being. The first book in many ways is still a favorite for me because I had the most to do with it, other than the selection of the poems. I chose the paper, I chose the typefaces, I chose the cover art—an etching by a black woman artist, Colette Delacroix. Once *Ceremony* came out, I began to look at those aspects of my work that Charles and other people had pointed out to me. I kept journals, and so forth. Then I began planning the next book. I planned *In These Houses* as a kind of companion volume to *Ceremony for Minneconjoux*, and many of the poems in *In These Houses* are poems that Charles had rejected *(laughs)* for *Ceremony*; I suppose it's not a smart thing to say, but many of these poems were rejects! And I see a third book in this series called *Sleeping the Mama Sleep*, and that would complete the *Ceremony* cycle. Some of the characters in *In These Houses* are characters who have been mentioned previously in *Ceremony*. I think that *Desperate Circumstance, Dangerous Woman* is a different volume entirely, and I did not plan it to be a single book-length poem; I thought I was writing a poem that might be twenty pages in typescript. I kept working on it and I realized that it was probably going to be a book-length poem. Thirteen chapters with a glossary. I started *Desperate Circumstance, Dangerous Woman* in New Orleans, or at least the idea of it came while I was in New Orleans. I left New Orleans; I stayed with Charles Rowell in Virginia for a few weeks; then I went up to Poughkeepsie and stayed with Moses Nkondo, and he read draft after draft after draft. He drove me up to Austerlitz, the Edna St. Vincent Millay colony, and I worked on it some more there. The first chapter of it was published in Switzerland in an annual called *Two Plus Two*. So I started working on it roughly in 1986, and I didn't finish writing it until 1990.

JL: Is that unusual for you, to take that long in reflection?

BMO: Well, there's one other poem that took that long; it's a poem that's a companion poem to this poem, *Desperate Circumstance, Dangerous Woman*. It explains the ancestry of Marie Crying Eagle, so that we see who she is and how the narratives of her life develop. That poem is called "Calcasieu," which means "crying eagle." It's not a very long poem—about a dozen pages. And I worked on that poem for seven and a half years! I worked on this one for four and a half years. But I was working on other projects as well, teaching and so forth. And I was ill while I was in Los Angeles—I had surgery, sports accidents, all kinds of things holding me up. But I finished it while I was out there and sent it off. I suppose *In These Houses* was the first planned volume. I had photographs taken, and I was actually pulling pages together. This one was planned as a single poem, and I have a genealogy chart for the characters, a timeline that shows when so-and-so was born, and when they lived, what they did, and who they were, and I have a list of landmarks and areas and things that I need and want to work around; I had planned that this volume would also have a map that would show the relationship between the French Quarter and the Faubourg Tremé, and between the Faubourg Tremé and the Faubourg Marigny. I never got around to it. Maybe a future edition will have a map in it, I don't know. But that, technically, is how the poems developed. For a long time I had the idea of a poem that would be called *Desperate Circumstance*. It wasn't until later that it became *Desperate Circumstance, Dangerous Woman*. When it was in its working form, while I was at the Bunting Institute in Cambridge in '86, I read a part of it, the first chapter, where the mother dies and Percy and Marie have their first big talk. Moses Nkondo asked a question about it when I read this chapter at a workshop. At that time it was called simply "The Percy Poem." The focus was primarily on how Percy was going to get himself healed, and whether or not he was going to die. The joke was, Moses Nkondo pointed out to me that none of my male characters ever spoke. I reminded him of one instance where one does, the little old man who tells the poem "Elvena" in *In These Houses*; I said, "Well, here's a man, he's the central character, he gets to tell the story," and Moses said, "Yeah, but he's old! The men in your poems never speak, and then when they do they die!" *(Laughs.)* But that was not intentional—so then I had to write poems where men got to live—and then I wrote a series of poems, some of them joke-poems, for Moses, which were later published. At the reading in Cambridge, I was reading a work-in-progress, and I asked the audience if I should kill Percy, and this little old lady sitting on the front row said, "Oh, just maim him a little bit!" *(Laughs.)* And poor Percy hadn't *said* a thing; he was just suspicious and conservative. *All Saints* is a new and selected poems collection, mostly new, and it has seven chapters, seven sections. I wanted to do something that would touch on several different aspects of black New Orleans life. I wanted to focus specifically on religion, especially on hoodoo and Catholicism combined; I wanted something that focused on women; I wanted something that focused on music; and I wanted something that was focused on the slave heritage, something set in the 1600s, 1700s. And I think I got all those things in. I'm sort of proud, I guess, of my Buddy Bolden poems, and of my Sarah Vaughan poem, called "Sarah Vaughan is Alive and Well in New Orleans." I also have a poem for Ellis and Dolores Marsalis; those selections constitute the music poems. What I was trying to do was to pull together several different aspects of New Orleans, and it's called *All Saints* not only because of the Feast of All Saints, but because of this tendency we have to deify—musicians become gods. We have this religiosity that I've already mentioned. But we have this focus on spirituality in the midst of what seems to be a great deal of corruption—and turmoil—and I wanted to get as much of that in as I could. So I really planned that book in step-by-step fashion, and it has the largest glossary by far, because it's a larger book. There are many historic figures, so I identify all of these people. Many people, surprisingly, don't know, for instance, who Bolden was. We know he's the father of jazz. Lots of people think that Louis Armstrong was the father of jazz. So I give a little brief bio of Buddy Bolden, and the purpose of that poem is to give a bio of Buddy Bolden. A poem that I like to think of as "Boldenesque" *(laughs)*; I tried to capture something about Bolden in the poem, without bothering to tell a story.

JL: Let me ask you something about that, because of course, your poetry is extraordinarily musical, more so than most poetry. And yet your last work, *Desperate Circumstance*, is an extended narrative, and I asked you when that first came out if you were moving in the direction of writing prose, and now you haven't done that *(laughs)*. I wonder if that has something to with music and what you just told me about musicians, because I suspect you see yourself as a musician of sorts, as a poet.

BMO: I would *like* to be a musician, I really would. I don't have any interest in writing fiction at all. I have a particular fondness for short stories; I really like the short stories of Henry Dumas. Now, if I could write Henry Dumas short stories, then maybe I *would* write short stories *(laughs)*. But I never tried my hand, except for when I was a little kid. But I'm not drawn to the writing of fiction, I suppose because I'm not that interested in stories; I'm interested in all the stuff surrounding the stories. I've seen some fiction writers—especially short fiction writers—who seem to have similar interests. I think Henry Dumas tells very tightly woven stories—they mean something. I like the short stories of Julio Cortazar—I *love* his short stories, in fact. I'm amazed by the short stories of García Márquez. I like Alice Walker's *In Love and Trouble*. So I really like short fiction a lot, but I'm not at all interested in writing fiction. I *am* really interested in the essay as a literary form, and I think that the essay has been badly neglected. I've learned that people don't even teach essays anymore—the essay is not taught. That's so sad—but I've been trying to write essays myself. The way I sort of wormed my way into getting up enough nerve to write essays was by writing for a black monthly in New Orleans, doing pieces on New Orleans culture and so forth. I'm constantly looking for collections of good essays, and I'm constantly annoyed by what is called "essay." I'm not interested in straight-up, didactic, expository writing. I'm interested in what people seem to be calling creative nonfiction. I'd like at some point to bring out a collection; I have this little plan for a series of three essays I'd like to write, and I've worked on each of them a little bit.

JL: Could you tell me about them?

BMO: *(Laughs.)* Some of the stuff you'd expect! There's one that's a humorous essay entitled "I Want to Die in New Orleans," and it's all about my ideal funeral. And I think it's a funny little piece *(laughs)*. But I've never finished it. I worked on it while I was out at Provincetown. It tries to talk about the importance of dying a good death and being well-remembered at the end.

But I intended it as a humorous piece. Another is one that takes a serious look at hoodoo as a legitimate religion and as a series of principles. The other one is just a kind of hodgepodge thing about New Orleans and writing about New Orleans, the image of New Orleans. I also worked for a short time on an essay called "Getting to Hip," which is about the decline of the hip element in black popular culture. What I wanted to do was to find a certain figure who epitomized hipness—somebody like, say, Ellington, who was the epitome of the hip in his day.

JL: What, exactly, is hip to you?

BMO: Oh, hip, I suppose, is a mixture of many things—a kind of sophistication—what people used to call "wise," a kind of wiseness, not just wisdom. A certain sophistication—a way of being comfortable in oneself that is physically apparent—as it is very physical. And it has to do also with reaching a level of coolness—and I mean coolness in the African sense. I know you're familiar with Robert Farris Thompson's *Flash of the Spirit.*

JL: Yes, and of course he has that essay on coolness in black culture, too.

BMO: Yeah, and coolness is clearly an element of hipness; and there's an element of funkiness. Ellington had a lot of that; I think that Larry Neal had a little of it. I think Dinah Washington had it *(laughs).* I *know* Dinah Washington had it—Dinah Washington was IT! And Sarah Vaughan had it in flashes—it was something that came in flashes. It's something that has been rather undefinable, at least in words. You recognize it when you see it but you don't know how to talk about it. And that's what I wanted the essay to do—I wanted the essay to talk about it.

JL: Let me ask you about this, because it reveals a lot of interesting things, but among them I see a concern you possibly have with authenticity. Earlier you talked about the problem of early black writers writing for a white audience, suggesting that that compromised their authenticity. Is that the way you feel about it?

BMO: Definitely. I think it compromised writers as great as Zora Neale Hurston and Langston Hughes. The fact that they had this patron who gave them assignments and withheld payments and so forth—they were often compromised. It's very easy to become compromised. I *do* worry about authenticity. That's what bothers me about what I read about New Orleans. Sometimes it's as simple as a travel piece that you pick up and read in a magazine, and you say, "Where the hell did they go when they were in New Orleans that they could write such tripe?" Or I'll look at something on TV that's supposed to be set in New Orleans and I don't recognize any of it—it doesn't say anything that I can recognize as New Orleans. So I'm always looking for the real—what is real about the place? What is real, what is true? How does New Orleans see itself, if there's any self, how does New Orleans present *our* selves? And of course, that's the other thing, that we're very good at masking. There's a whole Carnival culture—we're very good at presenting one face to outsiders and another face within.

JL: Which is another African and African-American tradition.

BMO: Uh huh. It's a multifaceted thing. So that I'm always trying to get beyond the surface of things. I want characters who sound real, who are recognizable. I'm happiest when black New Orleanians tell me that they see themselves, that they see a New Orleans that they recognize, and that they understand the stories, that they *get* it. And I worry about whether that little tiny group of New Orleans readers "get it." If *they* don't, then something's wrong. And then I know that what I'm doing is not good enough, and that I need to work on it. And that's especially important with voice. My students have difficulty, for instance, reading things written in plantation dialect, but they have less difficulty reading poetry by Hughes, or some of the poems of Sterling Brown, which are much closer to authentic black folk speech. They maybe drop word endings, but you don't get all the "funny spellings." I don't write in dialect, and I don't know anyone who does write in dialect. But I am trying to catch a real voice, without funny spellings or any of that stuff. I try to put the words together; I have my characters making words, making speech.

JL: But are you tempted sometimes to write stories or novels that cater to the popular taste? Because that's been a problem in southern writing from its inception, extending on up till today; there're so many lesser southern writers who obviously cater to stereotypes, especially in terms of things that are "grotesque," "typically" southern, or in the "New Orleans" line, replete with decaying mansions.

BMO: Like incest, strange kinds of doublings; there's a gothic something about it all. But no, I'm not tempted, because I guess I didn't become a writer because I thought it was going to make me a rich person *(laughs)*. I'm doing something that I really want to do, and I'm doing something that I think I'm pretty good at, and I hope that if I become less good at it I'll have the good sense to stop. I hope that someone who loves me will call me up on the phone and say, "Brenda Marie, please stop writing this garbage, it's really horrible and you need to stop now." I don't want to be like an opera singer who's past her prime up there warbling. I've been able to support myself as a writer, oddly enough, but I never thought I was going to make gangbuster money as a poet. That was never the reason behind it. And so I'm not tempted by that. But what happens is that people will often come to me to ghostwrite projects they're doing, that they wouldn't want their names attached to—and that I wouldn't want my name attached to either! *(Laughs.)* And people come to me with proposals and I say no—I don't have any problem with flat-out saying no. The thing that worries me more is dramatizations. People are always trying to get me to allow staged productions of poems. They see these characters and feel they can be acted out, blah blah blah. I worry about that a great deal, because I don't want my work reinterpreted that way. They always say, "But it will give you a broader audience," and I'll say, "But I'm not writing for a broader audience, I'm writing for an audience that reads poetry, or for an audience that *might* read poetry." So I'm not lured by so-called fame and fortune. I've set a series of problems for myself, and I'd like to be able to work through those problems. I have this thing about voice, and texture, and narrative, that I've been working on as long as I've been publishing. I'd like to see how many different ways I can develop a working voice, without ending up doing imitations or by repeating something I was doing earlier on. I'd like to do something that is authentically New Orleans. I'd like to do something that reflects the spirituality, the religiosity, things that I see as very southern, very New Orleans. So I have these goals that I work toward; these are problems I've set for myself. But no, I'm not drawn to that stuff, and I can't make myself read it. People give me books by southern writers, and they say, "This person's from the South, and their writing is so southern," and a lot of it I find offensive. Just like I don't recognize New Orleans in those Hollywood movies, I don't recognize the South in a lot of the fiction that gets published as southern. But on the other hand, I worry that we really do need to foster new generations of southern writers, and I think that there's still a lot of good material in the South—I don't think we've even scratched the surface—certainly not of the black cultural experience. There's the assumption that if you're from the South that you want to get away from it *(laughs)*. And that if you're in the South, you can't go anyplace else, you're bound by the South—there's this notion that life in the South is really horrible, and dreadful, and terrible. I found a lot of that in Cambridge.

JL: I just read an interview with Margaret Walker; she was asked why she lived in Mississippi. The question was framed in such a way as to indicate that it was astonishing that any black person—*especially* a black writer—would even think of living in Mississippi. Walker seemed to feel that she wrote best in Mississippi, although she said that she could actually write anywhere—and you've done that too, all over the states, and in Europe too—but Walker said that she was more comfortable and wrote better in Mississippi, because it was home. But to get back to the other kinds of writers we were discussing, who deal in stereotypes—what is it that keeps them from being true to the materials? Is it just catering to the audience, or is there something else at work?

BMO: It's catering to the audience, but there's also something that people have been calling, for some time now, "the new fiction." And a lot of "the new fiction" I'm not sure I understand. But there's a certain kind of MFA Writing Program fiction that seems to be very lucrative. And it breeds its own.

JL: Sort of designed to be published in *The New Yorker*?

BMO: Yes—and there's an MFA Writing Program poetry as well. There's a proliferation of these mass-produced writers, and I'm not sure what they read. I've just gotten to the point where I avoid it altogether. It's almost as though people are writing short novels that can be improved by being turned into movies. So people are writing for the movie market. If you write things that can be made into movies, then you have a secure income. And in fact, we're seeing a lot of things that *are* improved by being made into film. I think that we don't have enough writers teaching in the South.

JL: Not enough southern writers?

BMO: Exactly. And I suppose we have a generation of young southern writers for whom the topic of the South is taboo. Of course much of it has to do with slavery and racism. Then, too, people are always asking me, "Why did you choose to live in New Orleans? Why did you come back here?" And I always say, "I didn't choose to come back here—I always lived here. I was in other places but I never lived anywhere else. I didn't live in Cambridge—I stayed there for a year."

JL: It wasn't home.

BMO: Exactly! I was in Los Angeles for two years, but I lived in New Orleans.

JL: You came to see your family too.

BMO: Of course.

JL: I wanted to ask you about that. Unlike many practicioners of the "new fiction," you focus on ancestry; your first collection was dedicated to the memory of relatives. Do you consider your work elegiac, and is this southern?

BMO: Yes—I have a concern with elegy and remembrance. That volume was dedicated to my grandmothers and one great-grandmother. Sometimes I write poems for friends who have lost their parents. I wrote elegies when the parents of Clyde Taylor and Moses Nkondo and Charles Rowell died. As I said earlier, there's a peculiar sense of death in New Orleans. We see life as a continuum; there's really no end. We don't like endings in New Orleans. We never stop eating, drinking, or listening to music—it's always "one more, one more."

JL: I want to ask you about a writer who seems to meet many of the requirements you specify for southern writers, Ernest Gaines. How do you feel about his work?

BMO: Ernest Gaines definitely writes about Louisiana in a way I can respond to. He is the only black man writing today mainly about family. I like the way he relates the black family to wholeness, communal healing, reparation. Reparations and healing are priorities in his work.

JL: I agree with you, and I wonder why he doesn't get more respect and interest than he does.

BMO: Part of it has to do with the fact that he's southern—his work is *decidedly* southern. And there's a sense that that narrows his market, although I don't understand why. And because he writes about family and community it's possible to think about him as writing "like a woman," and that probably has something to do with it. He doesn't fulfill the stereotypes about what black men are supposed to write.

JL: Full of anger, and so forth.

BMO: Yeah, yeah. He's a quiet writer—even when there are violent interludes. His approach is not a passionate approach. He retains a certain amount of "dignity"; he also allows small children or seemingly insignificant characters to tell the story and forces us to acknowledge *their* dignity and *their* authority.

JL: *Miss Jane Pittman* is the perfect example of that.

BMO: Uh huh. (*Laughs.*) An old black woman—what could be more insignificant? And you know, I like his short stories very much—I like *Bloodline*.

JL: It's interesting that you particularly admire his interest in family, because Mary Helen Washington has just included his work in her anthology of black family narratives, *Memory of Kin*. I'm also struck by the interest in elegy that you seem to share with him. So many of the southern writers that we've named seem to be desperately trying to write down something about a culture that's vanishing before our eyes. Do you see your work as that kind of project? Is some of the material that you're concerned with disappearing as you write?

BMO: I don't know. I want to say, "No, it isn't!" I think in New Orleans it isn't so much that the material is vanishing—it's just being allowed to fall by the wayside. In the South in general, there are histories that have yet to be written, and nobody's writing them. The historic, archival materials we need to write from are 90 percent extant. You can go and look at records. In many southern cities, however, records were destroyed. That isn't the case here. People have family histories dating back to the antebellum period. Everyone has something on paper. What I worry about is oral history; I worry that all around us people are dying who have significant things to tell us. There are histories that we can't get in any other way, and we're not taking the opportunity to get them. There are the stories of the Zeno family across the street—three brothers and a sister. Their father was a famous jazz musician, and one of them has all of the father's memorabilia. I'd love to see somebody go and do a biography of their father. But they're old—here're all these wonderful people and their memories, but they're old. I'd like to see them donate those papers to an archive, but I also worry about not getting to *their* histories. We haven't had access to living people. I worry about all these musicians who die without ever telling us their stories. We have their compositions, but usually not their stories. Even when films are made about them, their biographers tend to be white; and even though I feel it's a good thing that we have those biographies, I really feel that *that's* the kind of work that young black writers should be exploring. They should be biographers. I know all these people right here in New Orleans who want to be writers, but I don't see them doing any writing. You have to start somewhere, you have to write, you have to mess up a few times. I have a friend like this who is so afraid of not doing the right thing that she won't write. So I worry about people not getting attention from writers; but I don't see this as a culture that's dying. I see us losing ground on a daily basis, unable to appreciate what we have. Sometimes we don't appreciate it until outsiders come in and see it for us. This idea of the South as a dying place—I think of Jean Toomer and *Cane*, and calling that book the swan song of the South. And I can see how the South that he thought was lost *was* lost. The rural towns he went to were losing their people to larger cities, so I can understand that. Yet there were those people who remained. Whenever people leave, there are those who remain. We have a tendency to see people who stay on as insignificant. You can walk down a street and see people sitting on their stoops, drinking their Friday night beer, and it's easy to trivialize their experiences. We do that too easily and too quickly. And that does mean that we're losing something. We may be losing our ability to talk with one another.

JL: It's partly related to our physical separation from one another too, isn't it? It's a hot day today, and we're inside enjoying the air-conditioning. If it weren't so hot we might be out on the stoop, or sitting in the garden.

BMO: (Laughs.) Well, the old-timers *are* out there! They're sitting in the shade, but they're out there! But that is a great part of it. I remember sitting out-doors as a kid—that's what we did. We sat on the porch and talked and drank lemonade. And you still see that in this community. People walk up and down and talk to each other. That's given me a sense of homecoming; it's like step-ping back into the past. Unfortunately, it's also related to poverty. Many of these people are poor, and things aren't getting any better for them. Gentrification is taking place all around them. It means the loss of a southern urban community.

JL: I also want to ask you about the many southern writers now, black and white, who strive to show black and white characters interacting with each other—writers like Ellen Douglas or Jack Butler in *Jujitsu for Christ*, say, where the racial identity of the writer isn't revealed until the last page. And of course there were earlier novels by black southerners like Richard Wright and Zora Neale Hurston that were focused on white characters. Have you ever thought about writing in this mode?

BMO: Now that I think about it, I've written only one poem where a white person is mentioned. I guess it never occurred to me to write about white characters. In particular, I don't pay that much attention to whites in New Orleans. In the New Orleans of my childhood—a part of the Seventh Ward, called Pailet-land—I was surrounded by black people, although there were some European immigrants on the fringes of our neighborhood. And there were a few Cuban families on one end, both black and white. We could go for days without seeing whites. We didn't count the Italians or non-English-speak-ing people as whites. I guess because they spoke with accents, were first- or sec-ond-generation immigrants, and had absolutely no power, no "white" power. They had small businesses in the black community, and we treated them as equals, on a first-name basis. They were dark like us, for the most part—most of the Italians were from southern Italy. We teased them about wanting to be white. We thought that was just the most hilarious thing in the world, that they wanted to be white people! White people were anglos. White people were city hall and the police. They [the Italians] were *people*. There were people, and there were white people. For us white people were a strange species, and we never knew what they might do. A white person might kill their own child, might go into a town and kill fifteen people he didn't know. Fifteen people who owed you money and wouldn't pay, we could understand that! White people were on television; they weren't like really real people. They were more like a problem than like real human beings. We saw white folk as a kind of a bad joke; we had endless funny stories about what white people had done. They weren't really real for us. And then we blackened those white people that we did have relations with. When we watched TV or went to the movies, for instance, we put on a filter that allowed us to see our favorite characters or actors not as white people, but people. They had qualities that we considered black qualities. I came of age in the 70s, so when the civil rights movement hit its peak, I was a little kid. Black Power was real, civil rights was the past. As a result, I never focused on race relations. I was interested in race, but not in race relations. My grandfather was what we called a "race man," and I had an aunt and uncle who were Garveyites. So race was always around me, and it was something that was always talked about, but race relations never really interested me. Also, I see New Orleans as a distinctly black space, and I see whites as marginal. I grew up in a very black New Orleans. Our doctors were black, our attornies, my school principals, all our authority figures were black. I've read these novels set in the 20s and 30s where some black child is forced to grovel before white authority figures. I never saw that. It never occurred to me to view blackness as a problem. It always shocks my students when I tell them that white racism is the problem, not blackness. I haven't anything to work out in terms of race relations, and that's why I don't write about it. There is a certain amount of pressure, however, both private and public, that says that white southern writers must struggle with it. I remember taking a Faulkner seminar when I was a graduate student and hearing Bob Hemenway talking about how Faulkner, writing a description of a black character as a mule, proved the perfection of black people, because Faulkner liked horses. And I remember how a black student in the class said, "But a horse ain't a mule!" *(Laughs.)* So I think that there's a pressure for whites that doesn't exist for black writers, because we don't feel responsible for the structure of race relations; for us, there isn't anything to work out. It's inconceivable for whites to write about the South without including black characters, but it's easy for me to write all-black poetry. If you're white and were born before 1945, it's likely that a black person changed your diaper. White southerners are drawn to something about blackness; there's something about blackness as an entity and a presence, but the reverse doesn't seem to be true for black southern writers. When I see a white woman walking down the street I don't see her as material for my work; I *do* see a black man or woman walking down the street in exactly that way.

JL: What do you make of the recent novels by northern black writers such as Toni Morrison and Gloria Naylor that are set in the South?

BMO: Milkman in *Song of Solomon* becomes more humanized the deeper he descends into the South. We see something similar going on in *Beloved*; many contemporary black writers see the South as some Harlem Renaissance writers did, as a kind of cultural homeland. If you consider it at all, you have to deal with all of it, slavery included, not just the pleasant parts. *Beloved* is a very painful book. Yet I don't understand why students should shy away from it or be ashamed or afraid of the history it explores. Morrison takes a moment in time and shows how people struggled for healing. You don't just move from point A to point B; you move through to life on the other side. There's that wonderful moment at the end of the book when Paul D. convinces Sethe that she's her own "best thing." Her act in killing her baby was unconscionable, but she has to choose to keep on living. She can choose to die or choose to live. In an act of supreme love, she decides, "I will have life beyond this." Morrison's work is true to life. We don't die because of things we cannot forgive. *Beloved* is one of the greatest books I've ever read. I like the way the South crops up there and continues to surface in other black fiction. The

South is the locale of memory, not only of the tortured past. Zora Neale Hurston, with her insistence on focusing on the black celebration of life and on the black self-sufficient community, helped us to see that. We need to see more of that in black southern letters. I'd like to see more work that focuses on the Caribbean as well. Many families migrated to the South from there; the South is also part of the Caribbean world.

9

JEFFERSON HUMPHRIES

The Discourse of Southernness

*Or How We Can Know There Will Still Be
Such a Thing as the South and Southern
Literary Culture in the Twenty-First Century*

*History is made up of wisps of narratives, stories that one tells, that
one hears, that one acts out; the people does not exist as a subject but
as a mass of millions of insignificant and serious little stories that
sometimes disperse into digressive elements. Generally, though these
are the stories that come together at least approximately to form what
is called the culture of civil society.*

Jean-Francois Lyotard, *Pagan Instructions*

Not just the past but the present and the future also are made up of "wisps of
narratives," and narratives about the future must inevitably evolve from
narratives of the past. History is just another word for temporal experience in
general, and in that sense it engulfs the future with the past and the present.
What this means is that before we can hope to say whether there might still be
a "southern" literary culture twenty, fifty, or a hundred years from now, we need
to say what we mean and have meant by the "South." What but a *story*, or several basic stories with an infinite variety of individual permutations, all of these
together making up one grand story of mythic proportions that all southerners,
to a greater or lesser degree, feel is *their* story? This must be the unarticulated,
perhaps even unadmitted premise behind all of oral history. Yet it is important
to note that it *has not* been admitted, least of all by most scholars working in
southern studies. Most southern writers—poets and novelists—have more or less
admitted it, however, though I doubt that any of them knew at the time or
knows it now, or would even be willing to admit it in so many words. I have
never heard of any "oral historians" specializing in the South—and almost all
of them in America do—who did not claim as their ground and premise the very
purest empiricism. I believe it is self-evident that they are wrong—not to do
what they are doing, but about why they are justified in doing it.

Whether slavery was or could continue to be economically feasible, whether it was more or less dehumanizing than the wage-labor system of the North, all these issues which empirical historians have debated and continue to debate, have nothing to do with what we mean by the South, with the South as an idea. The South, what we mean when we talk about the South, is not a geographical place and is only related to geographical place by pure arbitrary contingency. The South is instead nothing in the world but an idea in narrative form, a discourse or rhetoric of narrative tropes, a story made out of sub-stories, a lie, a fiction to which we have lent reality by believing in it.

Why do people invent stories? To make sense of something—themselves, circumstances—which does not make sense. This happens every day, on the smallest individual level, as well as on the plane of nations. People read the *National Enquirer* or *PMLA* according to what best responds to their personalized sense of how the world may be made to make sense, how it may best, *most satisfyingly*, be narrated. The most recondite scholarship is not any different in terms of the needs it reflects, expresses, and responds to than the endlessly repeated "journalistic" stories of Elvis's survival, of women being impregnated by ghosts and Martians, of men carrying fetuses to term in their feet. Soap operas and Masterpiece Theater are equally valid responses to the same need felt by persons of different educational and socioeconomic background. Edward Said has called this sort of narrative impulse as it operates between cultures "Orientalism." I will cite Christopher Miller's admirably succinct formulation:

> [*Orientalism*] analyzed the way in which such a term, conceived as a description of the world, generates concepts and categorizes thought until it becomes a massive screen between subject and object. From that moment on, perception is determined by Orientalism rather than Orientalism's being determined by perception. Said's book is part of a crucial reappraisal of European knowledge, possible only when the categories of thought—all "isms" and their attendant classifications—are recognized as arbitrary judgements made by discourse rather than real distinctions in the world. Said writes, "It is enough for 'us' to set up these arbitrary boundaries in our minds; 'they' become 'they' accordingly, and both their territory and their mentality are designated as different from 'ours.'
>
> . . . The Orient is a negative for Europe, conforming to the profile of what Europe thinks Europe is *not*; the opposition is therefore diametrical, producing a single, symmetrical Other. That Other always has a separate identity of its own, an "inferior" culture but a culture nonetheless.[1]

According to this paradigm, culture is a form of narrative or discourse. Cultural identity is a response to one's own compulsion to narrate, which in turn is almost always concomitant with the perception—accurate or not—of some *Other*'s attempt to impose a (negative, condescending, or otherwise undesirable) narrative order from without, or of the *possibility* of such a narration from without. No one likes to be hemmed in by the perceptions of others. Yet what we think are the ways others think of us—narrate us—whether what we think bears any relation to the reality of what others think or not—determine a great deal of our response, our defensive or offensive self-narration. So what matters historically is not how many abolitionists there were in the North, or how many northern politicians were committed to the eradication of slavery, but how many people in the South *thought* there were, and how this played on other factors that were involved in the nonsense which produced a narrative compulsion in the southern states, a desire to make sense which led to the invention of the Idea or Story of the South, which led in turn to the South itself.

The most important things that did not make sense to geographical southerners, to such a disturbing degree that they were obliged to invent themselves as metaphysical (rhetorical) southerners, was, first, the fact of being in a physical place quite remote from the European civilization from which they had come, and second, slavery, as well as the northern response to slavery (or narration about it).

It is hard to know which came first: Did the South invent the idea of itself in response to its own insecurities, or did those insecurities arise as a result of England's attempts to "narrate," to make sense of the southern colonies, and of the North beginning to articulate its own story, its own idea of itself, in opposition to the South's otherness, by making up, narrating the South's otherness? In fact, as Lewis Simpson has so brilliantly shown, North and South needed to invent each other in order to invent themselves. Neither story could come into being without the other; every culture must narrate itself not only in terms of what it is but also in terms of what it is not. The South is an amalgam of southern self-narrative, British and northern (more or less) negative projection, and southern counter-production. Thomas Jefferson's representation of the northerner as "cool, sober, laborious, independent . . . and hypocritical in . . . religion," and of the southerner as "fiery, voluptuary, indolent, unsteady . . . generous, candid, without attachment or pretensions to any religion but that of the heart"[2] is an early instance of the invention of the South as an idea and is openly dependent on a simultaneous narration of the North. By 1860, with the narrative impulse reaching fever pitch, George Fitzhugh would declare, "We alone are a new people. . . . New, original, and valuable combinations of thought will be suggested by our peculiar social organism, so soon as we dare to think independently, and to *justify ourselves before the world* [my emphasis]."[3] What Fred Hobson has called the southern "rage" to explain (to narrate) itself has been most vehement—most desperate—when responding to northern assertions, and inner doubts as well, that the northern "story" of North and South is superior to any of the South's own versions, and that northern literary culture or "story" in general is superior to that of the South. Thus William Hand Brown wrote to Paul Hamilton Hayne, on September 11, 1871:

And I rage internally when I see our Southern people—my brothers and yours—meekly admitting the Yankees' claim to have all the culture, all the talent, all the genius of the country. . . . And I rage tenfold when I see our people—aye, our women and maidens—taught to hanker after the works of Mrs. Stowe, that Pythoness of foulness; Lowell, the twice-branded hypocrite; Whittier, the narrow bitter Puritan; Alger, the dishwasher of maudlin mysticism, and the rest of that shabby crew.[4]

A similarly extreme anxiety in the face of encroaching northern narrative was expressed by Hayne in a letter to A. H. Dooley in 1876:

> No! I have not seen Walt Whitman's new book; nor to be *frank*, do I care a *"button"* about it! The world, or rather a few *artists*, English & American, have gone mad, touching the characteristics of this odd *Writer*. *One thing is certain*! If Mr. Walt Whitman really *is in any sense*, or to *any degree*, a genuine Poet; then, *all the canons of poetic Art must be reversed*; *and their most illustrious expounders* be consigned to oblivion, from Job to Homer; from Homer to Horace, from Horace to Shakspeare [*sic*], from Shakespeare to Tennyson.
>
> The admiration for this false, shallow, feculent *Eccentric*, is either *half affectation*, or *complete madness*! Were an Angel from Heaven to praise him to me, I would think it more probable that the Angel was a *false spirit* than that his commendation was *just*.
>
> Good God! My Dear Sir., think of *any mortal* cooly writing such ineffable stuff as this; —"*The scent of these arm-pits is aroma sweeter than prayer*!"—and *then*, the big, shameless *Beast* in his *"Leaves of Grass,"* actually *"apotheosizes,"* (if I may use that term), his own *genital organs*; falls down, & *worships* them (!), as if some visible deity glowed in the spherical beauty of his (doubtless) enormous testicles, and equally enormous *Penis*!! (Pardon such vulgar expressions; but *apropos* of *Whitman*, one becomes necessarily, & involuntarily vulgar!).[5]

The same deep apprehensiveness was expressed by Thomas Nelson Page in *The Old South*, albeit in somewhat more couth and calm language: "We are not a race to pass and leave no memorial on our time. . . . We must either leave our history to be written by those who do not understand it, or we must write it ourselves."

Most scholars are probably willing to admit that until well into the nineteenth century, the anxieties of alienation from Europe and slavery made of the South nothing more coherent than a group of individual states bound by common commercial, not ideological interests—ideology is a function of narrative, not commercial exigency (though the two may eventually overlap). The oil states of contemporary America, for instance, have no ideology in common. They do not because they have experienced no *narrative exigency* (the need to make sense of things that don't) in common.[6]

The south had no need to invent the "garden of the chattel" (by contrast with the "New Jerusalem" of the puritan North) until it experienced *narrative exigency*. It did not experience this in the way that New England did (because of the religious persecution of the Puritans in England) until, probably, the Missouri Compromise. Until then the South was simply several states and a lot of disparate individuals who found themselves in the same place with the goal of bettering themselves materially—of making money. At first, slaves were nothing but a means to make money, nothing more. Soon after that, however, they began to be perceived as a latent internal threat, and narrative exigency was born, giving rise to the "garden of the chattel," the "story" of the South as Great Civilization.[7] That story might be said to culminate in Lewis P. Simpson's deconstruction of it, though this is not to say by any means that it *ends* with Simpson's reading.

The need to make sense began as a response to physical displacement, continued as a response to slavery itself, and grew in proportion to the burgeoning northern and international sentiment against slavery, but it did not reach full tilt until the individual states of the Confederacy had known defeat. Nothing makes less sense than being utterly defeated and ruined, as an individual or a culture, and therefore nothing feeds the compulsion to narrate better. Thus Edward A. Pollard wrote in *The Lost Cause* that "the Confederates have gone out of this war, with the proud, secret, deathless, *dangerous* consciousness that they are THE BETTER MEN, and that there was nothing wanting but a change in a set of circumstances and a firmer resolve to make them the victors."[8] In 1906 the confederacy would be described by Walter Hines Page in this way: "—the horrid tragedy of it and the myths that were already growing over it, its heroes, its Colonels, its Daughters."[9] A myth of defeat. If nothing else, the South as a story had gained something perhaps essential to a successfully literary culture, which the North did not and perhaps still does not have: the circumstantial inflections of tragedy. Its story had now no choice but to include a horrible and tragic sense of loss. That sense of loss characterizes more than anything else what we know as southern literature worthy of the name; it happens to coincide—has had the good luck to coincide, quite accidentally—with an ethos that is characteristic of all great modern literature.

The element of accident, the fact of a long trail of concatenated narratives building quite haphazardly upon one another, shaping acts and thus events, and not in logical and orderly sequence, or as a mere transcription of event, but as a narrative intended at least to sublimate fact and more likely repress it entirely—this element of accident cannot be forgotten in considering what the South (or any cultural entity) means and has meant. The stories which southerners have told about the South, inventing and reinventing it in the process, have been shaped not only by internal circumstances and needs but also by the narrative that others sought to impose from without. Any regional or national identity (narrative) is the result of at least two conflicting attempts to narrate: negative, though self-avowed impartial ones, from without—in this case from England, and then from the North—and the attempt to recuperate a positive significance from these external narratives and from one's own experience of chaos. Both the negative and the positive may be, and probably are, entirely arbitrary and bear little relation to fact; when there is an attempt at moderation, if not objectivity, it usually falls on deaf ears on both sides because it appeals to neither's narrative desire, as for instance Daniel R. Hundley's *Social Relations in Our Southern States* in 1860: "Hundley called for the North to understand a South that deserved both praise and blame. In 1860 these views were not especially popular anywhere in the United States."[10] Fact, in the form of individual narratives (lives, desires) will, however, quickly begin to imitate these large narratives of cultural identity. So that it becomes difficult to tell which one came first. De Tocqueville's narrative of America is motivated by narrative exigency as I understand it: a compulsion to make sense of something that doesn't. The reality reacts to this story of itself by rejecting or embracing, but in either case it *grounds itself in the very narrative that is supposed to explain it.*

The many attempts to catalogue southern types—by W. J. Cash, Florence King, John Shelton Reed, going back to Daniel Hundley's *Social Relations in the Southern States* and *Flush Times of Alabama and Mississippi*—all dimly reflect this sense that the South is a narrative, a rhetoric of *stories* involving a relatively small set of stock characters or narrative tropes. At the same time, all of these works represent attempts to modify, to amend the narrative(s) according to present circumstances (narrative exigency). Implicit in all of these attempts, including mine, is the assumption that individual psychology is a kind of *narratology*, the very same assumption made by Freudian theory, in which the intervention of an analyst in a patient's self-narrative is of specifically *narrative* or *interpretive* order, a "critical," interpretive, and supposedly corrective intervention (or attempt at it) by an analyst in the patient's ongoing story of him- or herself.

What are the most basic narratives or characterizational tropes of canonical southernness? I will argue for seven though there are doubtless many other minor and ancillary ones.

1. Thomas Jefferson. Relentless introspection plus slavery equals the first stirring of southern mind (southern story) as Virginian mind and Virginian story, and also *national* mind and *national* story, for after all, four of the first five presidents were Virginians. The "southern" idea actually was dominant over the northern one for a brief period. Because it was dominant, however, its narrative compulsion lacked urgency, and the South cannot be said to have existed for Jefferson except latently until his last years, when he saw his and his state's, if not precisely his region's, political vision giving way to nationalism: "I regret that I am now to die in the belief, that the useless sacrifice of themselves by the generation of 1776, to acquire self-government and happiness to their country, is to be thrown away by the unwise and unworthy passions of their sons, and that my only consolation is to be, that I live not to weep over it."[11] This story, Jefferson's, is crucial because it is chronologically the first, but it is the one that is most remote from the narrative structure(s) of contemporary southern consciousness.[12]

2. Edgar Poe/Roderick Usher. The literary southerner as mysterious, dissolute, hypersensitive and, sometimes, effete; the literary ethos of defeat and

loss already prepared and ready, waiting for the fact (of defeat and loss). Defeat and loss were personal realities for Poe, which he was compelled to translate into narratives. His somewhat arbitrary identification with very early southern literary aspirations (after having signed his first book "a Bostonian"), and the accidental coincidence of Poe's personal narratives with the "tragic myth"of the post–Civil War South, made it possible for later southern writers like Allen Tate to discover a profound literary "kinship" with Poe.[13] The popular image of the writer in the South as benighted, alcoholic genius, prophet crushed by the burden of stewardship of the Fatherland's textuality, is one that William Faulkner certainly took seriously and some southern writers still believe enough to act out. This story is often used to represent the downside of southern "blue-bloodedness": its "decadent" tendencies.

   3. Sut Lovingood. The frontier southerner; redneck; *poor* or lower middle-class, as opposed to middle- or upper-middle-class, good old boy. This character embodies a narrative version of the frontier South that is still viable (on display at many gas stations throughout the South, and many a country saloon). Sut is the characterizational trope of the often comic, sometimes mean-spirited, always willfully ignorant and uncouth poor white (trash). Nowadays, and for some time, he or she may be middle-class in income—may own a gas station, rather than just work there—but this does not alter the type much, if at all. Daniel R. Hundley described the type in 1860:

> The chief characteristic of Rag Tag and Bobtail, however, is laziness. They are about the laziest two-legged animals that walk erect on the fact of the Earth, and their speech is a sickening drawl, worse a deal sight than the most down-eastern of all the Down-Easters; while their thoughts and ideas seem likewise to creep along at a snail's pace. All they seem to care for, is, to live from hand to mouth; to get drunk, provided they can do so without having to trudge too far after their liquor; to shoot for beef; to hunt; to attend gander pullings; to vote at elections; to eat and to sleep; to lounge in the sunshine of a bright summer's day, and to bask in the warmth of a roaring wood fire, when summer days are over, and the calm autumn stillness has given place to the blustering turbulence of hyemal storms. (262–63)

We would today have to include fanatical football and basketball (watching) among the recreational activities enumerated. The novelist Cormac McCarthy has elaborated this type in very uncomedic fashion.

   4. R. E. Lee. The Ur-narrative of southern heroism. The agony and tragedy of defeat and its bitter lessons (of which the rest of the United States will ever be ignorant). The narrative of Lee, incorporating that of Lee's family, is the one which most nearly approximates what every southerner since the Civil War—the Sut Lovingoods, the cotton snobs, the literati—wishes to accept as the *proper*, the *authentic*, instance of the idea of southernness. The story of Lee means all things to all southerners, and it even confounds the Yankee in his desire to find something contemptible in every story the southerner would tell

about the South: even northerners have never been able to deny Lee's heroic stature. This makes Lee's story a most fascinating one indeed, and one that has not really been examined as an instance, and probably the most important instance, of the South's invention of its own idea.[14]

Lee is represented by the same narrative techniques usually reserved for hagiography. Two instances from Shelby Foote's narrative of the Civil War will illustrate:

> In addition to the copies [of Lee's farewell message] made by Marshall's clerk for normal distribution, others were transcribed and taken to the general for his signature, and these remained for whose who had them the possession they cherished most. One such was Henry Perry, the young infantry captain. . . . Later he told how he got it and how he felt, then and down the years, about the man who had signed it. "I sat down and copied it on a piece of Confederate paper," he recalled, "using a drumhead for a desk, the best I could do. I carried this copy to General Lee, and asked him to sign it for me. He signed it and I have it now. It is the best authority, along with my parole, that I can produce why after that day I no longer raised a soldier's hand for the South. There were tears in his eyes when he signed it for me, and when I turned to walk away there were tears in my own eyes. He was in all respects the greatest man who ever lived, and as a humble officer of the South, I thank heaven I had the honor of following him."
>
> "You have disgraced the family, sir!" Ex-Governor Henry Wise sputtured when he learned that one of his sons had taken the oath [of loyalty to the Union]. "But, Father," the former captain said, "General Lee advised me to do it." Taken aback, Wise paused only a moment before he replied. "That alters the case. Whatever General Lee advises is right."[15]

Reynolds Price, in a poem published in 1982, attests that Lee is still, within the idea of the South, the story of everything good, describing him as like "old Chief Joseph or a captive pope," his "face as beautiful / As any human feasible vision / Of any god in charge of Fate / And Mercy—serene now, omniscient."[16]

5. Uncle Remus and Aunt Jemima/Nat Turner. These are two faces of one coin. The mysterious, apparently benign but *possibly* dangerous (even murderous) and latently tricky heart of darkness, or, as Henry Louis Gates has described him/her, the Signifying Monkey:

> The Signifying Monkey is a trickster figure, of the order of the trickster figure of Yoruba mythology, Esu-Elegbara in Nigeria, and Legba among the Fon in Dahomey, whose New World figuration—Exu in Brazil, Echu-Elegua in Cuba, Papa-Legba in the pantheon of the *loa* of Vaudou in Haiti, and Papa La Bas in the *loa* of Hoodoo in the United States— speak eloquently of the unbroken arc of metaphysical presuppositions and patterns of figuration shared through space and time among black

cultures in West Africa, South America, the Caribbean, and the United States. These trickster figures, aspects of Esu, are primarily *mediators*: as tricksters they are mediators and their mediations are tricks.

. . . The Afro-American rhetorical strategy of signifying is a rhetorical practice unengaged in information giving. Signifying turns on the play and chain of signifiers, and not on some supposedly transcendant signified. Alan Dundes suggests that the origins of signifying could "lie in African rhetoric." As anthropologists demonstrate, the Signifying Monkey is often called "the signifier," he who wreaks havoc upon the "signified." One is "signified upon" by the signifier.[17]

The idea, the story, of the black man as fable-spinner *par excellence*, the source of all narrative, is central to the South as idea and story. The black storyteller is no less than the keeper and the arbiter of (the story of) canonical, predominantly white southern identity; the character of Elgin in Walker Percy's *Lancelot*, and virtually all of the black characters in the fiction of Reynolds Price, are modern enactments of this same narrative.[18]

This is not to suggest that this is the only characterization accessible to black southerners; far from it. To whatever extent blacks consider themselves *southern*, all of the other tropes or types listed here are equally accessible. There are also within *black southern* culture a number of types that operate within the larger narrative of the South but are not part of the way in which white southern culture views or has viewed the black (or blackness). This may be changing, as critics like Gates bring more of black southern literature and culture into the southern canon.

6. The belle—Scarlett O'Hara or, as she exists in the twentieth-century consciousness, Blanche DuBois. The idea of southern woman, as distinct from northern (or any other kind), came about as a relatively insignificant and ancillary part of the effort to argue (to narrate) the supremacy of southern civilization, but quickly grew as large or larger than the story from which it had spun off. Many young southern women still act as though the antebellum narrative of femininity were the only *proper* one; they continue to act that narrative out, with variations according to new circumstances such as contraception and recent narrative exigencies such as feminism.

There is a variant of the belle corresponding to each socioeconomic gradient; the differences are superficial, however, amounting to little more than the amount and quality of clothing, makeup, perfume, and hair treatment, and the degree of attention and care with which these are applied. Both the wealthiest and the poorest belle will tend to paint their nails (toe- and finger-) and wear enough makeup and perfume to suit any northern clown or prostitute, but the difference between them is nonetheless clearly visible: there might be chips in the nail paint of the less well-off exemplar, and her accent and vocabulary will resemble Sut Lovingood's more, and Lee's or Poe's or Jefferson's less, the less well-off she is. The belles of more economically prosperous family, moreover, are less and less likely to be pure prototypes, but rather crosses of the belle with various female representations current in the popular national culture, on situation comedies, or in women's magazines. The effect of mixing the belle with various non-southern tropes of femininity is to render the whole effect more subtle (and also perhaps less stifling and more likeable—see, for instance, Clyde Edgerton's novel *Raney*), but it is doubtful whether the southern core will ever disappear entirely. (The same is true of all the other types described here.) One could ask for no more thorough or sensitive high literary use of the traditional belle character-trope than that to be found in the works of Tennessee Williams.

Of course, this is not the only narrative of femininity operating within the larger story of the South. Each of the other narratives or types may be female as well as male. A not uncommon type is that of the "bohemian belle" (one who has attended college in the North or California), an intermingling of the Poe and belle tropes, often with some smidgen of foreign spice sprinkled in. (Intellectual southerners of both sexes often feel compelled to go far outside their native region—in mind and body—long enough to dilute their southern selves with some extra-southern cultural tropes.) Reynolds Price's celebrated female character Rosacoke Mustian, in *A Long and Happy Life*, is an extremely subtle (and winning) admixture containing at least a pinch of virtually *every* southern character trope listed here.

7. The southern middle class, as defined or narrated by the Alabamian Daniel Hundley: the model storekeeper, the southern Yankee (southern in birth but northern in spirit), the southern bully (the middle-class counterpart of Sut Lovingood, another, perhaps even more offensive sort of good old boy, and the one that is perhaps the most common type in today's South) and the cotton snob. The southern Yankee and the model storekeeper are generally overlapping categories, as are the cotton snob and the bully. Hundley described the southern Yankee as follows, in a style worthy of Dickens or Balzac:

> In [Georgia] they grow to enormous sizes, and seldom stand under six feet in their stockings, often, indeed, reaching six feet and a half. Muscular, heavy-jawed, bettle-browed, and possessed of indomitable energy, they are well calculated to command respect almost any where, did one only have it in his nature to forget that SELF is the only god they worship, and MONEY the only incense that ever ascends as a sweet-smelling savor to the nostrils of their idol. (157)

"The Cotton Snob," on the other hand,

> is frequently to be seen in the Free States, and when seen is pretty sure to make himself a "shining mark," for he assumes to be the very tip-top of the first families, and as such considers his individual corporosity a thing too sacred to be touched even by the hands of Northern *canaille*, "greasy mechanics," or what not. He also seeks every opportunity to talk about "my niggers," (observe, a Southern Gentleman [a Lee, for instance] rarely if ever says *nigger*) endeavors to look very haughty and overbearing;

sneers at whatever he considers *low*, and "their name is legion"; carries a cane not infrequently; affects a military step and manner. . . . By such and other similar displays of vulgarity and ill-breeding, the Cotton Snob pretty soon renders himself both ridiculous and contemptible; and, what is more and worse, brings a reproach upon the true Gentlemen of the South. (170)

And the Cotton Snob verily, if persuaded it was *the thing* to have a juvenile African served up whole on state occasions, stuffed like a young grunter or prepared like a baron of beef, would never hesitate to have young Sambo served with parsley and egg-sauce, or whatever else might be the taste of the hour; and what is more, he would pretend to enjoy the delicious repast with as much gusto, as he at present evinces while discussing the mysterious compounds served at the St. Charles or the St. Nicholas—not one of which, in most instances, he would be able properly to translate into his own vernacular. (186–87)

The cotton snob, the bully, the model shopkeeper/southern Yankee are characterizations or narratives that resulted from (1) certain persons having profoundly misread the story or idea of southern aristocratic pretensions, and of that misinterpretation going on to become a narrative all of its own, eventually to be transcribed in parody by Hundley, and (2) certain other individuals having totally, though probably not really willfully, ignored the cultural narrative that was evolving around them, and having kept right on thinking of nothing but their own material betterment, as the first "southerners" (pre-southerners?) had in arriving in the colonies. All of Hundley's types still exist, as anyone who has lived in the South for any time knows. Which is to say that these narratives are still functioning as models of desire and comportment—positive or negative, to be emulated or reacted against—among members of the present-day southern middle class.

Every one of these stories responds to a counterpart that would impose itself from without, even in the case of Hundley, who was probably much harsher on the southern middle class than most northerners were—reflecting a narrative tradition of self-castigation and lampooning continued by many contemporary southern writers (James Wilcox, for instance, in *Modern Baptists*). Both the northern and southern versions of the South respond arbitrarily and in an extremely contingent manner to actual fact. Neither is motivated by any high-minded empiricism but rather by desire, narrative desire, narrative exigency, the wish to make sense of what does not and is therefore frightening or disquieting or enraging. This happens in a dialectical fashion very much according to the paradigm proposed by Edward Said.

In much the same way, every individual, man or woman, who thinks of himself or herself as southern must make him- or herself, his or her story, out of the story-types listed above, taking more or less from each one, through projection (denial) or introjection (affirmation). Lewis Grizzard might represent a prototypical New South urban/suburban good old boy: maybe two-thirds model shopkeeper and one-third bully, with a pinch of Sut Lovingood. He would probably have liked to think he had a couple of pinches of Lee, too, but he won't get them from me. The traditional southern homosexual is easy to make up using, say, one part Roderick Usher to two parts belle. The typical southern politician has always been and is still comprised of varying proportions (from all of one to equal parts of all) of the following: cotton snob, southern bully, Lee, model shopkeeper, and/or Sut Lovingood, with *perhaps*, and I only suggest the *possibility*, of a little Jefferson. This may be the recipe for the basic average southerner, give or take the occasional Roderick Usher/Poe, who probably will feel compelled to spend some time up North or abroad in order to leaven himself or herself with some northern or European affectations, thereby throwing some real kinks into the formula.

From *I'll Take My Stand* to present-day postsouthern writing, all writing about the South has been a variation on these themes, and motivated by the same narrative exigency. Why did it take so long—until the Agrarians—for there to be a mature *literary* expression of *southernness*? Because the compulsion to narrate comes before the narration itself, and the first narration always occurs on the level of historical consciousness. Once the basic story has been told, it can begin to serve as a model and as a subject for literary expression. The same delay has been true of South American literature, whose vitality is due to exactly the same sort of *narrative compulsion*, though the stimuli, the specific historical circumstances which made so disturbingly little sense that people felt compelled to make a story about them that *would* make sense, were different.

> To know (before we know) what narrative is [the narrative of the future, as well as the abstract possibility of narrative in general, I would add], the narrativity of narrative, we should perhaps first recount, return to the scene of one origin of narrative, to the narrative of one origin of narrative (will that still be narrative?), to that scene that mobilizes various forces, or if you prefer various agencies or 'subjects,' some of which demand the narrative of the other, seek to extort it from him, like a secret-less secret, something that they call the truth about what has taken place: 'Tell us exactly what happened.'
>
> Jacques Derrida, "LIVING ON: Border Lines"

If we would know what the narrative of southernness is, we must first admit that southernness itself is a narrative, an expression of the compulsion to narrate. That it is, in effect, a pure fiction, a rhetoric. That it was not born as a reflection of reality, or an attempt to describe it, but rather in dire response to it, in response to something *missing* from the real, as an attempt to deny that something which was missing, to repress it, to obliterate it. Our cultural identity as southerners is not then, or not only, the logical expression of certain physical and circumstantial factors, but rather a hysterical and, one might even say, superstitious refusal to accommodate those physical and circumstantial factors, a refusal either to run away to some other reality or to attempt to confront the unruliness of circumstances honestly and directly; this refusal, this denial, is expressed as a narrative. That narrative appears to reflect reality because, first, it may happen to resemble it, and second, having invented the story, men proceed to imitate it, to model their desires and opinions according to it.

We are southerners because we, and our ancestors, and the rest of the nation, have felt a compelling need to make up stories about southerners and because we then chose to act as though those stories were as true or truer than fact itself—to *imitate* those narratives, to model our desires, our behavior, our thoughts, and our lives according to them. We are then southerners by a perverse accident, which we have denied, repressed, exacerbated, and enshrined in a narrative that we are still in the process of telling. As long as we keep responding to this narrative exigency—and it is very difficult, in light of the past that comprises our present, to imagine that we could do otherwise—there will still be a South, and a literature that can with justification be called "southern."

Many scholars have suggested that we are in a "postsouthern" period, that the time of a coherent southern identity, and therefore of a viable and truly southern literary culture, is past. I would ask not only the scholars who have made these assertions, but any reasonable person who knows any part of the South today, if they can deny that the types, the narrative characterizations I just listed, continue to determine and therefore describe accurately (or to describe accurately and therefore determine) much of the appearance, comportment, and ideology of persons living today from Virginia to Texas? I certainly cannot deny it.

Moreover, the fact of a generational dispute regarding the viability of southern literary culture (Walter Sullivan and, to some extent, Lewis Simpson speak for those who assert that the "renascence" is over and "will not come again") is probably best interpreted as a struggle over who will have stewardship over southern discourse for the years to come, and this is a struggle in which the younger writers will inevitably prevail, so long as they continue to want to.

There is a parallel dispute between the elders of the southern (critical) literary establishment, whose critical ideology is more or less that of the New Criticism of Brooks and Warren, and the younger critics and scholars like myself, who would bring recent European philosophy and theories of literature to bear on southern texts and the text of the South. The elders appear to believe that the introduction of European theoretical discourses into the rhetoric of southernness will adulterate the latter beyond any possible redemption, contributing to an already inexorable progress toward extinction. In fact, this cannot be so if Lewis P. Simpson was right in saying that "after the First World War the South entered the modern world in a special sense: Southern writers joined the Great Literary Secession. So doing of course they reentered an old world—that is, the literary realm of Western High Culture."[19] I believe that Simpson was absolutely right in making this assertion, but I disagree with him when he asserts that the crisis of letters in the West is over because the "motive of literary attention—

the keeping alive of 'the spirit of the letter' — is draining away." (254) It seems self-evident to me that in fact European modes of literary theory such as deconstruction (as articulated by Jacques Derrida, Michel Foucault, and Paul de Man) are *symptoms* of the ongoing crisis of letters in the West and reflect both a steadily deepening sense of literary alienation and an indomitable commitment to keeping alive "the spirit of the letter." This means that there must be an enormous common ground—and, again, if Simpson is right, a *history* of common ground going back to the First World War and, before that, to Jefferson — between the rhetoric of southernness and European modes of literary discourse. This critical debate between the generations of southernists must be the same sort of struggle over *who will continue to narrate the (idea of the) South and how they will do it* as the one between the generations of southern novelists and poets. Of course the idea will go on being narrated as long as there is anyone who continues to experience narrative compulsions like those which "invented" the South in the first place; the fact of a debate on the question is alone ample proof that such compulsions continue to be felt, in and about the South. The elders' attempt to write *finis* to the tale before the next generation can wrest it from them must be futile: the end of *this* kind of narrative can only come when no one cares whether the story is ended or not.[20] It seems quite safe to assert that many will go on caring for at least another century.

Notes

This paper owes a great debt to four scholars whom I would like to thank here for their friendship and their work: Christopher L. Miller, whose work in intercultural discourse theory is without peer; Henry Louis Gates, who has done so much to bring black southern culture out of its traditionally repressed status and into the canon of southern letters and southernness; Fred Hobson, who has assembled and told an enormous chunk of the South's story of itself in *Tell About The South*; and Lewis P. Simpson, who has been modestly and elegantly deconstructing the idea of the South for years, since long before the term "deconstruction" was coined.

1. Christopher L. Miller, *Blank Darkness: The Discourse of Africanism in French* (Chicago: University of Chicago Press, 1985), p. 15.

2. Quoted in John Alden, *The First South* (Baton Rouge: Louisiana State University Press, 1961), p. 17.

3. George Fitzhugh, "Disunion within the Union," *De Bow's Review* 28 (January 1860), pp. 1–7.

4. Quoted in Fred Hobson, *Tell About the South: The Southern Rage to Explain* (Baton Rouge: Louisiana State University Press, 1983), p. 85.

5. Rayburn S. Moore, ed., *A Man of Letters in the Nineteenth-Century South: Selected Letters of Paul Hamilton Hayne* (Baton Rouge: Louisiana State University Press, 1982), p. 133.

6. See John Blassingame, "American Nationalism and Other Loyalties in the Southern Colonies, 1763–1775," *Journal of Southern History* (February 1968), 49–75; Carl N. Degler, "The Beginnings of Southern Distinctiveness," in *Place Over Time* (Baton Rouge: Louisiana State University Press, 1977), pp. 27–66. Alden, *First South*, argues for the opposite conclusion.

7. See Lewis P. Simpson, *The Dispossessed Garden: Pastoral and History in Southern Literature* (Athens: University of Georgia Press, 1975) and *Mind and the American Civil War: A Meditation on Lost Causes* (Baton Rouge: Louisiana State University Press, 1989).

8. Quoted in Hobson, *Tell About the South*, p. 85.

9. Walter Hines Page, "The Autobiography of a Southerner Since the Civil War," *Atlantic Monthly* 98 (July, August, September, October 1906), pp. 1–12, 157–76, 311–25, 474–88.

10. William J. Cooper, Introduction to Daniel R. Hundley, *Social Relations in Our Southern States* (1860; reprint, Baton Rouge: Louisiana State University Press, 1979), p. xxv.

11. Quoted in Noble Cunningham, *In Pursuit of Reason: The Life of Thomas Jefferson* (Baton Rouge: Louisiana State University Press, 1987), p. 335.

12. Lewis P. Simpson has read Jefferson's story more closely and astutely than anyone; see his *Mind and the American Civil War*, pp. 1–32.

13. I have explored these issues in considerable detail in *Metamorphoses of the Raven: Literary Overdeterminedness in France and the South since Poe* (Baton Rouge: Louisiana State University Press, 1985).

14. Thomas L. Connelly, *The Marble Man: Robert E. Lee and His Image in American Society* (New York: Knopf, 1977) comes the closest.

15. Shelby Foote, The Civil War, A Narrative, III: Red River to Appomatox (New York: Random House, 1974), pp. 956, 1049.

16. Reynolds Price, "The Dream of Lee," *Vital Provisions* (New York: Atheneum, 1982), pp. 6–9.

17. Henry Louis Gates Jr., "The 'Blackness of Blackness': A Critique of the Sign and the Signifying Monkey," *Critical Inquiry* 9 (1983): 687–89.

18. See my "Remus Redux, or French Classicism on the Old Plantation: La Fontaine and Joel Chandler Harris," in *Southern Literature and Literary Theory*, ed. Jefferson Humphries (Athens: University of Georgia Press, 1990), pp. 170–85.

19. Lewis P. Simpson, "The Southern Writer and the Great Literary Secession," *The Man of Letters in New England and the South* (Baton Rouge: Louisiana State University Press, 1973), p. 241.

20. This essay began as an attempt to understand what I had meant by a poem I wrote several years ago, called "Poe as Cause and Effect of the Civil War, or Why the South Is a Nation of Liars," *South Carolina Review* 20, no. 2 (Spring 1988), pp. 2–3. The poem says (I think) all of this in considerably fewer words.

10

JAMES OLNEY

Autobiographical Traditions
Black and White

M y first inclination when I undertook to think and write about a possible tradition of autobiography in southern literature (or at least a tradition of autobiographical writing: there is an important distinction to be drawn, I think, between the substantive "autobiography" and the adjective "autobiographical," which I will return to later)—my first inclination was to deny that any such tradition exists or has existed and that hence I had no subject to write about. But then on second thought I came to feel that this was not altogether accurate and was also not something that I really wanted to say, particularly in light of the fact that I have written more than one essay in which I argued for a very strong tradition of autobiography among southern writers—or at least a tradition that began with specifically southern writers and that then, but without ever ceasing to be a tradition of southern writing, reached out to inform the work of writers not of the South in any literal, geographical sense. Perhaps it was this regional dislocation that first caused me to respond (mentally) that no tradition of autobiography existed in southern literature. In any case, what I now feel to be a more correct and more complex answer to the question of whether such a tradition exists in this two-headed response: No, there is not a tradition of autobiography among white writers in the South; but, yes, there is a tradition of autobiography among black writers coming from the South. Now, with this as my thesis, what I would like to do is, first, to consider what constitutes a tradition of writing; second, to look closely at two exemplary instances of southern autobiography, Richard Wright's *Black Boy* and Eudora Welty's *One Writer's Beginnings*; and finally, to speculate on possible explanations for why *Black Boy* situates itself in a tradition that stretches back one hundred years into the past and forward forty-five years to the present—a tradition that moves and changes over time but that remains nevertheless one and continuous—while *One Writer's Beginnings*, as fine and as moving as in itself it is, does not take its place in any discernible, definable tradition of southern autobiography.

What does it mean to speak of a tradition; more specifically, what does it mean to speak of a literary tradition; most specifically, what does it mean to speak of a literary tradition of autobiography? I'm going to avail myself of the time-honored crutch of a dictionary definition here, because Webster's New Collegiate seems to me awfully good on "tradition," at least for my purposes. According to that source, tradition is (1) the handing down of information, beliefs, and customs by word of mouth or by example from one generation to another without written instructions; (2) an inherited pattern of thought or action . . . ; and (3) cultural continuity in social attitudes and institutions. As we are specifically considering a *literary* tradition—that is to say, a tradition that for the most part manifests itself in written form—I think we can safely disregard the phrase "without written instructions," and we might further say that the "inherited pattern of thought or action" of the second definition is inherited precisely in the form of written texts—written accounts of one's own life, in the case of autobiography. Borrowing from Aristotle, could we not say that as Sophoclean drama is the imitation of an action, so autobiography is the symbolic, written imitation of a life; and that the handing down of information, beliefs, and customs, the cultural continuity in social attitudes and institutions that constitute tradition, are achieved exactly in and through this written imitation of a life? The individual autobiographies that corporately form a tradition are thus particular outcroppings or realizations of a whole people's beliefs and customs, and they provide for the cultural continuity in social attitudes and institutions that define this people. The give-and-take from one account of a life to another, or the call and response from text to text and from life to life ("call" and "response" are Robert Stepto's terms in *From Behind the Veil*), provide the dynamics of tradition-making. And what I will argue is that this dynamic process, this ongoing shaping of a tradition by one call and response after another, is present in and crucially important to black autobiography from the South, while, conversely, it plays little or no part in autobiography by southern white writers.

There are so many reasons for choosing Richard Wright and Eudora Welty as my exemplary cases that the choice might seem overdetermined. There is first of all the quality of the books themselves: vastly different as the two books are, they seem to me, individually and in each case, as fine as any book we have from Wright or Welty. Then there is the circumstance, which makes it natural to pair the two books, that Wright and Welty were born within a year of one another (Wright in 1908, and Welty in 1909) and lived their formative years in the same city—or relatively small town, as it was then (some 20,000 people): Jackson, Mississippi. And finally, either book could bear some such subtitle as *A Portrait of the Artist as a Young Man/Woman*, or, in the Wordsworthian manner, *The Growth of a Poet's Mind*, altering the formula only to the extent of substituting "Fiction Writer" for "Poet": thus, *The Growth of a Fiction Writer's Mind*. There are no doubt other ties or incidental similarities that one could discover between the two books and the lives they recount, but the real truth is that *Black Boy* and *One Writer's Beginnings* are about as different as two books written in this century could well be—which, of course, is another reason (and really the most important one), among all the overdetermining reasons, for bringing the two books together. It is just exactly this utter contrast that serves to make the points that I would make: that autobiography by black southern writers is altogether different from autobiography by white southern writers, and one of the crucial differences—perhaps *the* crucial difference—is the relationship of the individual talent of the autobiographer to a tradition of writing in this mode.

Moreover, to turn directly now to *Black Boy*, it seems to me altogether reasonable to argue that no American writer of this century has produced a more important book than Wright's autobiography. It is not a perfect book, but one of its greatnesses is precisely that it is *not* perfect; and indeed one of the greatnesses of autobiography itself, as a mode or as a genre, is that it is never perfect—it is never, one might say, *finished*, in all the senses of that word. Again, one thing (though not the only thing) that makes *Black Boy* so important is that it is solidly within a tradition of autobiography from the black community, the central term, one could say, or the central text in a progression that extends from Frederick Douglass's great *Narrative* of exactly one hundred years earlier (1845) down through Wright and others to *Invisible Man* and *Go Tell It on the Mountain* and *The Autobiography of Malcolm X* and *The Autobiography of Miss Jane Pittman*. That three of these latter titles are novels (*Invisible Man*, *Go Tell It on the Mountain*, and *The Autobiography of Miss Jane Pittman*) and the fourth is a generic anomaly, since it should properly be *The Autobiography of Malcolm X* by Alex Haley, in no way tells against the point that I would make about a tradition of autobiography in the black writing community. On the contrary, this fact of generic continuity into and through Afro-American novels of the past three decades, a generic continuity capable also of creating and sustaining an anomalous authorial mix in the Haley/Malcolm X book, reinforces rather than confutes the strength—one might say the inevitability—of the tradition of autobiography for black writers throughout the history of Afro-American literature. The same argument could be made equally well out of *The Narrative of the Life of Frederick Douglass, an American Slave, Written by Himself* or out of *The Autobiography of Miss Jane Pittman* or any of the other books named and many more in addition, but the central position of Wright's book, midway, as it were, between Douglass's *Narrative* and Gaines's *Autobiography of Miss Jane Pittman*, makes it particularly effective as demonstrating the continuity of the tradition that informs all three of the books and a dozen more besides for each one of these three.

John Blassingame has argued, and I believe altogether correctly, that two distinct but intertwined traditions of Afro-American writing—the one a tradition of history, the other of literature—began with the slave narrative. If we think of Douglass's *Narrative*, which I take to be fully representative of the entire body of slave narratives, and of the thematic triad of literacy, identity, and freedom worked through with such concentration in the *Narrative*; if we then think of *Black Boy* and its virtual repetition of this three-in-one theme and try simultaneously to recall the variations on the same three-part, single theme in Washington's *Up from Slavery* and Du Bois's *Souls of Black Folk* and *Dawn of Dusk*; and if once more we think of the place that literacy, identity, and freedom, as lived thematic experiences, play in *The Autobiography of Malcolm X*, I think we will have some enhanced understanding of what a literary tradition is—a greater understanding, that is to say, of what the informing presence of a tradition of autobiography has meant for Afro-American writing. Going a step further, we should observe that these autobiographies are as thematic as any novel—*Black Boy* is thematically as intense and as controlled as *Native Son*—and that the themes of Afro-American fiction and poetry are these same themes of literacy, identity, and freedom, born ultimately out of the experience of slavery, and out of narratives recounting that experience and also recounting escape from it. This is a tradition simultaneously of history and of literature, and here, as with autobiography in general, it is the dynamic, generative tension between history and literature that would have made the act and the text of autobiography so unacceptable to the New Critic of the old school but that makes that same act and text so fascinating to us today.

Throughout *Black Boy*, various individuals and groups—the principal of the school, employers, fellow employees, members of his own family, and so on—attempt to impose numerous identities on the young protagonist of this "record of childhood and youth," all of which he finds false and all of which he resists furiously. It is as if he were involved in a story that he could not understand, with a role to play that in no way fitted his own character. "The white South said that it knew 'niggers,' and I was what the white South called a 'nigger.' Well, the white South had never known me—never known what I thought, what I felt. The white South said that I had a 'place' in life. Well, I had never felt my 'place'; or, rather, my deepest instincts had always made me reject the 'place' to which the white South had assigned me." Naming him with a name that was not his, "placing" him where he did not belong, the white South was in effect telling a story of itself and of him that was utterly alien to Richard Wright, and the project of *Black Boy* might be said to be the wresting of that story from the white South and the telling of it as Wright knew it should be told—with the white South now a character, however, and with Wright as the storyteller. Nor is it only the white South that weaves tales that entangle the boy in plots that he can neither understand nor adapt himself to. There are the stories told of their lives, which involve his life too, by the young Richard's Granny and Aunt Addie, by his Uncle Tom, indeed by everyone around him; and the boy finds these stories constantly baffling—he finds them, in a term Paul Ricoeur uses in *Time and Narrative*, "unfollowable." He tries to "read" the stories of others around him and to interpret them but he regularly fails in the attempt, precisely because they are stories told by others and not by himself. This need to interpret the essentially uninterpretable, to follow the unfollowable, as Wright makes clear in *Black Boy*, finally forced him to shape his own story, emplot it as he would, and tell it in his way. "The tension I had begun to feel that morning," he says of one incomprehensible experience—a tension that required resolution in a story that could be followed—"would lift itself into the passion of my life." The genius of *Black Boy* is that the emplotting of the

book, taken as a whole, is Richard Wright's doing, and included within that
encompassing act of emplotment are always the incomprehensible, baffling,
unfollowable plots or stories created by others. *Black Boy* is thus the followable
story of a string of unfollowable stories.

Wright's determination that he *will* tell his story, and tell it in the individual way that it demands to be told, is one thing (though not the only one) that
keeps his telling from becoming merely conventional or formulaic. For all the
similarities that can be observed between *Black Boy* and other books in a
clearly discernible line of black autobiographical writing, Wright was fiercely
individualistic both in his thought and in his writing. Like Douglass before
him, Wright fought furiously against any attempt to impose an identity on him
or any attempt to tell him what or how he should write. And the difference-in-
sameness where *Black Boy* and the Afro-American autobiographic tradition are
in question is to be explained also in part by the fact that Wright was first and
last a writer — an imaginative writer, with nothing of the mechanical write-to-
a-formula about him, for whom traditional forms were a great strength precisely
because they could be bent and shaped to his specific ends: in this case, the
specific end of telling his own followable, indeed compelling, story.

The power of story is both a theme and a fact of *Black Boy*, and the overwhelming need to tell one's story is surely the motive, one way or another, of
all autobiography. In the first volume of his *Autobiographies*, called *Reveries
over Childhood and Youth*, W. B. Yeats tells of the doings of people in western
Ireland, and he goes on to say, "All the well-known families had their grotesque
or tragic or romantic legends, and I often said to myself how terrible it would
be to go away and die where nobody would know my story." That Wright's story
should be told and known is unquestionably the moving force behind *Black
Boy*; what sets it apart from the story told in Yeat's *Autobiographies*, or from
the story told in *One Writer's Beginnings*, for that matter, is that Wright's story
is, *mutatis mutandis*, so very much like the story of Frederick Douglass in the
Narrative and so very much like the story also of the protagonist of *Invisible
Man*. *Black Boy*, in other words, while being stamped throughout with
Wright's unique character as a writer, is also and at the same time at the very
heart of a tradition of autobiography that extends from the beginning of Afro-
American literature right down to the present time.

Meanwhile, across town, the same cannot be said of *One Writer's Beginnings*. Eudora Welty's book, while it is as much devoted to the making of stories
as *Black Boy*, tells of *one* writer's beginnings, *this* writer's beginnings; it is not the
generic tale of a white girl growing up in the South, as one might fairly say that
Wright's book is the generic tale of a black boy growing up in the South. I use
the word "generic" deliberately to suggest that the story that Wright tells is
generic — it is the story, oft-repeated, of a group of people — and to suggest also
that in the end that story discovers a form for telling that makes it virtually a
genre of autobiography unto itself. Whether the autobiography is largely fictional, as it is with *Invisible Man* and *The Autobiography of Miss Jane Pittman*,
or whether it is largely nonfictional, as it is with *Black Boy* and *The Narrative of*

the Life of Frederick Douglass and *The Autobiography of Malcolm X*, seems formally to make very little difference. I cannot, on the other hand, think of any other books from the South that I would put together with Eudora Welty's book and claim that, taken *ensemble*, they form a distinctive genre or a coherent tradition. *One Writer's Beginnings* is very much a book by Eudora Welty; it takes its place in the whole corpus of her work rather than taking its place, as does *Black Boy*, in a line of generically similar books by other writers.

Consider how *One Writer's Beginnings* begins:

> When I was young enough to still spend a long time buttoning my shoes in the morning, I'd listen toward the hall: Daddy upstairs was shaving in the bathroom and Mother downstairs was frying the bacon. They would begin whistling back and forth to each other up and down the stairwell. My father would whistle his phrase, my mother would try to whistle, then hum hers back. It was their duet. I drew my buttonhook in and out and listened to it—I knew it was "The Merry Widow." The difference was, their song almost floated with laughter: how different from the record, which growled from the beginning, as if the Victrola were only slowly being wound up. They kept it running between them, up and down the stairs where I was now just about ready to run clattering down and show them my shoes.

Thinking of these two books—*One Writer's Beginnings* and *Black Boy*—together, it strikes me that, dangerous as it is to dispute Tolstoy, we might have to reverse the famous dictum with which *Anna Karenina* begins: "All happy families resemble one another, but each unhappy family is unhappy in its own way." I wouldn't want to deny the distinctiveness of the Wright family's unhappiness, but I do believe we would have to say that, at least as Eudora Welty presents it, her family was happy very much in its own way. And this is what her book is about: how, out of the unique set of legacies conferred on her by her mother and father and more distant ancestors, Eudora Welty came to be the fiction writer that she is. Toward the end of her book she will say,

> It is our inward journey that leads us through time—forward or back, seldom in a straight line, most often spiraling. Each of us is moving, changing, with respect to others. As we discover, we remember; remembering, we discover; and most intensely do we experience this when our separate journeys converge. Our living experience at those meeting points is one of the charged dramatic fields of fiction.
>
> I'm prepared now to use the wonderful word *confluence*, which of itself exists as a reality and a symbol in one. It is the only kind of symbol that for me as a writer has any weight, testifying to the pattern, one of the chief patterns, of human experience.

It is the confluence in herself and in her memory of mother and father and many others that makes Welty the particular artist that she is. *One Writer's*

Beginnings is a return in memory back to times in the past before the streams had flowed together, before the confluence had formed itself, to discover the individual and familial sources of her talent and her vision. "Of course," Eudora Welty concludes,

> the greatest confluence of all is that which makes up the human memory—the individual human memory. My own is the treasure most dearly regarded by me, in my life and my work as a writer. Here, time, also, is subject to confluence. The memory is a living thing—it too is in transit. But during its moment, all that is remembered joins, and lives—the old and the young, the past and the present, the living and the dead.

Opposite this passage in my copy of *One Writer's Beginnings* I see that I have scribbled "cf. St. Augustine on memory," as, in a similar way, in some early pages of the book when Welty is describing very early sensory experience that played its part in her becoming a fiction writer, I have jotted down "cf. first pages of Joyce's *Portrait of the Artist*." By contrast, at various places in my copy of *Black Boy* I find notations like these: "cf. Douglass," "cf. *Invisible Man*," "cf. *Nobody Knows My Name*." What this suggests to me is that in reading *One Writer's Beginnings* one is not reminded particularly of other writing from the South, whereas in reading *Black Boy* one thinks constantly of other books by black writers who, whether they were actually from the South or not, draw on a tradition that in its origins was profoundly southern.

At the outset of this essay I remarked that there is a distinction to be drawn between "a tradition of autobiography" and "a tradition of autobiographical writing," and I promised to return to the question later. I want to fulfill that promise now looking first at the adjectival form of our subject. There is a great deal of "autobiographical fiction" by southern writers—Faulkner might be cited as a prime example—and I imagine it might be possible to trace a tradition of autobiographical fiction from the South. White writers from the South seem for the most part unwilling to write autobiography without veiling it or presenting it as fiction. Let me hasten to say that this is not unique to southern writers: Dickens is the classic case, and one has only to mention the names of Virginia Woolf, Marcel Proust, and James Joyce to see how widespread the practice of autobiographical fiction has been in this century. Nothing surprising here. But think by contrast of what happens so often in Afro-American writing, where what we have is not autobiographical fiction but fictional autobiography: *The Autobiography of an Ex-Colored Man, The Autobiography of Miss Jane Pittman, Invisible Man, Their Eyes Were Watching God*, and in variant ways we might include *The Color Purple* and *Go Tell It on the Mountain*—these books, these fictional autobiographies, are, in addition to all the straight autobiographies, produced in such profusion by black writers: three by Frederick Douglass, two or three by Booker T. Washington, two or three by W. E. B. Du Bois (two or three in either case depending on how you define autobiography), two by Langston Hughes, four or five (is it?) by Maya Angelou, and so on down to the flood of autobiographies that came out of the civil rights movement of the 1960s and 1970s. Autobiography, straight and fictional, has been the heart and soul of Afro-American literature from the beginning to the present time; no similar claim could be made about the literature of the white South.

Why should this be so? I want to try to sketch briefly two or three possible explanations without claiming that one of them is correct to the exclusion of others. Wole Soyinka, the Nobel Laureate from Nigeria, when asked why autobiography seemed to be so prominent in African literature, responded that he thought that it might be because the African writer, unlike the European or white American writer, lived at different times in his life in two radically different sociopolitical worlds, the traditional world of the home in which he grew up and the colonial world that he had to learn to cope with upon growing up. "When the colonial or ex-colonial writer wants to express or to really record this divide in his experience," Soyinka said, "he makes it more frankly autobiographical because he is trying to recapture something which is so totally different." Soyinka's analysis reminds me of nothing so much as this passage early in Du Bois's *Souls of Black Folk*:

> The Negro is a sort of seventh son, born with a veil, and gifted with second-sight in this American world, — a world which yields him no true self-consciousness, but only lets him see himself through the revelation of the other world. It is a peculiar sensation, this double-consciousness, this sense of always looking at one's self through the eyes of others, of measuring one's soul by the tape of a world that looks on in amused contempt and pity. One ever feels his twoness, — an American, a Negro; two souls, two thoughts, two unreconciled strivings; two warring ideals in one dark body.

I think it may well be just exactly this "twoness," this "double-consciousness," that accounts, at least in part, for the frequency with which Afro-American writers have had recourse to autobiography. What is it to be both an American and a Negro, to be possessed of two souls, two thoughts, two unreconciled strivings? "What's it like? Let me tell you. Let me tell you my story," has been the response of almost innumerable people in that state of double-consciousness and twoness. "It's a complex fate being an American," Henry James declared; how much more complex to be, in Du Bois's phrase, "an American, a Negro" — to say nothing of the horrendous complexity of being, in the violent paradox of Douglass's title, "an American slave." I should remark that the tradition of autobiography that I have been at some pains to trace here is quite consciously a dual tradition: Douglass, Washington, Du Bois, Wright, Ellison, Malcolm X, Ernest Gaines, besides writing autobiography within a black tradition, write also within a general American tradition of autobiography descending from the Declaration of Independence — they write within it by way of challenging the tradition.

Another reason the tradition of autobiography has been such a coherent one among black writers, I believe, is that it has been most often an act of testifying, of bearing witness. Testifying in this sense is something that is not done individually but is rather the revelation of a whole group experience; or perhaps we should say that in the individual experience is to be read the entire group experience. Douglass testified individually, communally, historically, and with great rhetorical power to what slavery was; Wright testified, not on behalf of himself alone but on behalf of "black boy" or "black boys," to what it was like living the ethics of Jim Crow. This sort of testifying is an attempt to fix a historical reality, and just as the reality was remarkably consistent, so the testimonial response from decade to decade and generation to generation displays much the same consistency.

I want to introduce here an idea that is rather off to the side of my subject but that I find fascinating to contemplate all the same. I have seen it suggested that "the captivity narrative [is] the prototype for American autobiography by women and minorities." Now, I do not mean to say that this is the way in which Eudora Welty and Richard Wright, or white autobiography and black autobiography from the South, can be brought together, for in the sense intended I don't think that Eudora Welty writes in *One Writer's Beginnings* specifically as a woman. She writes instead as a *writer*. Hence this formulation does not really include Eudora Welty; but I wonder if it might not be that women who wrote consciously and intentionally as women, black writers who wrote consciously and intentionally as a minority (and very few do not), would be inclined to adopt a kind of paradigmatic form that would make their individual autobiographies sound very much alike, thus establishing a generic tale and a tradition of autobiography. This is only speculation, however, and it is as such that I offer it.

I want to conclude these speculative and fugitive thoughts by returning to the question of the southernness—or otherwise—of southern autobiography. Robert Penn Warren, whose credentials as a southern writer, I take it, are pretty well impeccable, has said, in some meditations on the nature of autobiography, that "poetry is a kind of unconscious autobiography," and, therefore, Warren implies, since he has produced a good deal of poetry, he has no reason to write an autobiography. "For what is a poem," he asks, "but a hazardous attempt at self-understanding? It is the deepest part of autobiography." Though Warren himself may be southern, however, there is nothing particularly southern about this claim, and it does nothing to establish a tradition of specifically southern autobiography. On the other hand, the pattern of bondage, flight, freedom that David Dudley finds in virtually all black autobiography bears witness to something specifically southern in the history of our nation, and, for better or worse, it is the South's to claim as its bittersweet own. And if one were to hazard a projection into the future, the logic of the situation seems to me to suggest that the historical, cultural, and literary dynamics that conspired with the talents of Richard Wright and Eudora Welty to produce, respectively, *Black Boy* and *One Writer's Beginnings* will continue to make black autobiographies appear to be momentary instances and manifestations of a long, coherent tradition, while autobiographies by white writers from the South will appear here and there, from time to time, separate from one another and not part of anything that one could call a tradition of southern autobiography.

11

DAVE SMITH

Speculations on a
Southern Snipe

In the stretched heat of summer nights we propped open doors and windows with sticks to catch the least breeze. We moved nearly breathless in that humidity so like a blanket of water, the delicate promising fullness of azaleas and daffodils and dogwood already gone, grass becoming brittled by ceaseless sun, the greenest lacy trees drooped, thick. School was forgotten. We played in the safe communal dark. We darted, squibbed like the bats just overhead, our cries known to the adults lingering to speak low in yellow light over supper tables. A few—the luckier ones, we thought—moved before a ghostly Truetone television. In this hour came older kids, maybe smoking a smuggled cigarette, who asked suddenly, "Did you see it?"

At first, puzzled, we wouldn't answer. Then we said, yes, we saw it. Next we permitted ourselves to be frightened by *it*. Even the small shadows of lilac and snowball bush contained it. It went with us into our night's sleep, though we drifted from it upon waking into the bright day.

What was *it*? We took the word of our elders for its shape, effect, cause, or nature. We assented. We believed in it because we wanted the truth firm, theirs and ours. In fact we experienced the great absence of *it*—which they said was the proof of it.

This was not exactly a snipe. *It* hunted us as much as we hunted it. When I think of what we have written about southern poetry I remember my critical elders and an *it* that is as present as undefinable. Putting aside the question of whether any writer wants *southern* stitched on his jacket, the question arises: What is southern writing that they have been telling about so long?

Mr. Poe, perhaps the first southern poet, little troubled himself about that adjective. The syllabus for the now-ubiquitous course in southern literature, in the South anyway, locates the quarry's kin in unanguished document makers, nature bards, and boostering apologists. They were, essentially, Euro-Americans. The War Between the States drew more than one line in the dirt with its incipient nationalism. To be "southern" was a geographical description which metamorphosed into being *southern*, a mythical and cultural tag which meant more than anyone might contain in a few words. Southern writing, by definition, became the *it* produced by those who were *there*. In the word if not in the fact.

In William Gilmore Simms and Henry Timrod before the Civil War, in Sidney Lanier afterward (more so among the fictioneers), the *South* was a "community." Or it was an image of a community, a sort of *polis*, which they bequeathed us: a nice place for slaves to live in, run by gentlemen schooled in Greek who could quote Homer, ride bareback races, bring in fine crops human and otherwise, but who knew evil in the world, and who apprehended the world's place in God's program. Its women, like Mormons, were epitomes of grace, silence, suffering, courage, and fertility. They produced. In *A Shaping Joy* the eminent Cleanth Brooks speaks of this definitive community and its "sense of religious wholeness, . . . concreteness of human relationships, . . . tragic dimension of life." What was *southern*, he and many others indicated, was the continuous and coherent system of values evident in that homogenous society in that rural place.

The war forced the industrial half of the nineteenth century to do battle with the agrarian half. This happened in that "community," which was and is an image warped to the extent it conceals its "others." These are the slaves, the yeomen whites whom Bell Irvin Wiley's *Plain People of the Confederacy* calls "shiftless, ignorant, undernourished, and depraved." That community, the historical evidence shows, was often rapacious, self-tormenting, and brutal. Partisan criticism of the Southern Renascence is prone to praise that "community" of agrarian self-reliance by contrasting it to contemporary consumerism, following the Tate/Brooks juxtaposition of what is concrete and what abstract. But Louis D. Rubin Jr. is helpfully candid:

> The society of the Old South was given to a devotion to leisure, which some have called laziness or hedonism, and others have called freedom from materialism. The Old South placed a less than Calvinistic importance upon the Work Ethic. The whites tended to feel that too much work was degrading, while the blacks were opposed to it because the fruits of their labor generally went to someone else. Southern society tended to cultivate the amenities. It placed considerable emphasis on manners, believed in noblesse oblige, cultivated the paternalistic concept of role. . . . the Old South was precapitalistic and even feudal, and its symbols of aristocratic distinction were land and slaves, not money. (*The Writer in the South*)

If being southern meant much to admire, it seems also to have offered a sort of posturing Camelot founded on dandyism, laziness, class superiority, condescension, and rank cruelty—all possible only when one has resources sufficient to translate into applicable power over another man. Rubin says of the southerner, "He belonged." Some did. The Fugitive poets John Crowe Ransom, Allen Tate, and Robert Penn Warren imagined themselves in flight from magnolia-and-moonlight poetry, which perpetuated a pre-modern and false image of the South. They created what we now define as *southern* poetry by that break, which simply engineered another image of the South. They also engendered our tribes of temple chroniclers, enthusiasts and critics such as the Society for the Study of Southern Literature. The tale of southern poetry is the flight from a dead-hand past of lies to modern art; but it is also a backward stare for the truth, a truth as often moribund as it is monologic and pastoral.

Ransom and Tate were modernists with the gloves on. Warren, too, early on. But he became a bare-knuckled contemporary with *Promises* in 1957, the year of Sputnik and the onset of civil rights change. In seeking to escape provinciality, these poets had to leave home in heart and in fact. They also had to discover that all significant art is rooted in the regional. In what does their *southernness* manifest itself? To answer that is to tell about the South, as we know, endlessly. Practically speaking, their poet is born in one of the eleven southern states and takes home (in all its dimensions of meaning) and history as primary subjects, is male, classically educated, demonstrates in and out of the poem a village gentility, a love of nature, and a hunger for spiritual stability in a world of phenomenal flux.

Even that limited silhouette excludes a further distinctive feature. The southern poet *felt* intensely connected to what Robert Penn Warren once called the only other nation on U.S. soil, the long-erased Confederate States of America. And his reader *felt* it as well. However falsely or accurately rendered, the South, for southern writers coming to maturity in the generation of the Fugitives, was a real place with real human survivors and real experience. In 1990, only five years ago, my *Richmond Times-Dispatch* carried the following: "Miss Josephine C. Sherrard, one of only five area 'real daughters' of the Confederacy, died yesterday at her home in Richmond. She was 94 . . . and the daughter of Joseph Lyle Sherrard, a second lieutenant for the Liberty Hall Volunteers in the Civil War." Born in 1895, Miss Sherrard would not have known drum rolls on her family's land, the rifle fire that felled forests; she would have held no slaves. But her parents knew an occupied war zone merely a generation away from colonial life in the New World. She straddled worlds through kin and friends, as did Robert Penn Warren, who often wrote of his Confederate cavalryman grandfather. This *feeling* for the South, for home, is a dual awareness of change and stasis. Home keeps off chaos — just as it embodies our values, self-image, and definitional base.

For those poets who are not products of the last gasp of old South passion, home is no less definitive and no less complex, but it is a different subject. Charles Wright, of Tennessee and Virginia, says bluntly, "Everybody's a product of Hollywood, every one of us." When the southern poet goes looking for truth, he looks at home, looks for home, looks into home and, frequently now, it looks like a Hollywood set, all surface, making definition impossible.

If we cannot define *southern* in any useful and agreeable way, then there should be a resounding *no!* heard when James H. Justus asks in *The History of*

Southern Literature, "Is there such a thing as a distinctly [contemporary] Southern poetry?" The publication of three major anthologies in the last four-teen years; the continual and scrutinizing testimony of special issues of such journals as the *Southern Review, Georgia Review,* and *Sewanee Review;* the con-ferences, books, courses, and poems; and the testimony of the poets say *yes* in thunder. Charles Wright, having lived much of his adult life in California and having never been critically tagged, says, "I've always considered myself a southern writer—always will, whatever that means." Justus provides us with our poet's personality sketch:

> . . . a recurrence of rural subjects; a residual fondness for conservative forms and techniques; an easy habit of incorporating emotional diction and syntax into a poetic discourse that is otherwise received Standard; a penchant for order and control even in experimental efforts; a preference for the visually concrete and aurally sensuous image over abstract medi-tation; the importance of memory in altering, deepening, and extending compulsive scenic recall; and, unlike more aggressive postmodernists of their generation, a lingering reliance upon pattern, design, and wholeness despite a resigned recognition that both life and art are resolutely frag-mented, disjunctive, and discontinuous.

Despite fitting perfectly Robert Frost, Richard Wilbur, or Howard Nemerov, even Joseph Brodsky or Derek Walcott, this catalog generates an identity emphasizing poetic practice rather than subject matter. To that extent the poet is not southern as the Fugitives were, or even, arguably, as current fic-tioneers Reynolds Price, Lee Smith, Josephine Humphreys, or Richard Bausch are. Yet the shape does fit the poets Justus chooses to observe: Donald Justice, Dabney Stuart, George Garrett, Miller Williams, Fred Chappell, and others, though in the way a baggy, used suit from Goodwill fits.

The southern poet, that slippery *it,* seems surely defined by biographical origin, subject matter, attitude, community of values, and formal poetics. But poet James Applewhite not long ago made his definition the "art of musical, emotional, rhetorical intensity (from Poe to Faulkner to James Dickey) that is unable to state its premises and propositions as clearly as writing of other regions." I confess this sounds vague to me. He appears to agree with Justus, defining according to manner, not matter, a quality he calls "southern alle-giance" (hinting choice, not inevitability). Applewhite tells us he grew up in a homogeneous rural environment that had "a collective emotional miasma which left no space for individual speech." If I understand him, he contends that the southern poet emerges from a vortex of powerful and unlocated emo-tions which reappear upon stimulation and define a poetic discourse that is dominantly "tone, landscape, atmosphere." The southern poet, then, he implies, tends to confusion, psychic effusion, and sentimentality. Applewhite says the "quintessential southern poet" can't speak clearly: "Whether through climate, history, or mythology, we southerners are heir to a tradition that assigns rich feeling and expressiveness to our region, clear rationality somewhere else."

For Applewhite southernness is a style, a rhetoric that is reinforced by our "oral tradition of language." This view identifies a tribal, fabular, anachronistic culture surviving to tell its stories in an urban age. We are, he suggests in remarks about southern climate, psychogeological products of a murk not much removed from Poe's slime and Mitchell's wisteria. We are, Applewhite says, spirits possessed of "formative music" but in need of a "new capability for plain statement." What Applewhite says of southern colleges might well be his definition, and a Romantic one, of the poet: "They offer whatever hope there is of seeing, still, past the kudzu, used-car lots, fundamentalist congregations, and slumber of Sunday-noon dinners, that rare smoke of the soul's fire rising beyond the pines." Applewhite's contemporary southern poet is a visionary in style, a truth-seeker whose desired ends are both elegiac and apocalyptic. It sounds more like Robert Bly than James Dickey, yet he assumes continuity at home.

Biographical definition assumes continuity, or commonality. What is common to poets born in Virginia, Georgia, Texas? Less, I suspect, rather than more. What is common to poets born in 1905, 1945, 1965? On April 23, 1985, the Academy of American Poets held a "Southern Poetry Symposium," where Russell Banks, native New Hampshireman and author of *Continental Drift*, perhaps the most "southern" of recent novels, asked five birth-validated southern poets, "Where is the South and what are we talking about when we say southern poetry?" The answers were understandably anecdotal, wandering, evasive, and partial. David Bottoms, of Atlanta, said,

> The south is the only area of the country that held slaves and lost a war. . . . I think land is tied to all the other things. . . . There was a time in the South when a family belonged to a piece of the land, rather than the land to a family, simply because the economy was such that you couldn't move. . . . There's a strong sense of personal identity formed from a particular land that a family is raised on, which is tied to the sense of community, which is tied to the sense of church. And that's all going by the way now.

Charles Wright promptly answered Bottoms, saying "Sure. It's all gone, isn't it." William Harmon, Cleopatra Mathis, and Robert Morgan agreed. *It* was gone, vanished, poof. But Bottoms seemed to notice *some* of it was still around—because *they* were there. He replied, "It's not gone completely." The surfaces (subjects) of southern poetry appear to be changing much more rapidly than the poetry's attitude, style, or ability to receive change. This may mean the old South is simply buried, though not dead, under the visible habits of the new South—the ubiquitous strip malls with their chain stores and the equally commonplace imitations of southern-ness glossily spread in the pages of *Southern Living*—thus new matter, old manner. But southern poetry, if it exists, cannot be a function of matter, for that would be only sociological, not aesthetic definition. The poetry exists in the tone, the attitude, the structuring vision of the language, precisely where traditional definition of "the South" has focused its attention.

The single common characteristic of the poetry written by southerners is consistently an attitude of obligation, of piety, of something like a sacred respect. Not precisely a historical consciousness, it begins there. One grows up deeply aware of a past with daily consequences, though less aware of cause-effect relationships. We can, and most poets do, physically leave the geographical South, but we cannot abandon the historical, meaning-invested scenes in our memories. We are always *there*, in presence of and influenced by a matrix of experiences overlaid, entangled, ingrown. We know we exist in connection to the lives and deaths of others in that place, yet we do not know, increasingly as generations remove from the source, exactly how we relate to it, what the core is, or what it means to us. We have to dramatize that core, to drive it to "articulate statement," as James Applewhite says, though it may seem all we are up to is rapturous gurgle. I am speaking, of course, of *home*. To let go of home, however ugly or fine, means letting go of our histories, our sacred places. Home answers meaninglessness and the ultimate disappearance of our kind. We do not expect to find salvation in a Kmart or a mall or a downtown freeway, although Flannery O'Connor instructs us to look even there. Perhaps especially there.

Thus Robert Morgan says, "Couldn't you say that people are now writing about the South so much because they've lost it?" The salient characteristics of this loss show how interwoven a blanket it is: the effects of the Civil War (history), the face of slavery (society), the economy (farm/permanence), the community (family), the biblical witness (religion). None of these lenses reveals much without the overlay of the others, and the revealed "thing" remains impressionistic, known, felt. The word for it in all of our mouths is change. For any southern writer, poets too, will make, as Reynolds Price says, "private relation to a public thing, a place larger than France, inhabited by millions of people united by an elaborate dialect formed in syntax and rhythm (like the people themselves) by the weight of land, climate, race, religion, history (A *Common Room: Essays 1954–1987*).

If southern poetry exists (haven't we known *it*?), what is it to be? Are we going to describe an old private relation to a new public thing? William Harmon may be only slightly myopic: "I think the South exists more in writing than anywhere else. I mean you know this *is* the South, the southern writers. When you go there and what you see is shopping malls, and expressways and McDonalds, it looks just exactly like anywhere else." Unlike Applewhite, Harmon sees only the Hollywood set. But perhaps, as Bottoms says, "It's not gone completely." Any black person might argue much that was southern remains, among them poets such as Yusef Komunyakaa, Nikki Giovanni, Etheridge Knight, Sonia Sanchez, Al Young, and slyly, Gerald Barrax in "Body Food":

> *If then it is in the blood of some of us*
> *to lust after the ears the tails the snouts*
> *the feet the maws & even the*
> *chitlins of the filthy beast*

forgive us: with these
& the greens cornbread & molasses
that transubstantiated into the bones
brain & flesh of the black household gods
who brought us through the evil
rooted in this land.
*   we honor them*
in the heritage of their strength.

Harmon's prediction that the landscape in the poetry of the new South will be kitsch and, essentially, anonymous tells us only that what you see is what you get. But what you see will be God-haunted, history-haunted, and as volcanic to the poets as ever.

One distinction has already begun to emerge. Poets are de facto outsiders as truth-carriers. The southern poet will have to confront what Wendell Berry once called "the hidden wound," which is the omnipresent engagement of black life and white life. Daily existence in almost all large southern cities is monitored by a black city council, black department heads, black services, with a black-envisioned future. This is dominantly true of the South, which is now the most integrated part of our nation in a way untrue of the rest of our country. Poets white and black must write openly of racial heritage.

A similar, if less noisy, artistry is evident among the women of the South. Urged forward by social changes in recent decades, poets such as Betty Adcock, Carol Cox, Kate Daniels, Lola Haskins, Elizabeth Morgan, Martha McFerren, Dara Wier, Margaret Gibson, and Ellen Bryant Voigt have published already a body of work as visibly a part of southern culture as it is astringent, feminist, and formally challenging. No American poet writes more pointedly than Ellen Bryant Voigt in *The Lotus Flowers*:

"Try to get home," is what she says,
the closed vowel encompassing
our set of inland islands: ragged plug
of the Southern map, the house and yard
centered in the green voluptuous fields,
and all of my childhood, pocked reef
floating within me, relic of past eruption
now cooled, now temperate, populous, isolate,
from which I venture further and further
into this life, like a swimmer
still in training, aiming
for the mainland in the distance.

Future southern poetry will reflect the communal psyche and memory, disintegration characterized by nostalgic religiosity, a slave society still being ingested by a white society itself yet experiencing class division, a rural landscape increasingly bulldozed, crowded, urban and, consequently, more volatile

with change and resistance. We may see an exciting hybrid poetry from ethni-
cally layered cities like Miami, where almost literally everything is up for grabs,
even language. The rhetoric and circumlocution of our native speech will
inevitably dominate our poetic style, but that style will modulate toward American plainness unless influenced by Cuban Spanish and Haitian French.
Whatever its shape, the southern poem, like the people, will seek stability from
fearful change. The church, the family, the town, even the neighbor no longer
automatically answer. The poem must confront our various disenfranchise-
ments—poverty, drugs, violence, insularity, racism, meaningless work—and
must resist both smug chattiness and the escapism of false heroizing. If a chival-
ric community existed, our poet will tell us, *It's gone.* Or our language can't
make it true any longer.

Perhaps the only real way to feel that truth is to elect a change in perspective, to flee the South temporarily. Parallels between southern poets and
poets of contemporary Ireland and Scotland are instructive. Seamus Heaney's
subject is dominantly language, a medium of national identity, as it was for
James Joyce, whose Stephen Dedalus remarks of the Englishman: "How different are the words 'home,' 'Christ,' 'ale,' 'master,' on his lips and on mine."
John Montague, Paul Muldoon, Eavan Boland, and Heaney share with Joyce
the task of "forging the consciousness of a race" (each fleeing Ireland to do it).
The seismic grinding between past and present, family, church, tradition, manners, economy, language, home—these conventionally define the Irish poet.
But they appear as well in what Douglas Dunn, a Scott, says of St. Kilda Island
in the Inner Hebrides:

> *On St Kilda you will surely hear Gaelic*
> *Spoken softly like a poetry of ghosts*
> *By those who never were contorted by*
> *Hierarchies of cuisine and literacy.*
>
> . . . .
>
> *Here I whittle time like a dry stick,*
> *From sunrise to sunset, among the groans*
> *And sighings of a tongue I cannot speak,*
> *Outside a parliament, looking at them,*
> *As they, too, must always look at me*
> *Looking through my apparatus at them*
> *Looking. Benevolent, or malign? But who*
> *At this last stage, could tell, or think it worth it?*
> *For I was there, and am, and I forget.* ("St. Kilda's Parliament")

The contemporary southern poet lives neither with the economic nor the
religious threat common to Dunn or Heaney. Yet our poet shares their sense
of home's sacrality and violation. He knows himself language-possessed, if not
strangled in his garden. He is acutely aware of representing the Sahara of the
Bozart, which he will flee, but to whom will he (worse, *she*) turn for a vital
model? Who is our Joyce? Our Yeats? Like Dunn, we have a parliament of dis-

parate voices in the post-fugitive poets Donald Justice, James Dickey, Fred Chappell, A. R. Ammons, and Miller Williams, all distinguished but none who looms so grand as the later Robert Penn Warren. And like Warren, none of them appear to be producing the sort of work we might expect to change southern poetry. Yet they are carriers of and passers of attitudes and subjects that define southernness.

If it is no longer superfluous to say that there is, indeed, a distinctive southern poetry, it remains to say that our poetry is part of the national expression of the heart's turmoil. How can this be otherwise in a nation that television has turned into a series of linked villages? In a national experience which government has so standardized that the word of choice now is "generic"? Conventional wisdom indicates that literary art arises in the aftermath of, if not within the process of, the most significant social changes. Nowhere outside the borders of the historical southern states will there be found continuous and deep changes that exceed those within the South — just as there is no region of our country more inherently given to maintaining and celebrating the society of our past. Claims for artistic eminence are invidious and foolish and make all writers cringe. Nevertheless, Robert Penn Warren, James Dickey, A. R. Ammons, and Donald Justice have for two decades been among the major voices of American poetry. Yusef Komunyakaa, a black poet from Bogalusa, Louisiana, has recently joined this group of winners of the Pulitzer Prize in poetry. His poetry is in every respect as inherently southern as theirs and will make possible the necessary recognition of how inherently southern art is simultaneously black and white.

We have reason to imagine this heritage will be renewed and extended by southern poets to come, though that poetry must be anything but parochial. Factors wholly outside the poet's choice may prove determinant. In the late 1960s and through the 1970s congressional and state support for arts and artists successively expanded until it ranged from fellowship support for individual writers to support for independent small press book publication and distribution to enrichment programs in public schools. All such support activities had the effect of encouraging readership, writing, and an intersection of literary art with a public community on a scale never previously achieved. Unfortunately, the 1980s and 1990s have seen a parallel diminution of funding, activity, and political interest. The likely prospect is a reduction in the enthusiasm for serious poetry, if not a reduced quantity and quality. This is a national problem, not a regional one, and is exacerbated by rapidly diminishing interest in books of poetry at all publishing houses. To date, southern university presses continue to publish poetry, none of it chosen as specifically southern, while regional presses such as Algonquin of Chapel Hill and Peachtree of Atlanta have published no poetry at all.

If the situation of the poet seems grim, one can't help being reminded of President Eisenhower's remark that things are more like they are today than they ever were. The American southern poet will continue so long as there is a distinctive South for him to write out of, so long as change challenges that, so long as readers want to know who they have been and are. Such a poetry requires an informed readership, a tutelary criticism, and, I think, places certain obligations on the poets themselves.

There is no foreclosure of the necessary elements of surprise and delight in our poets by suggesting they will be compelled, as James Applewhite asserts, to mitigate the high lovely moaning of bluegrass and gospel in their blood, to make articulate and culturally provocative statements. They must resist corn and dialect and cute phrase, avoid the most mystic opacities of James Dickey and the more blatantly Christian pitchings of Wendell Berry, both as teasing and beautiful and evanescent as ground mist. To matter southern poetry must, as Warren suggests, pick off the scab of alibi. It must engage the centrality of black experience as it has not done. It will have to translate its fear of instability along with its effort to cling to whatever rocky-top and hymn-room history provides for stability—and translate it not to the converted but to those outside the drawl line.

This poetry will be the metaphor of regional and universal experience. It will be work by poets mentioned previously, by some yet unpublished, and by poets whose books and awards have won them substantial public recognition. Most of the younger men, women, and blacks cited in this essay were utterly ignored by 1985's *History of Southern Literature*, a woeful commentary on our criticism. Among those poets, Henry Taylor won the 1985 Pulitzer Prize in poetry for his collection *The Flying Change*. Taylor, a Virginian, writes with the civility, polish, and respect for traditional poetics of Tate and Ransom, yet his subject matter is patently contemporary whether it be homage to old ways, chainsawing his land, or college concerts, as in "Kingston Trio, 1982":

> *Nostalgia freaks unite. Our darkest fears*
> *trot out on stage: Shane's gray, his voice is gone,*
> *but substitutes for Guard and Reynolds clone*
> *the sound that goes back almost thirty years.*
> *Who are these guys? The grizzled, stoned crowd cheers*
> *The Grand Reunion: Guard and Reynolds join*
> *cracked voices to the rest, and decades run*
> *through fingers fluffing riffs that no one hears.*
>
> *This won't bring back a day in '61*
> *when crowds outside a gymn in Charlottesville*
> *crushed to a door that none of us could see*
> *sucking us through to hear how songs, until*
> *they crack, can breed sweet hope that anyone*
> *this time tomorrow reckons where he'll be.*

Taylor's witty echoes of Dickey's firebomber and the endless Confederate reenactments juxtaposed against the marijuana-tuned crowd of college veterans is a medallion of the contemporary South from the poet's eye. Inside the still younger Mississippian T. R. Hummer's often drummingly chorded narratives there is the sober voice that turns its astonishment and recognition upon us, as this fragment from "The Real" shows:

The winter John Kennedy died
some of my classmates cheered.
I didn't, but I didn't know
If it was right to grieve.

That's a hard thing to admit.
But I was confused. Those were confusing times.
The South had spent a century

Perfecting the purity of hate.
It was them or us, we said.
We hated the North, communists, Russians,
Catholics, Negroes, liberals and atheists.

Everywhere. How could I know what to love?
Everywhere I turned I found a world
I was afraid to touch,

Unreal. If there was truth
It was somewhere else.
I knew it. Everybody knew it.
But no matter. That was our idea of heaven.

We were dying blind, turning into permanent shadows
Caught in some meaningless moment
Of what we prayed was not

The only life: burned childlike
Out of ourselves at any given instant
Of grace: touched by the fire, etched white
Against a pure black wall.

Claudia Emerson Andrews, Judith Ortiz Cofer, Forrest Gander, Andrew Hudgins, Rodney Jones, Wyatt Prunty, Bin Ramke, James Seay, Ron Smith, and C. D. Wright are only a handful among numerous poets whose work might have been cited here with equal validity.

Somehow it is not entirely surprising that the most interesting and powerfully evocative southern voice, like the others ignored by southern critics, is Charles Wright. Perhaps because he has spent the parts of his life in Italy and in California, or because his is often the interior, meditational, imagist poetics of European practice, or because in many ways his poetry is the least congruent with our definitions he is not ordinarily thought of as one who writes southern poetry, our spooky *it*. Yet no one more wholly enfranchises place, race, and gender than Wright does. He makes himself and his reader citizens of Dante's town, and Dickinson's, and even Faulkner's.

It's linkage I'm talking about,
              and harmonies and structures
And all the various things that lock our wrists to the past.
Something infinite behind everything appears,
                        and then disappears.
It's all a matter of how
              you narrow the surfaces.
It's a matter of how you fit in the sky.

("The Other Side of the River")

Wright, Barrax, Voigt, Hummer, Komunyakaa, Taylor—these poets claim our attention by the quality of their art, not their birth certificates. They belong to the South. They say it. Their work says it. But they are individual men and women who write individual poems. Art read any other way becomes statistical and abstract. We all know what that bump in the night is. Don't we?

12

MICHAEL SARTISKY

Robert Olen Butler:
A Pulitzer Profile

Robert Olen Butler was awarded the 1993 Pulitzer Prize for Fiction for his volume of short stories A Good Scent from a Strange Mountain. *Born in 1945 in Granite City, Illinois, Mr. Butler served in Vietnam as a U.S. Army counterintelligence translator. That service and his subsequent residency in Louisiana where he serves on the faculty of McNeese State University at Lake Charles were the basis of stories about Vietnamese living in America. Prior to* A Good Scent from a Strange Mountain, *Mr. Butler published six novels that, while well-reviewed, were never commercially successful, though they have since been reissued. These include* The Alleys of Eden, Sun Dogs, Countrymen of Bones, On Distant Ground, Wabash, *and* The Deuce. *His most recent novel is* They Whisper. *This interview was conducted in a single two-hour session in New Orleans in the spring of 1994.*

MS: Robert, I gather that winning the Pulitzer Prize has changed your life. Can you talk a little bit about how?

RB: Yes, it has changed it in some obvious sort of surface ways and some rather deep and profound ways as well. On the surface, certainly my life has gotten extraordinarily busy. At first, after the prize was announced—I'm cursed with call waiting—about two hundred phone calls daisy-chained their way through my life in that first eight or ten days. The accumulation of phone messages and mail has been oppressive since the middle of April.

The deeper change, of course, is that for over a decade, I wrote six very good books in considerable obscurity. My last novel, *The Deuce*, published by Simon and Schuster, got a better-than-half-page rave review from Scott Spencer in the Sunday *New York Times Book Review* and then went on to get about eight more reviews: which is almost like not getting reviewed at all. I sold a little over a thousand copies.

This was my sixth novel. I always had an ardent hard-core following in important critical centers and also amongst readers, but it has been a small hard core. I've not been very widely reviewed, but I've been reviewed very well in certain places, the *New York Times* for instance. I have not sold very many books, and so as a result I learned long ago that to avoid madness all I could do was to go to my computer every day and do my work and not think about the prizes and not think about the reviewers and not think about how many readers there were.

So the change in my life now has been quite a shocking sort of thing to me. On the one hand, I have learned just not to think about it or expect it. On the other hand, it seems like the most natural thing in the world on some deeper level, but there is a strange dichotomy in that reaction. The important change is that people are now listening; that's very clear. I had a long-standing commitment to give a reading at Baylor University which was set for about ten days after I won the Pulitzer. They had scheduled me with elaborate explanations about what they always do with visiting writers. They had scheduled me for an afternoon reading as opposed to an evening reading, because, they explained, it was very difficult to get people in Waco to come out at night. They put me in a modest English department seminar room expecting forty people maybe, which would be a pretty good turnout for a literary writer for that kind of event. Well, as soon as I won the Pulitzer, they called me up and said, "We're changing to this big auditorium and we're going to have the reading at 7 P.M." I thought, "Oh no!" I had visions of forty people or less scattered out through the auditorium, because it would be nighttime in Waco. But the auditorium that evening was packed with 350 people who hung on every word. The campus bookstore sold a hundred copies of the book in ten minutes, and that is the difference in microcosm: people listening.

MS: Let me ask you this, then: What is the nature of the inquiries you are receiving at this time? Do they really want to know about Robert Olen Butler, or are we in Andy Warhol–land? Is it the sheer notoriety that is attracting the inquiries?

RB: The inquiries are an extraordinarily mixed variety. Everything from an offer of a speaking engagement at Harvard University this fall to a letter I just received from a twenty-year-old woman who is half Vietnamese, a sophomore at an Ivy League school, thanking me for writing this book, which she says is the book she has waited for all her life, to my best friend in high school, who I had not seen or heard from in thirty years, to somebody who is striving in great confusion and hopelessness to be a writer who sends me a manuscript and asks me to tell him what is wrong with it, to a guy who runs a laminating business and wants to know if I would like to buy a laminated copy of the Associated Press article on my winning the Pulitzer.

That is just a little sense of the variety. All of a sudden, the world that I have been observing has suddenly turned its head and is looking back at me. The writer is always fascinated with the variety of human experiences; just walk the streets of the town, walk through the French Quarter—that is what I love about New Orleans so much—the extraordinary cultural and personal variety of the people that you pass. They are all looking at me now.

MS: After all these years of looking at the world, the world is looking back now.

RB: That's right. That's right.

MS: Of course, you can take some comfort in the fact that Herman Melville sold less than five hundred copies of *Moby Dick* in his lifetime.

RB: And got terrible reviews too, that book.

MS: In this country. Actually, the English were aware of him, and English visitors came over looking for the great American writer that no Americans had ever heard of for many years. Another example was Jack London. In his auto-biographical novel, Martin Eden agonizes over the irony of a writer who has been working for years and years sending stories out and even getting stories published to an absolute overwhelming silence of response who upon suddenly being discovered finds himself in the limelight. He agonizes over what has wrinkled in the universe that would suddenly change, and the question "Why am I at this moment a better writer than I was the day before when no one knew my name?" I am interested in the question of being a writer in America or a writer in Louisiana. At this very extraordinary moment, as you say, you've written six books that you obviously feel have merit, that always did have merit.

RB: Yes, always did.

MS: Yet at this moment they remain unavailable, though your publisher is about to rerelease them.

RB: Right.

MS: Because naturally now people know who you are and you've received the imprimatur of quality. People are going to rush back and try to secure those as well. It must be difficult for what must have been a very private life up to now to retain a measure of balance and perspective, to maintain the quality of mind that has been the norm for you and has allowed you to produce your work.

RB: Well, I think that having waited this long has pretty much prepared me for that. For many years I wrote under very difficult circumstances. I was in a very difficult marriage trying to keep a son whole within it, of whom eventually I got complete custody. At the same time I was working an eight- to ten-hour job as the editor in chief of a business newspaper in Manhattan, and so, as a result, every word of my first four published novels was written on legal pads by hand on a masonite lap board on the Long Island Railroad as I commuted from Sea Cliff, Long Island, to Manhattan and back again.

MS: What were those books?

RB: *The Alleys of Eden, Sun Dogs, Countrymen of Bones,* and *On Distant Ground.* In fact, I wrote half of *Wabash* on my lap as well, but by then I had gotten my Ph.D. from the University of Knopf and so was able to get my tenure-track teaching job, which happened to be at McNeese State University. I couldn't have been smarter than to come down here, but it was not my decision; ultimately it was the job that was available.

It was probably even literally providential, because the man I replaced left the position three weeks after I called McNeese pimping myself upon them as I did with some number of colleges. I talked to John Wood, my colleague and friend now at McNeese. We hit it off wonderfully on the phone, but he had nothing for me because they had one fiction writer spot and it was filled. Three weeks later that writer came in to him and said that he was quitting because he was going into the priesthood; he had received the call.

By the time I got here my own work habits were so deeply ingrained in me that I think I've been able to resist and will be able to resist those traditional temptations and distractions that the big prizes often carry with them. I lost that first ten days with those two hundred phone calls, but on the eleventh day I went back to work and finished up some important rewriting that I was doing on the final touch-ups of my new novel, which will be out in January. So I'm confident that I will be able to take this extraordinary enhancement of tension that has come my way in stride. I will always have that two hours somewhere in the day. I've got my laptop computer now and am fully capable of working anywhere.

MS: Let's take a step back a little bit, if you don't mind, and fill in some of the details about who Robert Olen Butler is, about where you were born, about where you grew up, how you came to be who you are today.

RB: I was born in 1945 in Granite City, Illinois, which is a steel mill town of about 35,000 people on the Mississippi River bottoms, just across the river from St. Louis. St. Louis is a very interesting place because everybody north of St. Louis thinks it is a southern city and everybody south of St. Louis thinks it is a northern city. Granite City is particularly interesting because it is a place full of both northerners and southerners who are on the make financially but at the lower-class level. There are Kentuckians, Mississippians, Alabamans, and people from the upper Midwest who were drawn there for the steel mills. I worked in the summertime in the steel mills and drove a taxicab at times in that area, but I was the son of a university professor who was the chairman of the theater department at St. Louis University. So I have always been in a situation where the collision of cultures was an ever-present theme. I think that is one of the things that probably made me so receptive to Vietnam, but also particularly in this case to the Vietnamese in their plight here in America with the collision of those two cultures.

After I graduated from high school in Granite City, I went off to Northwestern University in Evanston and majored in theater, thought I would be an actor. I had some considerable success my first couple of years at Northwestern in acting, but then I decided that I would rather write than interpret and so I transferred into something called oral interpretation. Because I had been in a theatrical family and had been interested in the theater, I thought playwriting would be the thing I would do. I then went off to the University of Iowa afterward and got a master's degree in playwriting. But it really wasn't my medium. I was trying to force the way I saw the world into that medium, and it was inappropriate for it. There is a fundamental difference between playwriting and fiction writing in that the playwright is a collaborative artist. He is responsible for a limited number of things, and they are not the things that really involve the moment-to-moment sensual flow of the art object. All art objects, whatever the medium, are fundamentally sensual. The sensual moment-to-moment flow of the art object that is a play exists not on the page of the playscript but on the stage in performance. The artists who are responsible for the moment-to-moment sensual reality of that art object are the actors, the director, the various production designers. The playwright is responsible for two things basically: structure—that is primarily what he is responsible for—and to some lesser extent, he is responsible for dialogue.

But since I had the impulse—that is, the impulse of art, which is a deep but inchoate conviction that the world makes sense under its surface disorder or chaos—I wanted to write to articulate that vision. That vision was pressing on me—and this is something I learned far more clearly in Vietnam—it was pressing on me in a directly sensual way. Vietnam was a ravishingly sensual place and thoroughly taught me where my own focus was. I then understood that playwriting was not my medium. I had to create stories in a medium where I was directly shaping the moment-to-moment sensual flow of the art object, and that is therefore fiction.

MS: Talk to me a bit more about your formative experiences prior to being a literary creator. I would be interested to know because there are certain sensibilities and characters that appear. Richard Ford once wrote that being an author is putting into words other people's ideas, other characters' ideas. They are not necessarily autobiographical, they are not necessarily your own, they are creations of your imagination. Yet I think many of us assume that there is in the writer's own formative past the origin of the ideas or the sensibility and ultimately at least the background necessary, the context necessary for that fiction to eventually find its way into words.

RB: Well, I guess I would ask you to be somewhat more specific about what aspects of my writing you would like to trace, for a couple of reasons. First of all, I don't think of my own work in the kind of analytical or ideational way that would require the books to trace back to something. Second—and I think this is part of being an artist—is that the artist gets very uncomfortable with the translation of his work into other terms, especially abstract terms or summarized terms. Particularly in terms of autobiography. I often paraphrase to my students a notion that Graham Greene voices in his autobiography, his memoir, *A Sort of Life*, and that is that all good novelists have bad memories. He says what you remember comes out as journalism, what you forget goes into the compost of the imagination. So the things that are really finding their way into my work that are most important and really ultimately are most deeply reflective of who I am and how I see the universe are the things that I have blessedly and necessarily forgotten.

MS: Let's play it this way. Since the literature is the expression of what you've forgotten, let's talk about what you remember.

RB: Okay, not much. What would you like?

MS: Particulars.

RB: It's funny. I just spent a weekend with my best friend I mentioned from high school thirty years ago. He told anecdote after anecdote after anecdote about me. I remembered nothing, not a word, even after he reminded me.

MS: I'm just reacting to what you're saying. I don't mean to be imposing anything. Would you characterize yourself in that sense as being less introspective than observant of the world around you? Is that perhaps why?

RB: No, I think the process is one of an intense fusion of both those things. Where my introspection disappears—it is incredibly intense and active—but it disappears into the kind of ravenous sensual observation of the world around me so that they become a single process.

MS: In a sense, as Shakespeare says, you have to lose the self to gain the self?

RB: Yes. Yes. And you have to lose the self—the self of the literal memory—to gain the art that comes from the deeper self. But if you want specific things, I would be happy to try to work with that.

MS: Yes, I'm just trying to ask you about what I'm calling your preliterate period, before you try to give expression to those things you have forgotten, for example in your youth or your adolescence. When did you begin writing?

RB: Well, I began writing seriously on my twenty-first birthday, at the point where I had changed from acting as an ambition to writing. I began writing plays, which were not really getting at things I wanted to say, but at least I was writing. Before that, my ambition had been in acting. I was certainly influenced by the theater; I did a lot of acting.

I was influenced by some of the things I mentioned already: Granite City, Illinois. I was influenced by the steel mills, I worked in them, found them to be a place of great beauty, great intensity. I grew up within a couple of miles of the largest earthen artifact of pre-Columbian America—a fourteen-acre, ten-story-high Indian mound called Monk's Mound, which was the centerpiece of an ancient Indian city which flourished around the thirteenth century. It was larger than its contemporary London. Those were certainly strong influences.

I was influenced by music; my son is incredibly musical. I played the piano for a time when I was young, apparently really well, but again it is something I let go of and forgot. But I've always loved music, classical music, and in fact to this day, I tend always to write to music. I find appropriate classical music as a kind of background hook for my writing. It depends on the book. In my youth my favorites were always Aaron Copland, Claude Debussy, Maurice Ravel.

I certainly spent a period of intense reading, the obvious people, Faulkner and Hemingway and so forth, early Joyce, Graham Greene. *Winesburg, Ohio* was a very influential book for me. The river, the Mississippi River, St. Louis. St. Louis is a remarkable city in that it stands at the fulcrum of two internal cultures, the North and the South. And that great river. These are all influences.

Vietnam, of course, was a terrific influence on me. It was a preliterate influence. Because the writing I had done before Vietnam was ghastly awful, utterly unattached to my inner self. And in the wrong medium altogether. So, I didn't start writing in any full sense until I got back from Vietnam and began writing fiction.

MS: What was your term in Vietnam?

RB: One year. Essentially calendar year 1971. The year of 1970, I spent that entire year in a Vietnamese language school, seven hours a day, five days a week, with a Vietnamese native.

MS: Where was that?

RB: In Washington, D.C., and Arlington, Virginia.

MS: That one year was an immersion in the language?

RB: Absolute immersion in the language and in the person of this young woman. An immersion, too, into the culture in certain ways, and into a glimpse of, even at that point, a glimpse at the struggle of an exile. She was here voluntarily, seeking whatever.

MS: What was her name?

RB: Nghi. Ms. Nghi spoke to me once about what happened to her each evening when the cannon went off. It is a ceremonial cannon that was fired at Fort Myer, Virginia, which was very nearby. At dusk, they fired the cannon. Ms. Nghi often would weep at the firing of that cannon, weep with a kind of yearning for her home. The cannon fire was a sound of nostalgia for her. Because she had grown up virtually all her life in the midst of war and the sounds of war. So, that was the beginning. I got to Vietnam and I spoke the language fluently from essentially my first day there. I then had an opportunity to have very close contact with a wide variety of Vietnamese people. I spent five months working with military intelligence, out in the countryside, mostly northeast of Saigon and a few weeks down near the South China Sea. Then I spent seven months working as a linguist at Saigon City Hall.

MS: Before we go into that, if you don't mind, I want to stay for just a moment with how you came to become a translator. How did you happen to have been handed that particular assignment in the service?

RB: Well, my assignment in the service was really counter-intelligence special agent. When I was finishing up my master's degree at the University of Iowa, I was informed—this was just before the lottery draft—I was informed by my draft board that as soon as I got my degree in February, my student deferment would be null and void and they would draft me. So, I went to my local army recruiter to see what sort of choices I had, and I did have a choice. They would guarantee I would go into a certain military occupational specialty if I enlisted for a third year instead of allowing myself to be drafted. So I did that.

The specialty I chose was counter-intelligence special agent, which, as it was described to me, meant I would probably be in an American field office, doing background investigations on U.S. Army personnel who were seeking top-secret security clearances. It seemed a reasonable sort of thing to do. So I went off to Fort Holabird, Maryland, and when I arrived they put me in a holding company because recruiters all over the country had been feeding this line to potential army men and there were hundreds and hundreds of counter-intel-

ligence, neo-counter-intelligence agents just waiting for classes to open up. So
we sat in Baltimore for six months and painted rocks and then finally I got in
my class and sure enough I became a counter-intelligence special agent.

However, there was another possibility for CI agents which wasn't out-
lined, and I got orders to go to Washington to learn Vietnamese. Then I ended
up in Vietnam and I did work for five months in Intelligence.

MS: Okay, we're picking up there . . .

RB: Yes, then for seven months I worked in Saigon as a linguist. The influence there was the Vietnamese people. In the countryside I was in contact with
Vietnamese informers, with the U.S. Army, village chiefs, and rice farmers,
water buffalo jockeys, and whatever, an extraordinary variety of people there.
Then in Saigon my favorite thing in the world was at two in the morning to
wander out of my hotel and into the steamy back alleys where no one ever
seemed to sleep. I would crouch in the doorways with the Vietnamese people
there. The Vietnamese as a group are the warmest, most friendly, most gener-
ous-spirited people in the world, and they inevitably invited me into their
homes and into their lives, and into their culture. I fell in love several times. I
had wonderful friends that ranged from my favorite leper beggar on the streets
of Saigon—who was also, by the way, the most cheerful man I ever met in my
life—up to the highest Vietnamese government officials. It was my intimate
intense encounter with those people and my ongoing intense encounter with
the ravishing sensuality of Vietnam that turned me into a fiction writer.

MS: Did you obtain this access by virtue of your command of the language?

RB: Primarily. The jobs that I did gave me opportunities to have contact
with a wider variety of people than probably most army men could have had
contact with. Then once I had contact with them, obviously the quality and
nature of my communication with them was greatly enhanced by my command of the language. So, certainly it is the thing that opened the whole experience up to me in terms of my understanding and becoming immersed in it.

MS: Did you write about it while you were there or did it not start to form
itself until after you left?

RB: I wrote a lot of notes there. I kept notebooks and I wrote one of my
worst plays there in Saigon. But it didn't really begin to shape itself until later.
I had not yet forgotten. In my creative writing courses, I always read "Open
Arms," which is one of the stories in *Good Scent*. I read that story to them. It is
a very fully realized story. Then I read to them the passage from my notebook
which recounts a couple of incidents that were the initial inspiration for that
story. But then I read them a story that I wrote in about February or March of
1972, which was just a couple of months after getting back from Vietnam and
only six or eight months after the incident.

In fact it was the first short story, the first piece of serious fiction I ever
wrote, and it is a dreadful little story. I show my students how it was a perfect
example of all the things that they do wrong, that I once did wrong as well. It
is interesting to see that one of the reasons it went wrong is that I had not yet

forgotten. I was still bound to my literal memory. That is not the place to write from if you are going to write good fiction.

MS: What was your first published work of fiction?

RB: My first published work of fiction was a short story called "Moving Day" which was in *Redbook* magazine in 1974. I was really a terrible short story writer, too, but this was a good story. I wrote one good story, interestingly enough in the first person. It was about a couple of guys who are about to be shipped off to Vietnam, jogging in Central Park. There's a kind of little psychological game they're playing with each other, each trying to convince the other that he's in trouble, the other guy's going to be in trouble but he's not, over in Vietnam in their anticipated assignments. It is a good story.

I sold another story which was just kind of typical women's magazine stuff and I sold a story to *Cosmopolitan*. I did those in the space of about a year and a half and then stopped publishing. I wrote a lot of bad stories after that and stopped writing short stories. Then I finally got my first novel, *The Alleys of Eden*, published in 1981.

MS: Was this the first work in which Vietnam was central?

RB: That's it. The first one I got published. Now, I wrote five other novels. I wrote six novels from 1972 to 1981. *The Alleys of Eden* was the fourth of those six novels. The other five have never been published. But I was trying to figure out how to do this thing.

MS: Were they all Vietnam-centered novels?

RB: No, no, they were not. Some of them were centered in Wabash, which is the fictional town that I created as the doppleganger to Granite City. The first novel I wrote, a thing I called *What Lies Near*, was really the first Vietnam novel I wrote. I finished that in 1973. An incident from there and even a chapter from there became critical parts in *On Distant Ground*, which was my fourth published novel, my first book at Knopf.

MS: In your own assessment, what was the weakness or failure, or shortcomings of the first novel?

RB: *What Lies Near* was about half a novel; it was half the conception of a novel extended to novel length.

MS: By which you mean what?

RB: There wasn't enough there to really explore a vision of the world through the novel form. There was an incident in the book of a military intelligence officer seeing a bit of graffiti in an interrogation cell. A remarkably ironic bit of graffiti which to David Fleming, the intelligence officer, suddenly summoned up the sense of the person, the real person. He then finds out who was in that cell and through the novel just misses him here and there. He continues almost against his will to seek this man out while doing what for him is basically an irrelevant other investigation. Ultimately he finds the man on Con Son Island, where Thieu had his tiger cages, and he goes there and kidnaps him and sets him free. That is the novel. There wasn't enough there to explore, number one. Number two, I was still writing too much from my head, which is where you go when you write from literal memory. The place art is created from is much deeper than that. The compost heap that Graham Greene speaks about, the artistic unconscious which most people talk about, that deep amorphous well of your sensual memory, your sensual self. I wasn't in that place; I was writing too much from my head. That is the other major thing wrong with that book. I didn't know how to get in there, didn't know even then that is the place I had to go. I was content to create from my head. Nobody had ever told me otherwise.

I would not have written that many bad novels, misbegotten novels, if I had had somebody to spend just six hours, eight hours with me and tell me the things that I tell my students in the first six or eight hours, but I had to learn all that for myself. That is why it went bad. I finally found my way with *The Alleys of Eden* into that place and I never wrote that other way again. Well I did. The fifth and sixth novels are not so good either, because then I was really getting desperate to get published and I started doing things willfully and from my head again. But finally my best novel got published after twenty-one rejections.

MS: Which was?

RB: *The Alleys of Eden.*

MS: You consider that your best novel?

RB: Of the first six. Of those six unpublished books, that was my best one. It was the only one I really wrote from the place where I should be writing, and forever thereafter, I knew I should stay in that place. I knew where to go. So, by the time I wrote my fourth published novel, *On Distant Ground*, I knew where to write from and I also knew how to go back to the partial conception of my first novel manuscript and give it a whole other element. That other element still exists, but that book picks up with the court martial of David Fleming after he had set free that prisoner. Fleming is married, and as the court martial begins, his first child is born during the trial. During the trial, memories are brought up, particularly of a Vietnamese woman he had a brief affair with in Vietnam. She had broken the affair off mysteriously after a couple of months, and through several factors, not the least of which is the birth of his son, Fleming becomes convinced that the woman broke it off because she was pregnant. With this newfound love for his son, based on the fact that the son looks like him, just as he finally learns that that fragment of graffiti reminded him of his own mind, he becomes obsessed with the notion that he has a son in Vietnam. Without getting into too much of the plot: he goes back to try to find him.

So it was that; it was the deeper and richer conception and the overlapping pattern of what was really behind this obsession about the writing on the interrogation cell wall and what is really behind his obsession with finding his child, this putative child. It is the dual conception and reinforcing conceptions of those two patterns that really made for a fully realized novel.

MS: The protagonist Fleming in that novel . . .

RB: Was a minor character in *The Alleys of Eden.*

MS: And the novel was written from the point of view of Fleming, I presume.

RB: Yes, not first-person, but a limited third-person omniscient narrator, which is strictly Henry James's central intelligence. Yes, it is limited to Fleming.

MS: Which was the first published work, if you will, in which the point of view was that of the Vietnamese?

RB: *The Deuce*, in 1989, my sixth published novel. Though *The Alleys of Eden* has a very fully developed, equally important Vietnamese character, Lanh, a former bar girl, lover of Cliff, who is a U.S. Army deserter who deserted in Saigon. It is a story of a U.S. Army deserter and the bar girl he has lived with for four and a half years in the back alleys of Saigon, and it picks up on the night that Saigon has fallen. Lanh is a very fully realized character and we see her entirely through Cliff's eyes, but he sees her as whole and complete, so we see her too. As far as writing within the point of view of the Vietnamese, *The Deuce* is the first book. There I actually write in the voice of a sixteen-year-old Vietnamese boy.

MS: What made you decide—if in fact decision is quite the word—why was it that in this sixth novel you brought Vietnamese consciousness so much into the foreground?

RB: Well, I think he brought himself there, in a sense. I was thinking about a new book to write. I had become intrigued with a notion of David Fleming's life after he brings home his son, the kid who might be his son, though not in any obvious way. So I thought I would write a sequel to *On Distant Ground*, but when I started thinking about it, the kid himself really took over and then became a kid of his own, really somebody new. Once I knew I was going to write a book about this boy, he just insisted on speaking for himself without the mediator of that third-person narrator.

MS: You say he insisted on speaking for himself. In what sense of your own consciousness do you phrase it that way?

RB: When you have a book to write, a story even, for me at least—I'm sure it is this way for many writers—what you have really inside you is a character, somebody who is there. He is somewhat like his real world counterpart but probably because he doesn't really exist, he is even more real to you. He is a different, distinct, and very clear real person who is just there somewhere in the shadows whispering to you, and you have to listen to him, go to him, and pull him out of the shadows and into the light. That is the way it was with Tony in *The Deuce*. That is the way it was with all the others in *Good Scent*. That is the way it was with the other books, too.

The question is always whether the author is a voice and eminence apart from but close to that person or whether you in fact enter into that person's own consciousness and sensibilities and voice. But this kid would not let me mediate. I had also been reading at the time—my wife Maureen and I had been reading to each other each night—a book that I really like to think helped nudge me in the direction of the first-person voice as a narrative medium. Indeed, its influence carried forward just as strongly if not even more strongly into *Good Scent from a Strange Mountain*.

MS: What book was it?

RB: A book about baseball called *The Glory of Their Times*, by Lawrence Ritter. But it is not by him. It is by his tape recorder. He went out in the early '60s and interviewed maybe sixteen, eighteen, twenty players from the very early days of baseball when they were all very old men. It is in the voices of Rube Marquard and Sam Crawford, for instance, and Fred Snodgrass. These guys were so wonderful and strong and personal and full of the sense of exile. In a way, they had lived in another country. They had lived in the country of youth and of baseball and now they passed out of that country in their thirties and had lived forty or fifty years in exile from that country of their youth. I think that book had a real influence on me.

MS: You mentioned several times, voice and sensuality. Would you elaborate a bit more on both those dimensions in your writing? They seem to be very central.

RB: Fiction exists as a mode of discourse separate from all others, because it is sensual. It is the one mode of prose discourse that is trying to articulate a vision of the world through the senses. Fiction is trying to communicate primarily by going back to that flux of sensual experience out there that is life on the planet Earth, pulling bits and pieces of it out and shaping them and reshaping them and giving them back to the reader as experience itself in its own form. I see this as the primary characteristic of literary fiction.

I think then the corollary is that those nascent artists who are destined to be literary fiction writers are probably uncommonly conscious of and open to their senses and are uncomfortable trying to communicate, just as I am now, important things about the world in any mode other than a sensual mode.

MS: Define sensual.

RB: Sensual? The direct rendering of the things that we touch, smell, taste, hear, and feel on our skin.

MS: The direct experience, in a total physical and emotional engagement?

RB: Right. Where a man is feeling fear of the jungle and someone nearby that would kill him, we don't say he is full of fear, that is abstract. We don't say he moved quietly out of the jungle because that is summary. We don't say he leaned against the tree and because his father used to beat him and he'd hide in the barn from him this was a particularly difficult moment and he listened and he thought about his father; that is analysis. If the father is important, the man leans up against the tree and then we see his father bring his face into the candlelight and it is as if the man's nose flares with light and his mouth opens; his mouth opens but did not close again and the jaw hangs slack and now the man leans back against the tree and shakes his head and he's breathing only from the lip up. That is moment to moment, through the senses, as opposed to abstraction and generalization and summary and analysis. A literary fiction writer's impulse, primary impulse, is to write in that sensual way.

MS: To convey the raw experience itself?

RB: To draw the reader out of himself into the sensibilities of the character. If you don't—because we're writing about human emotions—and human emotions are felt only through the senses, all the other stuff, our labeling of those emotions, our understanding of them in some abstract way, the willful flow of rational discussion about our feelings in our heads, the analysis and interpretation we put on it, those are not the emotions themselves; those are ways of not having the emotions. That is its usefulness to us in daily life. But if you use those nonsensual devices as a fiction writer you end up throwing the reader back into himself to fill in the sensual blanks.

It is like the difference between masturbation and making love. Nonliterature relies on abstraction and analysis and summary and cliché, which is the same as abstraction. Look at all the Harlequin Romance readers who weep real tears or who actually get physically excited about this man taking this woman in his arms and "her heart beat wild with passion." They read sentences like that and they get excited, physically excited. Why, though? Because they're filling in those sensual blanks. The fundamental experience of nonliterature is you are thrown back into yourself. It is self-referential, masturbation. In literature you are drawn out of yourself, just as in making love. You become part of an other and the only way you can do that is by rendering the other's inner sensibilities, the way that unique person, and his or her unique body encounters those emotions directly through the senses. If we entered into that process, then we can feel those feelings too. Not as ourselves, but as part of this other person, which is what literature is all about.

MS: Very nicely said. In the same respect, what about place or setting? What if we were to go through the novels. *The Alleys of Eden* is set primarily in Saigon?

RB: Yes.

MS: *Sun Dogs?*

RB: Northern slope of Alaska.

MS: *Countrymen of Bones?*

RB: Alamagordo. Desert.

MS: *On Distant Ground?*

RB: Saigon, Baltimore, Maryland, and Saigon again.

MS: *Wabash?*

RB: Wabash, Illinois. Steel mill town in the St. Louis area.

MS: *The Deuce?*

RB: New York City.

MS: *Good Scent from a Strange Mountain?*

RB: The two Vietnamese communities, one in New Orleans and one in Lake Charles, mostly New Orleans. Places were very strong. The locations are a very strong element. I think it was Henry James who said, "Landscape is character," and I'm very much influenced by places. I travel a lot, and it is absolutely critical to my creative process; places are inescapably and comprehensively sensual, and they are always shaping us. Since our emotions are sensual, and one of the sensual ways that we express our emotions and experience them is by the selectivity of the sensual cues around us. There are hundreds of sensual cues surrounding us, any of which we might respond to.

But at any given moment only a very small number are really present in our consciousness.

How is that comprehensive world of sensual possibilities selected down to that very few that we're conscious of? This is happening every second of our lives. Well, the answer is, very rarely do we do so on an intentional basis; it is done for us by our emotions. Our emotions are constantly choosing what it is that we respond to sensually. So it is a reflection of and an expression of that emotion. If that is true you can understand then how landscape is character, because everything that surrounds us is constantly picking up and gaining valence, an emotional valence from our perception of it.

MS: Is that something that you perceive as an insider to those landscapes or an outsider? You speak frequently of exiles.

RB: The exile probably stands in relationship to his landscape as an artist does to life and that is as both an insider and an outsider.

MS: The places in which you have located your fiction, are these places which are important to you personally?

RB: Sure. Of course, they have to be. All places are important to me personally. Every place I go is important to me personally. Those are the ones I find particularly rich in metaphorical possibility, sensual possibility for the characters that I have.

MS: I see, now that you secured the Pulitzer Prize, Louisiana is eager to claim you for its own; I'm sure St. Louis is probably making a bid on much the same ground; New York will take a quick scan at your recent biography and at the ten years you spent there compared to the eight you spent in Louisiana and put their bid in.

RB: Chicago, I had about six years in too. They're doing their bid.

MS: There you have it. But for you, as a writer, in terms of where you locate and identify yourself, sometimes that is not a function of time.

RB: No.

MS: Would you agree that the place you might most strongly identify with might be, as in the case of Vietnam, a place where you actually spent only a year of your life?

RB: Sure.

MS: Is there any place that you identify with most closely?

RB: I would say at this point, and it can change for a person too, so I would certainly say that at this point my personal identification is unquestionably with Louisiana. Particularly southern Louisiana.

MS: And that is what gave rise to *A Good Scent*?

RB: Yes, certainly. It was deeply rooted here. If I had been in southern California instead of southern Louisiana I probably could still have written this book, because there are Vietnamese communities there as well.

MS: Was it your acquaintanceship of these specific communities which created that correspondence with and the setting for those stories?

RB: Yes. The places I knew were southern Louisiana. I don't think the book would have been quite as rich in southern California, say, because there is an interplay here with landscape and climate and in the southern Louisiana cultures too. The voodoo, too. For instance, "Love"—which is one of my favorites in the book—would never have been written in southern California. So, that book is deeply rooted here. I would have written a book about Vietnamese expatriates if I had not had the opportunity to come to Louisiana, but this particular book, the book that won the Pulitzer Prize, is deeply and inextricably rooted, bound up with southern Louisiana. On a personal basis, this is where I feel most at home, and where I intend to stay. I certainly have a lot of options now, but my firm intention—as long as the legislature doesn't destroy the university system in the state, which at times seems like a possibility—my intention is to stay in Louisiana. Because I really feel like a Louisianian now.

MS: Gee, how would you characterize that?

RB: Not in abstract terms. It is a very sensual thing.

MS: Why don't we leave it at that.

13

STEPHEN A. SMITH

The Rhetoric of
Southern Humor

Writing an essay for this book is, for me, like robbing a bank for Thomas Crown. Crown, you will recall, was a brilliant fellow (played by Steve McQueen in *The Thomas Crown Affair*) who recruited and instructed a group of folks to rob a nearby bank. He conceived the idea and knew exactly how it would work. The recruits had never seen his face, had some sense of their purpose but no idea how it would relate to the roles of the others, and had never met their partners in crime; nevertheless, each did his assigned part, and the robbery was almost perfect. In a sense, I am robbing the wealth of my nearby heritage for this essay, and the rest of the analogy plays fairly well. In the movie, the robbers get caught, and Crown gets Faye Dunaway. Southerners Rhett Butler and Jefferson Humphries can appreciate the irony of this situation.

The South, of course, has always been rich in irony, because it has always been a land of contrast and juxtaposition—black and white, rich and poor, mountaineer and planter, religion and violence, unregulated development and a sense of place, greed and grace, illiteracy and great writing. In an essay entitled "The Irony of Southern History," C. Vann Woodward noted the special problems of and requirements for interpreting the meaning of such a society: "In the nature of things the participants in an ironic situation are rarely conscious of the irony, else they would not become its victims. Awareness must ordinarily be contributed by an observer, a nonparticipant, and the observer must have an unusual combination of detachment and sympathy." One must, he said, "be able to appreciate both elements in the incongruity that go to make up the ironic situation, both the virtue and the vice to which pretensions of virtue lead." The sensitive writer "must not be so hostile as to deny the element of virtue or strength on the one side, nor so sympathetic as to ignore the vanity and weakness to which the virtue and strength have contributed."[1]

The interpretation of the irony of southern society has benefited from the works of Woodward, George Tindall, John Shelton Reed, Louis Rubin Jr., and others in the academy, but it has also found explanation in the productions of the region's storytellers, singers, and writers. Perhaps nowhere has that interpretation been more successful or more enduring than in southern humor, a genre that lives and dies by its explication of the ironic and incongruous elements of life and society. In fact, as my contribution to this perspective on the future of southern letters, I will argue that contemporary southern humor is an enlightened heir to an old tradition, that it has a distinctive rhetoric, and that it will survive the cultural homogenization of the global village in an age where the mass media have become our electronic storytellers.

Old Times There

The southern frontier of the nineteenth century was, of necessity, an oral society. Isolation and illiteracy made it so, and both physical distance, which inhibited confirmation, and the prevailing romanticism of the era liberated the storyteller from the shackles of fact. The demands of wresting a living from the new soil and the loneliness of the frontier combined to make humor a psychological necessity. While the oral storytelling tradition would continue to exist, many of the tall tales, wild stories, and grotesque character sketches were soon captured, transcribed, and embellished by a group of writers who raised "local color" to a low art. William T. Porter's *Spirit of the Times* first provided a forum for this brand of "Southwest humor" as early as 1831, but the literary movement generally dates from the publication of Augustus Baldwin Longstreet's *Georgia Scenes* in 1835 to the publication of George Washington Harris's *Sut Lovingood's Yarns* in 1867.[2]

The early southern humorists were captives of the worldview of their class and time; however, they did establish a new and unique genre and did make literary contributions that have outlived the utility of their social attitudes and political philosophy. They understood the effectiveness of having their characters speak in dialect, the use of the outrageous to show the foibles of humanity, the techniques required to lead their audiences to suspend disbelief, the mental clarity and concrete depiction provided by metaphors and similes, and the creative construction of pretended insight for their readers but not for their characters. Most important, perhaps, they recognized and exploited the dialectic tensions that have always abounded in human nature but are especially prevalent in southern culture.

In a period when the South was fresh with the political footprints of Andrew Jackson, this first school of southern humor did not share in that vision. Their tales were rhetorical narratives that carried the same subtle messages found in the romantic Cavalier novels of the period, and their yarns revealed social attitudes similar to the congressional speeches of the anti-Jacksonian aristocrats of the planter class. Typically, the southern humorist "was a man of education and breeding who felt deeply and spoke with conviction. . . . Often a devoted Whig, he was convinced that if the nation was to be saved from chaos and degradation, only the honor, reasonableness, and sense of responsibility of gentlemen—Whig gentlemen—could save it." While the unwashed and unlettered mass of democracy often served as the subjects of their stories, few of these writers came from or shared the values of the plain folk of the Old South. One study suggested that the "writers' amused observations on the outspoken, crude, and often illiterate democratic man reveal a persistent if sometimes only half-conscious feeling that while these ring-tailed roarers had their virtues, they could not be trusted to run the country."[3]

Both the stance and the stories of these Whig writers revealed their politics. The author's persona was that of an educated, articulate, refined, and somewhat bemused observer, and each usually made an effort to identify with their readers while distinguishing themselves from the homegrown fools who populated their plots. Longstreet's "Ned Brace," Johnson Jones Hooper's "Simon Suggs," Harden Taliferro's "Ham Rachel," Francis James Robinson's "Lije Benadix," and Kittrell Warren's "Billy Fishback" often told their own stories of confusion and consequence, but the author and his imagined readers could forgo empathy and "safely indulge in unrestrained laughter, for the narrator [was] an aristocrat, describing from a superior social and moral position the antics of these peculiar specimens."[4]

Southern letters waned after the Civil War, but the neo-Bourbon redemption was followed by a resumption of literary efforts to resurrect the dream of an Old South that had never existed in fact. W. J. Cash, assessing the writing of the period and contrasting it with a rhetorical vision of his own, said, "What we really have in the literature of the Reconstruction era is . . . a propaganda. Its novels, its sketches and stories, are essentially so many pamphlets. . . . Their tone is definitely polemical and forensic. Often, indeed, their platform is simply that of the old rhetoric of stump and platform—the Southern oratory—brought over and set down on paper in all its native turigidity, bombast, and sentimentality; and in most cases the influence is plain."[5] The novels of Thomas Nelson Page, the editorials and speeches of Henry Grady, and the epideictic oratory at hundreds of Confederate reunions valued the past, plutocrats, plunder, and privilege over the messages of interracial populism.[6]

Southern humor reappeared after Reconstruction in the local color writings of Joel Chandler Harris, and once again it seemed to parallel the rhetoric of the general literary milieu of the period. *Uncle Remus: His Songs and His Sayings* was a translation of indigenous folklore; it employed black dialect and many other conventions of the genre, and it has remained a popular collection of stories, recast into the film *The Song of the South* by Walt Disney.[7] Uncle Remus was not Joel Chandler Harris; he was a docile black man telling happy stories about animals with conventional values. Uncle Remus was not Nat Turner; he was Joel Chandler Harris's vision of what blacks were in the Old South and should be in the New South. It was amusing, but it was not apolitical.

A Change of Mind

The South of today, however, is not the South of the nineteenth century or of any other yesterdays. The "bulldozer revolution" and commercial strip development have reflected our new "cents of place." The crossroads country store has been replaced by the Kmart. Pool halls have become video arcades. Mobile homes and air-conditioning have eradicated verandas and front porches, so storytellers have lost their favorite forum. The Grand Ole Opry abandoned Ryman Auditorium in downtown Nashville for a new plastic theme park out on the bypass. Our preachers have folded their tents and traded them for satellite transmitters. Our politicians have stepped from the stump and substituted slick spots. Hank Williams, Patsy Cline, Bazooka Bob Burns, Brother Dave Gardner, Senator Sam Ervin, and Kissin' Jim Folsom are dead, and Jeremiah John Egerton ain't feeling so good himself. It's not funny.

Like kudzu, however, the southern storyteller has survived and thrived, and the new strain may be the hardiest yet. The pure oral tradition is celebrated annually at the National Storytelling Championship in Jonesborough, Tennessee. The stories of family told by John Egerton in *Generations* and Shirley Abbott in *Womenfolks* are true local color. The novels of Larry McMurtry, Willie Morris, Donald Hays, William Price Fox, and Dan Jenkins make me laugh out loud. Plays such as Williams, Sears, and Howard's "Greater Tuna," James McLure's "Lone Star" and "Laundry and Bourbon," Ellen Byron's "Graceland," Larry King's "Best Little Whorehouse in Texas," and Preston Jones's Texas trilogy make it worth putting on a tie to hear their stories. The brilliant character sketches in Marshall Frady's *Southerners* and Roy Blount Jr.'s *Crackers* are real and really funny.

Even the new communications media appear to be more hospitable than hostile to the southern-style storytellers. Ted Turner's Superstation WTBS and Cable News Network provide access for southern voices in the electronic environment. The stories of Tom T. Hall, Don Williams, Johnny Cash, Alabama, Jimmy Buffett, and Loretta Lynn sound even better on compact disc. The birth of *Southern Magazine* and numerous state and local magazines provide a new popular forum for southern writers, and the growth and maturation of southern university presses hold even more promise for both prose and poetry.

Somehow, southern humor has endured the Great Depression, the Second Reconstruction, the election of Jesse Helms, the defeat of Jimmy Carter, and the fall of Jimmy Swaggart. It's different, all right, just like the South is now different; but it's still the same, just like the South is still the South. If that sounds like a contradiction, you obviously don't understand the South and probably won't understand its humor. Nonetheless, I will try to identify the unique characteristics of contemporary southern humor, illuminate the distinctive new rhetoric of the new local color writers, distinguish it from that of their literary progenitors, and explain the reasons why the genre will continue to be a part of the future of southern letters.

The evidence for my argument will be drawn from the works of four especially gifted and unusually insightful practitioners of the art—William Price
Fox of South Carolina, Larry L. King of Texas, Lewis Grizzard of Georgia,
and Florence King of Virginia. Besides being my personal favorites, they have
other things in common. They have the lucrative habit of writing feature
pieces for newspaper or magazine publication, and even their books have
enough popular appeal to do well in the trade market. They generally pro-
fess to be telling facts, but they always tell truths—even when their narrative
confessions flirt with fiction. They seldom make harsh moral judgments about
their characters, but they frequently expose those who do. When they address
politics, either directly or indirectly, they are closer to being democrats than
royalists. They have a keen understanding of language, much of which is
drawn, like their stories, from the southern scene. They all make me laugh,
and they all make me wiser.

William Price Fox

Fox has been spinning his yarns for more than twenty years. His books include
*Southern Fried, Southern Fried Plus Six, Ruby Red, Dixiana Moon, Moonshine
Light, Moonshine Bright, Dr. Golf,* and *Chitlin Strut & Other Madrigals*
(which I have taken as today's text), and he has contributed articles to magazines such as *TV Guide, Sports Illustrated,* and *Harper's.* His work is enter-
taining, but it is also argument. He writes in first person, a participant-observer
who presents characters engaged in everyday dramas and chasing everyday
dreams, and the reader needs to be neither a semiotics expert nor a Jungian
psychologist to interpret the inherent values in the scripts of these rhetorical
visions.[8] One might see, however, a bit of projection in his description of drive-
in restaurateur Doug Broome: "Like all great storytellers, he was a consum-
mate liar. A straight tale would be transformed into a richer, wilder mixture,
and the final version, while sometimes spellbinding and always logical, would
have absolutely nothing to do with the truth."[9]

Doug Broome is also representative of the antiheroes frequently found in
contemporary southern humor. He is a self-made hustler who "left school in
the fourth grade, worked his way up from curb boy at the Pig Trail Inn out on
the Broad River Road, to Baker's on Main Street, and finally to his own restaurants all over town." Fox portrays him clearly, allowing Broome the populist to
take a single shot at both Yankees and corporations in the best rhetorical tradition of the South. "One day he told me, 'Billy, these chain operations are ruining the hamburger. Ruining it. Most of them come from up north to begin
with, so what in the hell do they know about cooking?'" In the same essay, Fox
reveals his own affinity for the southern shuffle strategy in describing his own
"style" to a New York talk show host by talking about faking the production of
his first omelet. "I don't think he understood it, but I knew I did. I knew that
style wasn't an exclusive property in the aristocracy of the arts. A jockey, a short-
stop, a used-car salesman, or even a mechanic grinding valves can have it, and

the feather-trimmed hookers working the curbs along Gervais and Millwood are not without it."[10]

Fox further provides distinction between the voice of the contemporary writers and those of the past in telling of an interview with Satchel Paige. It is not the racist recollection of a condescending Whig or an interview with an Uncle Remus; it is conversation of mutual respect. He relates that they "talked about fast cars, fights, catfish, carp, redbreast, barbecue, Southern politics, and moonshine, and finally—baseball."[11] The range of subjects, a virtual liturgy of good old boyism, demonstrated the lack of racial barriers and the sharing of a topical community between the pitcher and the poet. It also serves as a catalog of many of the contemporary rituals that help define the South.

Southern culture is, in many ways, constituted by the unique traditions and rituals of the region. As long as these unique events continue, the South and its humor will continue to be distinctive. Fox identifies Labor Day as the highest of holy days. "In South Carolina, everything happens on Labor Day. The football season opens, the Darlington 500 revs up, and . . . more than a hundred official barbecues, okra struts, catfish stomps, and demolition derbies are all going on at the same time."[12] In discussing four of these sacred rites— dancing, dying, dining, and drive-ins—he displays a masterful command of language and a keen understanding of the congregation.

At an annual Chitlin Strut, a community excuse to celebrate life with fun and food, Fox was amazed by the contest dancing of a fellow named Jack West, and his description of West's performance might be equally applicable to his own flair for the dramatic prose. West, he said, "came on shimmying like a '54 Ford with a bad front end"; next he was "just this side of an epileptic fit"; then he "passed the point of spasm and, in the frenzy and froth you see only in the back of salvation tents and Pentecostal jubilees, he held his shaking hips and loins to the incredible beat for another thirty-six blistering bars." Finally, Jack "cut loose with the only finish possible—the long, dark, subterranean, unmistakable deep-swamp sound of a Carolina redbone who has treed a twenty pound possum."[13] Few can imagine this performance occurring in Iowa City or anywhere outside the South, and the same might be said of the writing. Jack West and his kind are going to be around for a long time; I hope this brand of description will, too.

Funerals and dying, frequent themes among the earliest southwestern humorists, have also become ritual experiences in the South and not infrequent topics of contemporary southern writers. Sure, death is a universal theme, but only the Irish appreciate the social ritual and cultural importance as much as we do in Dixie. Explaining the significance of funerals in a letter to a Yankee friend, Fox tells him that in the South we still have "old-fashioned screaming, and praying, and singing, and falling-down-in-the-dirt funerals. . . . Down here, it's just another excuse to bring over a covered dish and get together and hear some music out under the pecans."[14]

Foodways, which Fox discussed with Paige and which are related to funerals, are important cultural signifiers in their own right.[15] The importance of understanding food rituals to understanding the region is revealed to Fox as Max Gergel holds forth on the epistemology of chitlins: "Grease—that's the secret of the South. This is the hard lard belt down here. You go in a store and ask for something like safflower oil and they'll think you're part of the Red Menace."[16] Fox is less accurate, however, when he discusses the teleology of barbeque. He is almost speaking in tongues when he describes South Carolina as "the Garden of Eden of Barbecue" and testifies, "At the Springfield Frog Jump, I have seen serious men in business suits and full-grown women go into what is called a 'barbecue coma.'"[17] He correctly witnesses on the necessity of hickory wood and the false doctrine of Texas barbecue, but he is in serious error when he states that decent barbecue can be formulated without tomatoes.[18] Nonetheless, his writings reveal the thematic importance of foodways in southern distinctiveness and in the southern humor of the big brag. Neither show any sings of disappearing from the social or literary landscape.

The South often is seen as the bastion of conservative conformity, but one of the cultural contradictions that enhances the argument of southern humor is the extraordinary amount of personal slack we allow to oddballs and throwbacks. Rather than poking fun at the deviants to demonstrate social superiority as did the early local color writers, Fox and the other contemporary writers of humor, secure in their own personal and professional status, are more sympathetic and supportive. To demonstrate one aspect of the praxis of moral accommodation in South Carolina, even before the fall of Jim Bakker, Fox argues through drive-in movie owner Terry Holman, who realizes, "There's a lot of folks down here who would just as soon see what Linda Lovelace is doing, too." Then Fox explains in his own voice, "Down here where 'Jesus Saves' signs are thicker than rednecks at a white-sock sale, the fundamentalists and the pornographers have arm-wrestled to a draw."[19] Fox's humor has contributed to that latitude and other regional forbearances of folly by constructing a vision of a more tolerant society.

Larry L. King

Larry King has been writing for money since before I was born, and I have learned more from him than he'll ever know. He has written or coauthored three plays: *The Best Little Whorehouse in Texas*, *The Kingfish*, and *The Night Hank Williams Died*. He admits that *The One-Eyed Man* is a work of fiction, but he has published as fact books such as *Confessions of a White Racist*, *The Old Man and Lesser Mortals*, *Of Outlaws, Con Men, Whores, Politicians, and Other Artists*, *The Whorehouse Papers*, and *None But a Blackhead: On Being a Writer*. His essays have appeared in publications as diverse as the *Putnam News* and *Playboy* and everything in between worth reading.

Some of King's stories share an affinity with those of Fox, because they are writing of the same "place" and the same "people." Shades of Doug Broome can be seen in King's story of his brother Weldon ("the undisputed fried chicken king of Midland") in the Texas Fried Chicken marketing battle against

Kentucky Fried Chicken.[20] Where Fox tried to define his own style by relating the production of his first omelet at Doug Broome's, King related his style by hilariously recounting his own failed scam to market plaques made from the Eisenhower Inaugural Platform.[21] While Fox noted the Memorial Day rituals of South Carolina, King relates how Texans living in New York maintain their roots. "Many of us gather for chili suppers, tell stories with origins in Fort Worth or Odessa or Abilene; sometimes we even play dominoes or listen to country-western music. . . . We meet each March 2—Texas Independence Day—to drink beer, hoo-haw at each other in the accents of home, and honor some myth that we can, at best, only ill define."[22]

King also writes in the first person and identifies with the common folk, admitting to being part redneck and aspiring to be a good old boy; however, he still chafes at "being called a redneck, . . . especially when you know in your genes and in the dirty back roads of your mind that you *are* one—despite having spent years trying not to be." He distinguishes between "a 'Neck of the true plastic-Jesus-on-the-dashboard and pink-rubber-haircurlers-in-the-supermarket variety" and a a higher life form known as a good old boy. Fox's Doug Broome would fit King's definition of a good old boy: "He's a climber, an achiever, a con man looking for the edge and the hedge. He'll lay a lot of semi-smarmy charm on you, and bullshit grading from middling to high. He acts dumber than he is when he knows something and smarter than he is when he doesn't." Then, in what might be taken as an autobiographical disclosure of his own style, King says, "Such parts of his Redneck heritage as may be judged eccentric or humorous enough to be useful will be retained in his mildly self-deprecating stories and may come in handy while he's working up to relieving you of your billfold or your panties."[23]

A background in and around politics has furnished King with more political stories than the other authors discussed here, and he is more open in his political affiliation. By age seven, he said, "I realized that everyone save the Goddamn Republicans and inmates of insane asylums" was stomp-down for Franklin Roosevelt. King still is.[24] He has known and written about Sam Rayburn, Lyndon Johnson, Mo Udall, Nelson Rockefeller, Jim Wright, and Jimmy Carter, as well as Sheriff T. J. Flournoy of LaGrange, Texas. King's best piece, and one of the most sublime chunks of prose ever written in the English language, was a story about the nomination and election of Jimmy Carter that appeared in *Esquire* under the title "We Ain't Trash No More: How Jimmy Carter Led the Rednecks from the Wilderness." It utilizes regional dialect and insightful bravado to lead the Yankee reader through southern food, southern lifestyles, southern guilt, and southern power. It is the King James (Earl) Bible of southern humor.

King admits that he likes "to write about the underside of our society," because he finds those folks more interesting as well as more familiar. It had been his good fortune, he writes, "that my recreational habits helped me to get stories and gain new insights into the people I wrote about. I frequented the beer joints of the Southwest 'fightin' and dancin' clubs'—because I loved (a) country music, (b) beer, and (c) the kinds of characters to be found in those crazy places." Fox proudly claimed that "the feather-trimmed hookers working the curbs along Gervais and Millwood" in Columbia, South Carolina, had "style," and King, too, seemed to share that assumption. "I was always sympathetic to whores," he said, "and it was for more reasons than that they provided better services to mankind than do, say, most preachers and bankers. I think it was because I sensed something of the tough lives they led and didn't believe they needed to be harassed beyond the limits of the law." King expressed the inherent tolerance of his vision when he concluded, "The law is hard enough on outcasts without other people winking when those in authority step beyond it." This commitment to judgmental slack exceeds even King's Democratic Party loyalty, for he does not hesitate to upbraid the "rural Tory Democrats" of the Texas legislature for their "outraged orations almost comically declaiming against welfare loafers, creeping socialism, the meddling ol' feds, and sin in the aggregate."[25]

Although King has been in print for more than fifty years, neither his South nor his humor seem to be vanishing. Although he has wandered to New York, Princeton, Duke, Howard, and Washington, D.C., his mind still drifts back to Texas. It can be said of Larry King, as he once wrote of horse trader Alvin Lancaster of Dew, Texas, that he is still "whooping at his own folly, convinced that as long as the world stays crazy, he'll have a mighty good time."[26]

Lewis Grizzard

Lewis Grizzard was a nationally syndicated columnist who drew a regular paycheck at the *Atlanta Constitution*. Among his books, which you can find in paperback at almost any southern airport, are such descriptive titles as *Elvis Is Dead and I Don't Feel So Good Myself*, *Don't Sit under the Grits Tree with Anyone Else But Me*, *Kathy Sue Loudermilk, I Love You*, *Won't You Come Home, Billy Bob Bailey*, *If Love Were Oil, I'd Be about a Quart Low*, and *They Tore My Heart Out and Stomped That Sucker Flat*.

While almost all of Grizzard's collections are about the South and southerners, *Shoot Low, Boys—They're Ridin' Shetland Ponies* may be the best example of the rhetoric of southern humor. Drawing on the character of Rooster Cogburn, created by fellow southerner Charles Portis in the novel *True Grit*, Grizzard is quite clear about whom he considers to be today's real heroes: "Folks who have overcome overwhelming odds, have fought and won and fought and lost, have spit in the devil's eye, have soared with eagles despite being surrounded by turkeys, have been bloodied and bullied and tricked and tangled and peed on and pissed off." He eschews the morally superior stance of the Old South Whigs and New South Bourbons, and he takes sides with the common folks. "These are the people I have come to honor," he said. "Not those who bask in the spotlight, but the strong, the swift, the courageous who huddle among the masses. True grit comes in many different shapes and sizes, and it often turns up where you least expect to find it."[27]

Like Fox and Larry King, Lewis Grizzard speaks in the first person and narrates his own observations. His self-made persona is pure southern. "As for myself," he says, "I'm a beer drinker. We're usually honest, straightfoward people. We also are usually kind and quite sentimental and will get cryin'-about-our-daddies drunk with one another." Then, dropping the southern shoe, he adds, "That's just before we destroy the establishment in which we're drinking because somebody made an offhand remark about Richard Petty or the memory of Patsy Cline." Grizzard knows that some of the old traditions of the South are on the wane, but his writing of that vanishing past allows him to keep it fresh. Addressing the cultural impact of technology, he says, "Mandatory air conditioning not only did away with underarm sweat stains, it also led to the demise of a great tradition: the paddle fan." These fans, he notes with nostalgia, were closely linked with the important rituals of funerals, politics, and religion. "The fans generally were provided by either a funeral home or an ambitious politician, with their message on one side . . . and a four-color biblical scene on the other side (usually the Last Supper)."[28]

Grizzard does eulogize some of the southerners who live in the spotlight of fame and attention—the sort of folks, he says, who "just bounce through life like a pinball, taking the easiest path but lighting up things and racking up points all the way." He does so to emphasize their most human qualities, ones he would argue are important in his vision of the better southern way of life. Among his examples were two southern comedians with a brand of humor different from his own. After meeting the unassuming Jerry Clower on an airplane and stealing enough material to fill a column, he concludes, "Anyone who has spent much time with Jerry Clower has been blessed far beyond his due." Grizzard also writes of attending the funeral of Junior Samples in Forsythe County, Georgia, noting that Samples was buried in his overalls. The point he stressed was that Junior had survived the experience of television celebrity: Samples was a hero to the town because, in the words of a local reporter, "He was one of them right to the end."[29]

Other heroes in Grizzard's pantheon are probably less well known, but his attention to their lives makes them important, both as unique individuals and as examples of true southern grit. He tells of meeting Mikki working in "the sort of place I wouldn't want my mother to catch me in" and listening to her hopes of someday making it in Las Vegas. Cutting plenty of sympathetic slack, he whimsically surmised that "tattooed strippers have a right to dream, too."[30] In a barbershop in Macon, Grizzard met a sixty-two-year-old black man who "shines shoes all day . . . and then shines for a good part of the evening in a local jazz bar." At former stations in the Atlanta airport and at the White House bootblack stand, Eugene Ellis had shined the shoes of John Kennedy, Lyndon Johnson, Richard Nixon, Hubert Humphrey, Gerald Ford, Muhammed Ali, and Elvis Presley. In making his point, Grizzard says, "I asked him if it bothered his self-image that he was still shining shoes for a living. He answered my question by looking at me like I was crazy." Ellis told him that "when he's got a good pair of shoes to shine and his rag is popping just right, 'it's like I'm making music.'" Grizzard's response was, "Yeah, I think that's enough said."[31]

In addition to promoting slack by taking up for strippers and bootblacks, Grizzard also takes on the narrow-minded Moral Majority. Mythmakers have always employed the tactic of taking their audience away from the here-and-now to paint their visions, usually by reconstructing idyllic scenes of the past or hopeful ones of the future, where their stories are exempt from the constraints of reality in the present. To visualize his view of right in the present, Grizzard relates a dream wherein God gets a briefing from an angel on earth's state of affairs. As Grizzard tells it, the angel relates current controversies, and God responds:

> "First, tell both sides that I don't want to be any part of their political squabbles. Their forefathers had the good sense to leave me out of politics, and I don't see why they can't.
>
> "Also, tell Ronald Reagan to forget about school prayer for awhile and instead find a way to talk to the Russians before they find a way to destroy what I've created. Then tell that Falwell fellow to stop using my name to boost his television ratings and stop trying to run the country from his pulpit. Can you handle that?" God asked the angel.
>
> "Yes, ma'am," the angel replied.[32]

The old Whig local color writers might have had God coming down on Andrew Jackson, but Grizzard's rhetorical vision is quite different in several ways. Like most other contemporary purveyors of Southern humor, he holds a more tolerant vision of the South, one that respects and includes women, blacks, poor folks, and other democratic heroes.

Florence King

Florence King, unrelated to Larry L. King within the third degree of consanguinity or affinity, grew up in Virginia and worked in North Carolina on the staff of the *Raleigh New and Observer*. She has written numerous magazine articles about southerners and their ways, and she has written two books about them, *Southern Ladies and Gentlemen* and *Confessions of a Failed Southern Lady*. King serves as he own narrator and speaks in the first person as she relates her personal experiences and observations, claiming that only the names have been changed to protect the guilty.

King's style differs somewhat from that of the other southern writers discussed here. While they lean toward subtle irony, she peddles full-frontal satire, wielding her weapon sometimes as a scalpel but more often as a machete. While they generally hold up heroes, she usually knocks down villains, exposing pride and prejudice. Her first book, *Southern Ladies and Gentleman*, best illustrates the rhetorical nature of her humor. It is an excursion in "fraudian" psychology, a glandular analysis of the South as revealed in its genes and jeans, and she does a fine job of reconstructing and deconstructing the stereotypes southerners have of themselves, their friends, and their foes.

Florence King is one of the brighter stars in what she has called "the galaxy of women writers that the South has produced." It is a phenomenon produced at least in part, she says, by four forces. First, writing was work that required no heavy lifting and could be done inside the home, where women belonged, so it came to be seen as women's (or sissy boys') work. Second, resulting from a male-imposed expectation, "the Pert Plague has made the Southern woman a delightful raconteuse." Because of the required sense of the dramatic, "almost anything that comes out of a Southern mouth is bound to be a ringing line." Third, women have especially keen insights into handling the special contradictions of southern culture. The southern woman "is required to be frigid, passionate, sweet, bitchy, and scatterbrained—all at the same time. Her problems spring from the fact that she succeeds." Finally, women seem to have a special talent for using the language. Being forced to make dull subjects interesting or having to write society columns making each debutante party sound exciting as well as different requires a great vocabulary, so it is no surprise that many of the old ladies she grew up with "talked like the first edition of Roget's *Thesaurus*."[33]

King knows how to use the language and knows its importance. She uses the story of her Granny ordering "a mess of bagels" to define that unit of measurement, and later she quotes a customer of Johnny's Cash and Carry tavern to explain the absurdity of liquor laws: "Local option is kinda like states' rights. . . . Only it ain't as much fun." In drawing her characters in the book, King relates that the "Haut Good Ole Boy" often "uses bad grammar for protective coloration," and she uses dialect to develop the "Shucks Ma'am," a subspecies of the good old boy who allows as how he just wants to make sure "evrathing" is "aw-right," "thass all." King also applies her understanding of figurative language and the South to explain the environment, exemplified by her description of one summer evening as "one of those hot, sticky nights now associated with Rod Steiger movies, a race-riot sort of night in which not a breeze is blowing, a night so airless and hot that you can even smell the cockroaches."[34]

The sense of contradiction essential to the southerner is learned at an early age, and it has served King well, forming the basis for much of her humor. At some point, the southern child "snatches chaos from the jaws of logic," she says, explaining that she later realized, "I was not sane, I was a Southerner." Such a conclusion was only normal, she knew, because "sanity has never held any charms for us; in fact, we're against it." In that social environment, southerners develop "an internal gyroscope subject to capricious fluctuations," and King found she had all she needed for her special version of southern humor. "Once my regionalism was launched, there was no stopping the stockpile of Southern contradictions that built up in my mind."[35]

In the South's surface attachment to a rigid social and moral order, King sees much worth commenting on and much that needs debunking, and she uses a series of character sketches to achieve her ends. Beginning at home, she devotes a chapter to pretensions of royalty in the invention of famous ancestors by family genealogists and to establishing relative social standing by overcoming one's white trash roots or neighbors. Her Granny Ruding, née Miss Lura Virginia Upton, always spoke about "that trashy look," an appearance exemplified by "the heavy, bovine face with undefined features that look as if the Lord smeared them while they were still wet." Other physical features of trash were "slack mouths, weak chins, and something she called 'that pink-eyed look,'" and their spirit and manners were always inferior to those of superior aristocratic stock.[36]

Among the characters of which King seems to approve are "That Child," and the "Good Good Ole Boy." Each possesses certain attributes she clearly admires. For example, she says, "That Child is very easy to get along with. She puts everyone at ease and poses no threats, not even to the flakiest Southern outpatient. . . . She can *do* something, and she does it magnificently well." The Good Good Ole Boy, Earl, shows a simple courage and a direct, uncomplicated approach to life and relationships.[37]

Less admirable in King's view are other character types. She has some tolerance for "Little Eva," an old maid who "has come to enjoy making mud pies on the playgrounds of her mind." She has less regard for "The Poor Thing," whom she compares to "a *mean* ole Melanie," and she thinks, "Having a Poor Thing at a party is as bad as having the dean of women under the bed with a tape recorder." King's least favorite type is "The Pill," who was "president of every organization on campus that had the name 'Christ' in its title," and whose judgmental looks and lectures encourage only resentment.[38]

The Southern male type King sees at the lower end of the evolutionary scale is the "Good Ole Boy Jock." This one can be found driving between football games, listening to another game on the radio, and holding a beer between his legs. "He cannot seem to navigate without this aluminum truss and is able to drink one crotch-warmed beer after another with no apparent ill effects." One ill effect that King *does* attribute to the football culture is a certain type of intolerance. In King's narrative, the southern jock believes that "any male co-worker who does not spend coffee break talking about the great Stretch Malooski's forward pass is a queer. Any male co-worker who does not know who Stretch Malooski is, is a Communist queer."[39]

King exposes the southern "proneness to make snap judgments about people," but she also finds a certain benevolent irony in the exceptions to certain certainties. For example, in describing the "Town Fairy," she says, "Nobody minds him, and he is no threat to even the worst queer-hater." He is safe from the macho threat of the Good Ole Boy Jock, because "the ladies of the garden club would take up their pruning shears and call a charge" in his defense. She explains this contradiction by explaining, "Southerners have a genius for psychological alchemy. . . . If something intolerable cannot be changed, driven away, or shot, they will not only tolerate it but take pride in it. Conformists to the end, they nonetheless feel affection for any eccentric." In fact, she is personally thankful that calling someone an eccentric "is the nicest thing any Southerner can say about one of their own."[40]

Will these southern characters and the character of this South survive the forces of modernity? King thinks so, and she attributes that continuity to a tough persistence of pre-Copernican egocentrism in the mind of the south-erner. Furthermore, she says, "the ultimate Southern contradiction is *static change*."[41] Yeah, I think that's enough said.

The Last Laugh

The four storytellers discussed here each present artfully crafted narratives of southern life, and they help develop a collective rhetorical vision with heroes, villains, and fools who engage in public dramas that help us understand motives, values, accidents, our region, and ourselves. While all four are white, their visions of the South and of southern humor are racially integrated and gen-erally nonsexist. In telling of the way in which a southern woman in the pub-lishing center of New York can confront the Yankee stereotypes, Florence King prizes put-on interaction with a black male confederate. She says, "This can be great fun if you can find a black man with a sense of humor well laced with irony—and there are few blacks who have not had the opportunity to develop one."[42] All of these writers understand that blacks are an integral part of south-ern culture, and their humorous stories present a world where blacks and whites share common concerns and values. Unless one wants to read Florence King's biting satire of Good Ole Boys or Lewis Grizzard's whining about his ex-wives as sexist, sexism is difficult to find in contemporary southern humor.

This essay began with the question of whether southern humor might sur-vive the forces of demographic change and the ravages of time and then pro-ceeded to examine the nature of southern humor to help answer that question. One of the most apparent discoveries was that the rhetoric of contemporary southern humor was quite different from that of the past. No longer vehicles for demeaning poor whites or controlling free blacks, the stories of today's writ-ers present a much more egalitarian argument premised on the virtues of the common folks. The southern immunity to the forces of demographic change, especially in the categories of education and income, suggests that there will continue to be plenty of potential heroes, and the success of contemporary southern humor in getting itself accepted in the marketplace of paperbacks suggests the continued present of appropriate models for future writers. Fur-thermore, time is so easily ignored and reality is so elusive in the South that writers should easily be able to overcome at will the obstacles of change.

Rather than asking whether southern humor can survive the changes in the region, a better question is whether the social order of the region can sur-vive the changes in and changes wrought by the rhetoric of southern humor. In Umberto Eco's novel *The Name of the Rose*, Jorge of Burgos fearfully tries to suppress Aristotle's Second Book of *The Poetics*, the "lost" treatise on com-edy. William of Baskerville argues that the book may contain valuable knowl-edge. Aristotle, he says, "sees the tendency to laughter as a force for good, which can also have an instructive value; through witty riddles and unexpected metaphors, . . . it makes us say: Ah, this is jut how things are, and I didn't know it." Jorge knows, however, that comedy has "the power of a thousand scorpions," and he believes the manuscript is dangerous. It could cross "the last boundary," overturning the image of the world and the authority of the Church. Jorge reveals the greatest heresy of humor just before he destroys the manuscript, saying, "This book would have justified that the tongue of the simple is the vehicle of wisdom."[43]

The wisdom and virtue of the common folks of both genders and races has been one of the principle arguments in the rhetoric of contemporary southern humor, and its flanking action has helped win and secure the victories of the Second Reconstruction of the South. It insidiously undermined the old worldview and empowered the peasantry. The Bourbon oligarchy's blind, book-burning priests of social, economic, and moral hegemony did not understand its power, while the academy discounted it as frivolous popular culture, unworthy of the attention of scholars more concerned with serious literature and dead poets; nonetheless, it quietly and surely "justified that the tongue of the simple is the vehicle of wisdom." The South may never be the same again, but the prospects for the survival of southern humor are excellent.

Notes

1. C. Vann Woodward, *The Burden of Southern History* (Baton Rouge: Louisiana State University Press, 1968), 193–94.

2. Henning Cohen and William B. Dillingham, éds., *Humor of the Old Southwest* (Boston: Houghton Mifflin, 1964), ix–xi.

3. Ibid., xi, xxiii–xxiv.

4. Ibid., 29.

5. W. J. Cash, *The Mind of the South* (New York: Vintage Books, 1969), 146.

6. See Stephen A. Smith, *Myth, Media, and the Southern Mind* (Fayetteville: University of Arkansas Press, 1985), 23–24.

7. For a critique of the Disney version, see Alice Walker, "Uncle Remus, No Friend of Mine," *Southern Exposure* 9, no. 2 (1981): 29–31.

8. As a crutch, however, I lean throughout this essay on Ernest G. Bormann, "Fantasy and Rhetorical Vision: The Rhetorical Criticism of Social Reality," *Quarterly Journal of Speech* 58 (1972): 396–407.

9. William Price Fox, "Doug Broome, Hamburger King," *Chitlin Strut and Other Madrigals* (Atlanta: Peachtree Publishers, 1983), 18.

10. Ibid., 15, 17, 21.

11. Fox, "Leroy 'Satchel' Paige," *Chitlin Strut and Other Madrigals*, 155.

12. Fox, "Celebrity Golf," *Chitlin Strut and Other Madrigals*, 48.

13. Fox, "The Chitlin Strut," *Chitlin Strut and Other Madrigals*, 10–12.

14. Fox, "The Frog Jump," *Chitlin Strut and Other Madrigals*, 174.

15. The best discussion of this is John Egerton, *Southern Food: At Home, on the Road, and in History* (New York: Knopf, 1987); see also Stephen A. Smith, "Food for Thought: Comestible Communication and Contemporary Southern Culture," in *American Material Culture*, ed. Edith P. Mayo (Bowling Green, Ohio: Bowling Green State University Popular Press, 1984), 208–17.

16. Fox, "Chitlin Strut," 8.

17. Fox, "Frog Jump," 171–72.

18. This point has been authoritatively settled in Stephen A. Smith, "The Rhetoric of Barbeque: A Southern Rite and Ritual," *Studies in Popular Culture* 8 (1985): 17–25.

19. Fox, "The Drive-In," *Chitlin Strut and Other Madrigals*, 39.

20. Larry L. King, "Eccentric Americana: Of Kinfolk and Friends," *None But a Blockhead: On Being a Writer* (New York: Viking, 1986), 287.

21. King, "A Matter of Style," *None But a Blockhead*, 261–65.

22. Larry L. King, "Playing Cowboy," *Of Outlaws, Con Men, Whores, Politicians, and Other Artists* (New York: Penguin, 1981), 60.

23. King, "The American Redneck," *Of Outlaws*, 3–6.

24. King, "Remembering the Hard Times," *Of Outlaws*, 31.

25. Fox, "Doug Broome, Hamburger King," 21, and King, "Playing Cowboy," 71–73, 56.

26. King, "Gettin' Stung: Horse Tradin'," *Of Outlaws*, 136.

27. Lewis Grizzard, "Walk a Mile in the Duke's Boots," *Shoot Low, Boys—They're Ridin' Shetland Ponies* (Atlanta: Peachtree Publishers, 1985), 7–9.

28. Grizzard, "Never Go Camping With a Man Who Drinks Whiskey Sours," *Shoot Low, Boys*, 27, 30.

29. Grizzard, "The Bigger They Are, the More They Weigh," *Shoot Low, Boys*, 165, 169–70.

30. Grizzard, "Profiles in True Grit," *Shoot Low, Boys*, 13–14.

31. Grizzard, "A Heaping Helping of Grit," *Shoot Low, Boys*, 39–41.

32. Grizzard, "Sinning and Grinning and Knowing the Difference," *Shoot Low, Boys*, 58.

33. Florence King, *Southern Ladies and Gentlemen* (1975; New York: Bantam Books, 1976), 218, 50, 191, 32, 135.

34. Ibid., 5, 8, 112, 92–95, 53–54.

35. Ibid., 1–3, 16, 95.

36. Ibid., 29.

37. Ibid., 153–54, 101–2.

38. Ibid., 150, 143–44, 176–77.

39. Ibid., 110–11.

40. Ibid., 157–58, 170, 233.

41. Ibid., 240–42.

42. Ibid., 231.

43. Umberto Eco, *The Name of the Rose*, trans. William Weaver (1983; New York: Warner Books, 1984), 566–82.

Index